THE CRS TEAM AND THE BUSINESS OF ARCHITECTURE

NUMBER FOURTEEN
Kenneth E. Montague Series in Oil and Business History

Joseph A. Pratt, Jr., General Editor

▪ THE CRS TEAM AND THE BUSINESS OF ARCHITECTURE

Edited by

Jonathan King

&

Philip Langdon

Foreword by Ronald Skaggs

TEXAS A&M UNIVERSITY PRESS : COLLEGE STATION

First edition

The paper used in this book
meets the minimum requirements
of the American National Standard for Permanence
of Paper for Printed Library Materials, z39.48-1984.
Binding materials have been chosen for durability.

∞

Library of Congress Cataloging-in-Publication Data

The CRS team and the business of architecture / edited by Jonathan King and Philip Langdon ; foreword by Ronald Skaggs.

p. cm. — (Kenneth E. Montague series in oil and business history ; no. 14)

Includes bibliographical references and index.

ISBN 1–58544–206–2 (alk. paper)

1. Caudill, Rowlett, Scott—History. 2. Architectural practice—United States—Management. 3. Architectural services marketing—United States. 4. Architecture—United States—Decision making. 5. Group work in architecture. 6. Architects—United States—Interviews. I. King, Johathan, 1925–1997 II. Langdon, Philip. III. Series.

NA737.C3 C77 2002

720'.92'2—dc21 2002004964

FOR BILL CAUDILL

JOHN ROWLETT

WALLIE SCOTT

WILLIE PEÑA

TOM BULLOCK

ED NYE

CHARLES LAWRENCE

AND HERB PASEUR

■ WHO TOGETHER

MADE IT HAPPEN.

■ CONTENTS

■ ILLUSTRATIONS

■ FOREWORD

RONALD SKAGGS

In the world of architecture, the twentieth century was a time of exceptional transformation. The art and science of architecture and the construction industry, which once changed slowly and incrementally, mutated with dizzying speed throughout the century. One hundred years ago Art Nouveau was in vogue, but that was not the only game in town. The arts and crafts movement supplied an alternative, and there were also various revival styles: Gothic, Colonial, Italianate, and Beaux Arts.

Soon the headlong rush of the Industrial Revolution began to spawn a new attitude—one that pushed forward in the 1920s under the names of "Modernism" and "International Style." The decades after the Second World War produced many "isms": brutalism, postmodernism, neomodernism, deconstructivism, and so on. The twentieth century was a stage on which those who were admired in the architectural profession acted the part of individualist. Most often they were the products of the École des Beaux Arts in Paris or Ivy League colleges in the United States.

In the second half of the twentieth century, however, a new paradigm was established in the practice of architecture. It was created not by celebrated individualists on the East and West Coasts, but by a group of young architects and one engineer who came mainly from two middle-American land grant colleges: Oklahoma State University and Texas A&M University. The firm of Caudill Rowlett Scott—later known as CRS—was established in College Station, Texas, in 1946. Almost from its start, CRS embodied what the practice of architecture would evolve into during the postwar decades.

As I think back to my early years with CRS, after the firm had picked up and moved to Houston, I see that much of the philosophy of architectural practice I learned at CRS has become the foundation for how my own firm operates today. Whether it is the problem-seeking aspects of programming, the use of concept cards in design analysis, or the team approach to project delivery, each is an idea that originated with CRS and that is commonplace in today's practice.

The idea of team design, which is best described in Bill Caudill's book *Architecture by Team*, may seem obvious now. But in the mid-twentieth century, that concept was foreign to most of the people in our field. Even today, much of the architectural media and many of our schools of architecture tend to emphasize the singular contribution of the individual architect. What CRS recognized was that architecture should be a group endeavor—a social art of sorts. Today, the architectural process is tied more than ever to a group of professionals with a wide variety of skills and preoccupations. The firm visualized the design process not as the work of an individual, to which others contribute, but as the work of a "collective mind" that could generate great architecture.

The core of the team was what Bill Caudill referred to as the troika: the designer, the manager, and the technologist. The emphasis was not on one person, but on achieving a balance, with each doing the best that he or she could. The emphasis on balance pervaded the firm's values. For example, equalization of form, function, and economy was the standard by which the firm evaluated the success of an architectural undertaking. That theory was essentially a modern-day reaffirmation of Vitruvius's dictum that architecture required an aggregation of firmness, commodity, and delight.

Caudill Rowlett Scott was a firm that embraced change and was driven by a pioneer spirit—reinforced, no doubt, by its Texas roots. The core values of the eight founding partners permeated the firm, fostering a belief in hard work within a nonhierarchical organization and providing freedom for individuals to take on as much responsibility as they were willing and able to handle. It was a firm dedicated to quality architecture supported by sound research.

It should not be any surprise that a firm rooted in research, dating to Bill Caudill's early years as a faculty member at Texas A&M's School of Architecture, would be recognized for its innovation in the industry. Many ideas conceived at CRS have become common practice among firms today. The programming approach that gave rise to the term *problem seeking* is now the prevailing method in predesign activities. Architectural firms nationwide use the "squatter's" approach, which calls for the architect to travel to the customer's home base for intensive on-site design sessions. Analysis cards are frequently employed for gathering information, organizing ideas, and communicating design concepts, even in this computer age. The term *fast track*, connoting the acceleration of the design and construction process through an overlapping of activities, is widely used today and credited to CRS. Twenty-first-century architectural firms consistently employ many other innovations discussed in this book, and the firm continues to have a significant impact on the way architecture is practiced.

The American Institute of Architects, which is focused on redefining the profession, points out that the world is undergoing fundamental changes in the ways it works, and architects practicing in this new world—one driven by technology, instant communication, knowledge-based economies, and tough competition on every side—are being forced to change with it.

They are far less concerned with maintaining professional boundaries than they were in the past; they are much more adept at forming alliances with other disciplines that can help anticipate and meet the needs of clients. The demands on architects go well beyond traditional architectural and engineering services. Clients are looking for long-term relationships with teams they know and trust—not just a one-project relationship. They are asking for a lifecycle-performance-based approach, with the design teams serving as facilitators and integrators for all their facility-related services, thus allowing the clients to concentrate on their own core competencies. Additionally, clients are increasingly asking architects to work on interdisciplinary teams where the design is the result of a collaborative process rather than an act of individual intuition and creativity. Throughout this book, readers will find examples of CRS having instituted methods well suited to the demands the world is making today. It has practiced these tenets from the beginning; its core values are as relevant today as they were during the firm's prime.

One may ask if it was Bill Caudill's inspiration that made the firm so great, or if it was the team of early founders and those they mentored. The answer may be both, as reflected by the American Institute of Architects bestowing its Architecture Firm Award on Caudill Rowlett Scott in 1972 and awarding its Gold Medal posthumously to William W. Caudill, F.A.I.A., in 1985.

As a firm with vision, CRS always seemed to be ahead of the trend lines, able to forecast new market demands and, as a result, be at the right place at the right time. The firm's principals emphasized the importance of operating in a businesslike manner. They accomplished their goals through solid project management, but they also realized that good architecture could be good business. Their simple credo was to do good architecture, make money, and have fun doing it.

The latter part of this book attempts to address the factors that led to the firm's dissolution after almost fifty years of phenomenal growth. Three interrelated factors are identified here. Since Bill Caudill organized many of his ideas in groups of three, it is appropriate to list these three possibilities. The first centers on the firm's going public in the early 1970s, a bold move for an architectural and engineering firm, and one that some believe shifted the focus from the client to the shareholder. Others believe that the increased emphasis on large international projects, particularly in the Middle East, took the firm away from its strong client relations in the United States. Lastly, there are those who believe that a change in priorities from architecture to construction management and heavy engineering had an impact. No one really knows. It is up to you the reader to draw your own conclusion. As a point of reference, it is worth reading a TIB (This I Believe) memo penned by Caudill on March 4, 1969:

CRS TEAM—DEATH OF A TEAM

When should a team die?
When should a leader resign?
With a firm like CRS, which has reached the age where some of us will be pushed out soon at one end of the pipe while at the other end new recruits are flowing in steadily, we must have answers to these questions.

Already there are three generations of architects in CRS. I'm a grandfather, so to speak. My former students in CRS have former students working for CRS.

We have yet to retire a principal partner, but the time is near. Even more concerning is the fact that CRS has reached "the age of professional hardening of the arteries." So far, we have been rather lucky. Instead of a 20-year firm, we may prove to be a 50-year firm. I have always said that CRS would be here when I am long dead.

CRS Is a 2000 Firm

It will be here in 2000, and it will reach 2,000 in number. This I believe. But there are some "ifs":

If we continue to bring in the best recruits—the most talented in America.

If we keep on top of the profession.

If we have an awareness of social change.

If we believe in Architecture.

If we believe in CRS's contribution to making this world a better place to live.

Certainly CRS lives on in the hearts and minds of those who worked there and among those it served. The firm developed individuals who are leaders in the industry all over the globe, in addition to advocating principles that are now widely embraced in the profession. The interviews contained in this book offer a fascinating insight into the launching, expansion, and transformation of one of the truly great architectural and engineering firms. The candor provided through open dialogue offers a unique insider's understanding of how a group of passionate people working together with common goals can achieve greatness in the annals of American architecture.

Ronald L. Skaggs, F.A.I.A.
Chairman and Chief Executive Officer
HKS Architects
Past President, The American Institute of Architects

■ PREFACE

This book describes, in the words of many of those who were responsible for it, the rags-to-riches evolution of a remarkable American architecture firm: Caudill Rowlett Scott, later known as CRS, and subsequently CRSS. From 1991–94, interviews were conducted with fifty of the firm's key employees—individuals who worked at CRS between 1948, when the organization was just starting, and the early 1990s, when it was nearing its final days. Some CRS people were interviewed several times. The sessions, ranging from as short as forty-five minutes to as long as fourteen hours (spread over several days), provide firsthand accounts of how CRS grew from a tiny operation in a central Texas town to the largest architectural/engineering firm in the United States.

The oral history was one of the first undertakings of the center that CRSS established at Texas A&M University in 1991 to explore leadership and innovation in the business side of the design and construction industry. The center, now known as the CRS Center for Leadership and Management in the Design and Construction Industry, has gathered and preserved audiotapes, videotapes, photographs, slides, articles, business and personal records, and other material documenting CRS and its influence. Complete transcripts and tapes of the oral history interviews may be read or listened to in the Center's archives.

When Jonathan King, Hon. A.I.A., joined the Center as associate director in August, 1992, the interviewing, conducted by a number of individuals, was near the halfway point. After reading the transcripts of all the interviews that had been done up to that time, he conducted the remaining interviews himself. Jonathan was a prominent figure in architectural research in the United States. As vice president and treasurer of the Ford Foundation's Educational Facilities Laboratories in New York from 1958 to 1970, he fostered innovation in school architecture. He was a partner at CRS from 1970 to 1976 and professor of architecture and director of the University of Michigan Architectural Research Laboratory from 1976 until 1983. He was enticed out of retirement in 1992 to join the Center's staff, and became its director the following year.

As Jonathan conducted the final interviews, he felt more and more strongly that the histories together told an extraordinary story. They revealed a corporate culture that was not only unique, but which also reflected important changes occurring in architectural practice and business in the postwar era. He realized that this massive body of recollections included the answers to gnawing questions about CRS: how it had grown so fast, how it had become so influential, and why it had failed.

In their raw form, the histories were cumbersome, uneven in length and focus. They would likely end up underused or forgotten. However, Jonathan saw that if they were gathered into a coherent whole, with extraneous and repetitious passages removed, they would tell an important story, one that would be of value to the profession and would interest many people in the design and construction fields, as well as students. Thus was born the idea of turning selections from those interviews into a book. He raised the idea with Tom Bullock—they met frequently to discuss the aims and operations of the Center—and with Walter Wendler, who was dean at the time. Both responded enthusiastically.

Jonathan worked on the book over a period of approximately three years while he was director. After he turned the directorship over to Bob Johnson in January, 1996, the work progressed more quickly. He finished the manuscript at the end of May, 1997, shortly before he retired.

He planned to cull the archives for visual material to be included in the book. He knew precisely what he wanted, and anticipated spending one or two days a week in the next month doing this. However, he became ill, and on the first day of July, 1997, he had a series of doctors' appointments. He never returned to the Center. The manuscript was his last major piece of writing. He died of cancer at his home in Houston, November 19, 1997, at the age of seventy-one.

Jonathan had been proud of his final draft of the manuscript and optimistic about its prospects for publication. During the next year, the Center asked several critics to read it. There seemed to be agreement that although the story was important, it needed to be set in a broader historical context. In January, 1999, the Center commissioned Philip Langdon, a New Haven–based author of books on architecture and design, to make revisions and additions that would answer that need. Twenty years earlier, when Phil was a National Endowment for the Humanities Professional Journalism Fellow at the University of Michigan, studying architecture and urban planning, he had met Jonathan, and the two became friends, staying in touch over the years. Phil wrote the book's opening and closing chapters and the introductions to the twelve chapters in between. He used some of Jonathan's language and material but added much elaboration and explication. He also selected excerpts from the prolific writing of CRS founder Bill Caudill to intersperse throughout the text, and he interviewed a number of former CRSers to provide additional perspective; those sources are identified in the footnotes.

While looking through the CRS archives at Texas A&M, Phil found a typewritten oral history of CRS produced in 1971 by the Graduate School of Business at the University of Texas at Austin. Though less comprehensive than the history undertaken at Texas A&M in the 1990s, the 1971 document contained interesting interviews with the three founders who had died: Bill Caudill, John Rowlett, and Wallie Scott. Phil incorporated parts of the 1971 document into the opening chapter and into introductions to other chapters. Phil cut some nonessential passages from what was a long text, but otherwise made no substantial revisions to the oral histories Jonathan had assembled. The heart of the book remains as Jonathan intended.

The aim of the oral history was summed up in a statement Jonathan wrote shortly before his death: "This book is an attempt to portray [a] corporate culture which sought to forge a passion for new and better architecture and a deep commitment to finding better answers to client problems while improving business success and client communication, increasing experimentation in design, and redefining the established building delivery process. Consequently, it may contain valuable lessons for architects and others who are today grappling with similar problems in establishing or expanding their own firms."

■ ACKNOWLEDGMENTS

The oral history interviews with former CRS staff members were conducted by a number of people, including Michael M. McCarthy, who at the time was dean of the Texas A&M College of Architecture and director of the CRS Center. Kevin Noon, who was then a doctoral candidate at Texas A&M, also did some of the interviews. John Only Greer, Texas A&M's Wallie E. Scott Professor in Architectural Practice and Management, and Allen Commander, then executive associate director of the CRS Center, participated in some of the interviews as well. In addition, I conducted about half of the interviews. Dean McCarthy interviewed me long before I joined the CRS Center.

The Center's Barbara Anderson and Marty Benthul transcribed most of the interviews. Emily Staples, a member of the dean's staff, also transcribed several. All of the tapes and transcripts are part of the CRS Center Archives and are available to the public.

I had help from a number of people in the CRS Center while preparing this book. Shana Hutchins, the Center's executive assistant, was of great assistance. She also identified a number of good statements in the oral histories that are now part of the book.

Barbara Anderson, Tom Bullock's long-time executive assistant, keeps a complete CRS history in her head. She, too, was helpful—both on CRS history matters and by identifying good interviews and cogent quotes.

Tom Bullock, a founder of CRS, was enthusiastic about this project from the outset. Walter V. Wendler, dean of the College of Architecture, was encouraging throughout, and the current Center director, Robert E. Johnson, provided invaluable support and advice.

Regarding errors, if there are any, there is no one to blame but me.

Jonathan King, editor

Thanks to the many former CRS executives and staff members who patiently answered my questions. Two individuals, Center director Robert E. Johnson and Cynthia "Toni" King, Jonathan King's widow, provided information and advice that helped me immeasurably in producing the opening and closing chapters and the introductory sections to the twelve chapters of oral history. Special thanks are due to Willie Peña. My greatest debt is to the late Jonathan King, who left such a vivid, lively manuscript, and whose wisdom and wry wit were a delight to us all.

Philip Langdon, editor

■ THE CRS TEAM AND THE BUSINESS OF ARCHITECTURE

■ CHAPTER 1

PIONEERS

■ TIB: 23 MAY 1983

Everyone must know that 90 percent of all architectural firms are under 10 people. I do remember when CRS had five full-time people:

- That sweeping out the office wasn't very efficient;
- That since there was not a genius like Frank Lloyd Wright among us, we worked together as a team;
- That each of us had to specialize doing what he liked to do best;
- That to be competitive, the firm had also to specialize to be better than other firms in certain aspects of practice;
- That since we started our practice in a very small town, we couldn't make a living at home;
- That since we all had kids, or hoped to have kids, CRS had to grow so that we could send them to college;
- And that if we were going to stick together throughout the years, we had to have common goals.

What goals? No great manifesto, nor philosophical elaboration. Our goals then and now are pretty down-home stuff:

TO PRODUCE GOOD ARCHITECTURE, MAKE SOME MONEY, AND TO HAVE SOME FUN WHILE DOING IT

■ This was one of thousands of pithy memos that Bill Caudill wrote to help communicate his values, philosophies, and beliefs to what was becoming a large company. From 1964 until 1983, Caudill distributed approximately four thousand such memos, which he called "TIBs," an abbreviation for "This I Believe."

■ "I believe progress is made by doing things even if they are wrong," Bill Caudill observed more than once.[1] The future, asserted the leader of what became America's largest architecture and engineering firm, belongs to people who act—despite their youth or limitations. "I get quite disturbed at the perfectionist," Caudill said, "the person who closes himself in a shell of perfection; the person who cherishes perfection to such a degree that he won't do anything. . . . How can improvement be made unless something is done? . . . Everyone needs to do something. If not, he can never learn."[2]

If you had walked into the offices of Caudill Rowlett Scott—later known simply as CRS—in the spring of 1950, you would have seen a firm that was destined to bring important innovations to the practice of architecture. Was there a way for architects to push buildings from drawing board to finished construction faster than ever before? Then CRS would find a way to accomplish it. Could architects in a remote community design schools across much of the United States? Then CRS would devise a system to do that. Could teams of designers, managers, and "technologists"—including specialists trained in fields other than architecture—produce buildings? Then CRS would accomplish that, too.

But in the spring of 1950, the future of this path-breaking firm looked much more mundane. Caudill Rowlett Scott was, despite Caudill's confidence, a struggling young enterprise in an out-of-the-way location. The firm had set up shop after World War II in College Station, Texas, an unprepossessing place of 7,925 inhabitants on the flat, hot prairie about ninety miles northwest of Houston. College Station possessed one reason for being: the Agricultural and Mechanical College of Texas (Texas A&M), an institution that had attracted young men desiring a highly practical education since it was founded in 1876. The men (A&M was a male-only school until the 1960s) came from throughout Texas to learn disciplines connected mainly with the land and what could be grown on it, built on it, or extracted from it. Petroleum engineering, civil engineering, agronomy, and animal husbandry were among the leading livelihoods taught at A&M.

Texas A&M had a small architecture department, and it was there that William Wayne Caudill, John Miles Rowlett, and Wallie E. Scott Jr. first got to know one another. Caudill was the unforgettable one: a passionate man utterly dedicated to his work. A journalist described Caudill as a "fidgeter, a gesticulator, a diagrammer, a stammerer, an interrupter, a theorist, and a man of relentless ambition"—all true—but he was, in addition to that, a man of great warmth and enthusiasm, which was one of the chief reasons for his profound effect on the people around him.[3] All his life, Caudill had suffered with the remnants of a stutter, but it never seemed to stop him from expounding on his myriad thoughts—in the classroom, the office, or anywhere else. He had taught at A&M since 1939, except for wartime service in the U.S. Army Corps of Engineers in Nebraska and as a carpenter's mate in the navy, and had distinguished himself as both a researcher and teacher.

Rowlett was the perfect foil to Caudill. Unaggressive, always considerate, willing to let his more fervent and flamboyant partner grab the limelight, Rowlett was a pleasant man who possessed first-rate drafting skills. "He could just brush the plans onto a sheet of paper; he knew exactly what he was doing, they were very detailed," a colleague marveled.[4] A native of Georgetown, Texas, the tall, lean Rowlett joined the A&M faculty a year after Caudill, went into the navy as an officer in 1944, and, after his discharge, tried to establish an office in Austin for the two-man firm first known as Caudill and Rowlett. The market for architectural services ought to have been more promising in the state capital than in an outpost like College

John Rowlett, *left,* was thirty-two, and Bill Caudill was thirty-one when this photo—the first picture of the newly formed firm's two principals—was taken in Caudill's office at Texas A&M in March, 1946. Rowlett was still in his navy uniform and had to borrow a jacket for the photograph. *Photo courtesy Harold Jordan.*

Station, but success proved elusive, so by the end of 1946 he was back in College Station with Caudill, mixing teaching and practice.

In 1948, Caudill and Rowlett rented a two-room office above the Southside Food Market in a nondescript brick building next to the campus's south entrance. The front room was just large enough for a big drafting board and a secretary's desk—although the firm could not yet afford a secretary. The second room accommodated three drawing boards. By summer, air conditioners were humming in the windows. Caudill and Rowlett still had little money, but they splurged on air conditioners because without them, the architects' forearms would sweat in the sultry Texas atmosphere, smearing the drawings and making them unpresentable. Wallie Scott, who had grown up in Port Arthur, Texas, and studied under Caudill and Rowlett, joined the firm that year as the third partner, contributing a small sum to the young enterprise. The following year, William M. Peña, an A&M graduate originally from Laredo, became the fourth partner after serving as one of the firm's first employees. By 1950, the firm was gaining ground, but it was still an untested little enterprise, one of hundreds of such postwar outfits across the United States that subsisted principally on designing houses.

All four men possessed ability. Caudill had been singled out early for attention, being named "Outstanding All-Around Male Graduate" at Oklahoma A&M in 1937. He headed east a year later to pursue a master's in architecture at the Massachusetts Institute of Technology (MIT). The late 1930s was a transitional time in architectural education, the fade-out of a long period of deference to established traditions. Beaux Arts schooling methods, which called for learning how to recreate architecture's classic forms, persisted, but students and faculty alike were beginning to embrace modernism. The year that Caudill arrived in Cambridge for classes at MIT, Walter Gropius, founder of the Bauhaus, became chairman of Harvard's Department of Architecture and soon revolutionized its curriculum. Although MIT still used Beaux Arts methods, Lawrence B. Anderson had begun introducing European, and especially Scandinavian, modernism to his classes after joining the faculty in 1933, so Caudill obtained an education that, although hardly radical, did nothing to quash his impatience with old ways of doing things.

By the end of the 1940s, the self-confident Caudill, then in his second stint of teaching at Texas A&M, felt ready for bigger undertakings, but as yet there was only a limited supply of projects on which to work. Like most practitioners in their twenties and thirties, Caudill and the others above the

Southside grocery looked to the future with more hope than assurance. Until commissions became plentiful, Caudill and Rowlett would rely on their faculty positions at A&M to remain solvent.

The 1950s changed everything, as CRS speedily ascended into the ranks of highly admired and respected architectural firms. Popular magazines such as *Collier's* (starting with an article in September, 1950, entitled "The Little Red Schoolhouse Goes Modern") and *Life* enthusiastically presented CRS's school ideas to the public.[5] Education journals brought CRS's innovations to the attention of school officials. Architectural journals spread news of CRS's school expertise among fellow practitioners. The attention lavished on CRS's educational work was invaluable, generating many commissions for elementary and secondary schools, which constituted the firm's strongest field in the '50s. By the end of that decade, the firm had progressed to college and university buildings and to campus master planning. As one of the partners, Charles Lawrence, observed, "We followed the baby boom from elementary school to high school to college."[6] Caudill Rowlett Scott also expanded into other specialties, such as manufacturing and research facilities for clients like 3M. The firm cultivated its strengths with such zeal that it outgrew College Station and the neighboring city of Bryan. By 1960, CRS was based in Houston—a rising metropolis of 1.2 million with a busy airport that made it easy for CRS personnel to fly to job sites throughout the country. The largest architectural firm in the largest city in Texas, CRS was an organization that architects around the country had begun to watch. In about ten years, the caterpillar had turned into a butterfly and the firm's ambitions continued to expand. By 1970, CRS was one of the leading American architectural firms not only in schools, but also in the rapidly growing field of health facilities design.

Tasks that were rarely undertaken by architectural firms attracted CRS, which explored new ideas in all kinds of areas: management, design, engineering, and finance. In 1971, the firm became the first sizable publicly traded architectural corporation, its stock offered on the National Association of Securities Dealers Automatic Quotation (NASDAQ) system stock exchange, later on the American Stock Exchange (AMEX), and eventually on the New York Stock Exchange (NYSE). In 1972, CRS, having won dozens of awards, received the American Institute of Architects' (AIA) Firm Award, the highest honor the AIA can bestow on a company. By the early 1980s, CRS had become, at least for a while, the largest architecture and engineering firm in the United States and one of the most successful American firms in the Middle East.

The firm became known for the quality and innovation of its designs, but what truly set it apart from others in its field were the advances it pioneered in the process of design and construction. The firm knew how to analyze problems and devise systems that would enable architects to do things better, cheaper, or faster—and sometimes all three. A favorite saying at CRS was that "the process is as important as the product." The firm shared its innovative procedures with the architectural profession as a whole, helping to improve buildings and building processes throughout the United States and the world.

Long before CRS was formed, pioneers of the Modern Movement had propagated the idea that architects should be free to shape buildings around their functions rather than around preconceived notions of what a building should look like. Although modernist leaders invoked functionalism in their rhetoric, in reality they had a hard time designing buildings that satisfied the full range of functional requirements. The results thus often fell far short of the aspirations.

Part of the difficulty was that modern architects, for all their talk about logic, still tended to design in an intuitive fashion. Try as they might to get useful information and guidance from clients, in the end they pursued a primarily esthetic vision, if only because there seemed to be no surefire way for designers to identify the problems they were trying to solve. What was needed was a process that would make it easier for designers to identify and understand the issues that should be addressed.

Designers at CRS argued that an architect should not start sketching what a building might look like before the problems had been fully diagnosed. The designer first needed to find answers to many questions: What qualities did the clients need in their spaces? What was the nature of the activities that would take place in and around the buildings? Did the buildings' users need privacy, seclusion, or opportunities for social encounters? Which people or activities needed to be close together? Which needed to be kept apart? There were a potentially large number of issues to be investigated, and CRS insisted that the results be summarized before the designer could begin trying to give the building its shape, layout, and character. Architects at CRS, though they found inspiration in new forms, wanted to be certain that clients and users received a practical creation, one that would enable people to accomplish their tasks as conveniently, flexibly, economically, and pleasurably as possible. Through years of trial and error (or, more accurately, trial and success) CRS learned which questions to ask, when and how to ask them, and how to convert the answers into concise statements that would be useful to designers. The name for this discipline was programming.

Programming requires considerable self-confidence. If the architect is afraid to engage the client in the process of defining the problems, if the architect fears that an in-depth study of the client's needs will constrain creativity, programming simply will not work. Not every architect is eager to make the client so central to the process or to delay working on "schematic design" (the initial phase of designing a project). But CRS had faith that good architects could remain the masters of the process—probing the client, listening intensely, and, at the appropriate time, turning those requirements into a work of the imagination.

The twentieth century, with its never-ending cycle of modernization, was a fertile time for these techniques. Scientific and technological progress was forcing buildings to become increasingly complex and to combine many sometimes highly specific functional requirements. Nobody designing technically sophisticated buildings such as laboratories and hospitals could get by for long by relying on an undisciplined gathering of facts and a sudden leap of intuition. Nor was the advent of technically complicated buildings the only reason why the profession was moved to adopt rigorous methods of predesign analysis. Society was developing increasingly varied and precise expectations even for common activities, pursuits that had existed for centuries. Education is an example. From 1900 to 1940, thousands of elementary and secondary schools were built in the United States, many of them based on the idea that the school should be a civic monument, an impressive two- or three-story building in which teachers presided over students who sat at immovable rows of desks, all facing the front of the room. By the 1940s, however, educators had begun to devise new theories about how to teach, and the purposes and content of education gradually became more elaborate and humane. Progressive educators saw that instructors might do better by sometimes teaching small groups, sometimes teaming up with other instructors, and sometimes asking students to carry out independent projects or collaborate with a number of classmates. Such variations suggested that the school and its spaces should be flexible, providing the teacher with an expansive open classroom one day and small areas another day, as needs shifted. Architects at CRS paid close attention to the new thinking among educators and discarded every custom and convention that seemed obsolete.

The firm tried to assimilate the most advanced thinking of the fields in which it was involved. Fortuitously, Rowlett had earned a joint degree in education and architecture at the University of Texas in Austin, and Caudill's MIT thesis project was a long-range plan for the schools in Stillwater, Oklahoma, so the two partners had a base of knowledge that helped prepare them for school design. In 1941, as a junior faculty member at A&M, Caudill wrote a 120-page booklet, *Space for Teaching,* which examined the conditions and needs of Texas' elementary schools. "We are building schools today that are obsolete before they leave the drafting board," he declared. "The majority of our schools are being designed without recognizing new methods of teaching, without analyzing community needs, and without considering economy."[7] Caudill further asserted: "The scope of the curriculum has broadened. 'Learning by doing' is replacing 'Learning by listening.' . . . Educators need modern structures, structures that are flexible enough to conform with the changing needs of education."[8]

The booklet was packed with documentation of Texas schools' deficiencies: Only two of every ten Texas elementary schools had modern toilet facilities. Only three of ten had adequate lighting. Only one out of seven had the five-acre or larger site that authorities deemed necessary. Caudill's booklet called for charting the community's growth patterns so that new schools would be the right size and in the right location and, if appropriate, would serve not only the children but also the community at large. Photographs and plans highlighted examples of the best recent schools throughout the nation. Caudill recommended arranging rooms, circulation, and seating so that teachers (implicitly understood to be progressive, nonauthoritarian educators) could carry out activity programs that would help youngsters learn. This forceful and authoritative publication from the Texas Engineering Experiment Station established Caudill's credentials in school design and laid the foundation for CRS's expertise.

"Caudill believed in information. He believed in communication," recalls Peña.[9] That faith propelled the firm and ultimately made CRS renowned for its ability to compile and succinctly summarize facts, trends, statistics, and recommendations. Caudill wrote constantly. He was good at it—phenomenally good by the standards of architects. Architects often write in a terse, jargon-ridden manner or, at the opposite extreme, fall into flowery expression. They do this in some cases because writing is not where their talent resides but, more crucially, because they view writing as something that does not matter much. For a visual person, what really counts is the drawing, the model, the building—not words on a sheet of paper. Caudill, by contrast, seemed to be both visually oriented and word oriented. He recognized that successful designs grow out of effective communication, and so he found ways of "hooking" the reader, making the reader want to find out what he was going to propose. In his hands, even that most mundane form of writing, the office memo, sparkled with originality.

Because Caudill revered research and because he recognized that buildings were becoming too complicated to be mastered by any one individual, he argued that architectural firms should have access to experts—either specialists on staff or experts who were available for consultation. He believed that architects with specialized talents should be sought out. In some instances, the firm would hire nonarchitects who were experts and place them in positions of responsibility on a par with members of the close-knit fraternity of architects.

Besides wanting contributions from experts, CRS avidly sought information from clients and users of the buildings it was designing. The firm welcomed suggestions from the grassroots. Long before such procedures were common, Caudill would meet with a group such as the local Parent-Teacher Association to solicit parents' ideas about how to design their new school.

After CRS conducted studies, the firm freely disseminated the results to other architecture firms and to people in relevant fields such as school administration or health care—giving away what it had invested much time and money to learn. Caudill and others at CRS realized that openness, which was common in the academic world but rare in business, burnished the firm's reputation. The firm's leaders wanted their staff members to be regarded as people who "knew their stuff." Publishing the firm's knowledge was also a good practice because it forced CRS to continue searching for new insights and techniques. This pushed the company toward the frontiers of knowledge, and helped the architectural profession move forward. Many of the innovations conceived or honed by CRS staffers have become common practices, in part because of the firm's insistence on sharing information.

The company was created at an opportune moment. World War II had lifted the country out of the long depression of the 1930s, and the economy continued to strengthen in the postwar years. The population was booming. Communities were expanding. Demand for schools, hospitals, and business and cultural facilities far outstripped the sluggish prewar pace of construction. As a result, opportunities blossomed for architects, especially those who could adapt to a newly vigorous mass market.

In the 1920s and 1930s, American architecture had principally been a small-scale, genteel enterprise. Men of good breeding—and a few privileged women—designed houses, churches, civic buildings, and other structures in their own community or region. Few architectural firms practiced nationally or grew to great size. The largest American architectural firm in the 1920s, Albert Kahn's office in Detroit, had two hundred to three hundred employees.[10] After World War II, however, tremendous undertakings proliferated. At CRS, the goal that evolved was to do good work for clients across the nation and eventually across the globe. The firm influenced entire categories of buildings, including schools, hospitals, hotels, commercial buildings, and performance halls.

None of CRS's leaders came from wealthy or powerful families. "Every one of us started from scratch," Scott observed. "Nobody had any backers. All of us had to work our way through college."[11] The very plainness of the founders' backgrounds helped them to respect rather than look down upon everyday problems and ordinary needs. They were enthusiastic about how their buildings would improve conditions for large numbers of people.

Caudill and his partners strongly believed in balance, and thought something was out of kilter if an architect created a handsome building but lost money on it. Caudill liked to say that the firm wanted "to produce good architecture, to make some money, and to have fun doing it." Such a philosophy helped CRS avoid being carried to extremes. The firm evaluated the success of projects by grading them on a three-part standard of function, form, and economy. Function referred to how well the building served its purposes. Form referred to whether the building had a satisfying shape, one that was appropriate to the site, the task, the desire for symbolic expression, and the potential of space. Caudill defined economy in his 1971 book *Architecture by Team* as "maximum effect with minimum means," a criterion frequently used by modernists.[12] In practice, economy was also understood in a less intellectual way: as construction without undue expense.

Central to the firm's approach was "architecture by team." Caudill viewed the firm as being made up of individuals with differing strengths and weaknesses. If they collaborated as a team, they would learn to maximize each person's strong points and avoid or control each person's weaknesses. The team concept did not come to fruition immediately. In the first few years, almost every partner imagined himself a designer. That, after all, was the creative, prestigious role, the one that was held up as the most important during a typical architectural education. In truth, however, some individuals were better designers than others. Of the eight partners in the firm in the mid-1950s, Charles Lawrence was, by general agreement, the best designer, and he ultimately became chief of design. Willie Peña left design to concentrate on specifications and color, and developed a national reputation in the psychology of color. Later, Peña became synonymous with programming, the field in which his national reputation endures. Tom Bullock gave up design to concentrate on management, becoming managing director in 1957, later president, and finally chairman of the Board of Directors. Wallie Scott specialized in design development. Gifted with the ability to put a school board or a group of hospital trustees at ease, he later shifted into sales. John Rowlett, who also got along well with people, concentrated on client relations.

The rudiments of the division of labor were devised in 1954 when Caudill, presiding over the firm from an office in Bryan (CRS had by then outgrown its office above the grocery store), realized that too many people were trying to do the same job. "None of us is a genius," he wrote. "But all of us working together can be a genius." Caudill himself sometimes designed, and loved doing it, but he was better at orchestrating the talents of others. That was the role he ended up playing most consistently. He coached, criticized, stimulated, and philosophized, bringing out the best in a diverse crew and getting them to operate as a team.

As CRS's work across the country grew, the firm devised procedures for partnering with local firms. During the rapid inflation of the 1970s, CRS saw that the speed with which projects were designed and constructed was becoming critically important. This was especially true of public projects, because it was often impossible to obtain a budget increase after a project was approved. The firm realized that through "fast-track" construction (a term attributed to CRS), crews could start laying a building's foundation while other construction details were being drawn up. It was not a comfortable process—the time available for any one operation was tight—but it brought substantial benefits for clients, enabling them to get more building for their money.

To counteract poor organization in the construction process, which came to be recognized as a serious problem in the 1960s, a new field called "construction management" came into being, and CRS entered that arena in 1971 by establishing CM, a subsidiary that provided construction management services. The subsidiary grew enormously, surpassing CRS's architectural activities in volume of business and profit.

In 1964, CRS was asked whether it would be interested in building a campus in Saudi Arabia. The firm had done master planning and design for campuses in the United States, beginning in 1959 with Ohio State, one of the largest universities in the country, but the Saudi Arabia opportunity made everything previous seem small. It was selected to design the College of Petroleum and Minerals (later the King Fahd University of Petroleum and Minerals) in Dhahran, near the Persian Gulf, an undertaking that took more than two decades in a harsh climate and an unfamiliar culture.

The firm's most lasting contribution to the architectural profession—aside from many good buildings—has been the discipline of programming. More than any other firm, CRS refined the procedures through which architects defined the problems each building was meant to solve. Its influence on architecture continues even though the firm itself is gone.

Much can be learned from CRS's history. That history is told mainly through the words of the disparate individuals in College Station, Houston, and CRS's other far-flung locations who made or carried out the decisions that put the firm at the forefront of the profession. Each chapter from 2 through 13 looks at a particular activity, period, or aspect of CRS—first with a brief introduction and then with edited interviews. Chapter 14, the conclusion, tells about the firm's dissolution and its place in American architecture.

■ CHAPTER 2

ABOVE THE GROCERY STORE

■ TIB: 17 APRIL 1964

When I was a boy my mother used to tell me that I could do anything I wanted to if I worked hard enough. At that time I was naive enough to believe it. . . . Today, as I look around and see what has happened to people I have known for years, including myself, I definitely believe that my mother was right. I do recognize that there is a great difference in talent and intellect. But I am convinced that a man can achieve most anything he wants to, even with limited talent, if he has the dedication and the motivation.

'Give me a motivated, dedicated person over a highly talented but not so industrious person any day. He'll make a better architect.'

■ The firm that became CRS got its start in March, 1946, when John Rowlett settled in Austin, Texas, and rented an office above an old grocery store at Lavaca and Fourteenth Streets, two blocks from the capitol. The quarters were fairly primitive. "It was an unpainted building and it leaned sideways," Rowlett recalled in a 1971 interview.[1]

Rowlett was a lieutenant junior grade in the navy, and William Caudill was a navy enlisted man (the military had rejected him for officers' training because of color blindness) when they first laid their plans while stationed in southern California during World War II. Neither Caudill, who was discharged

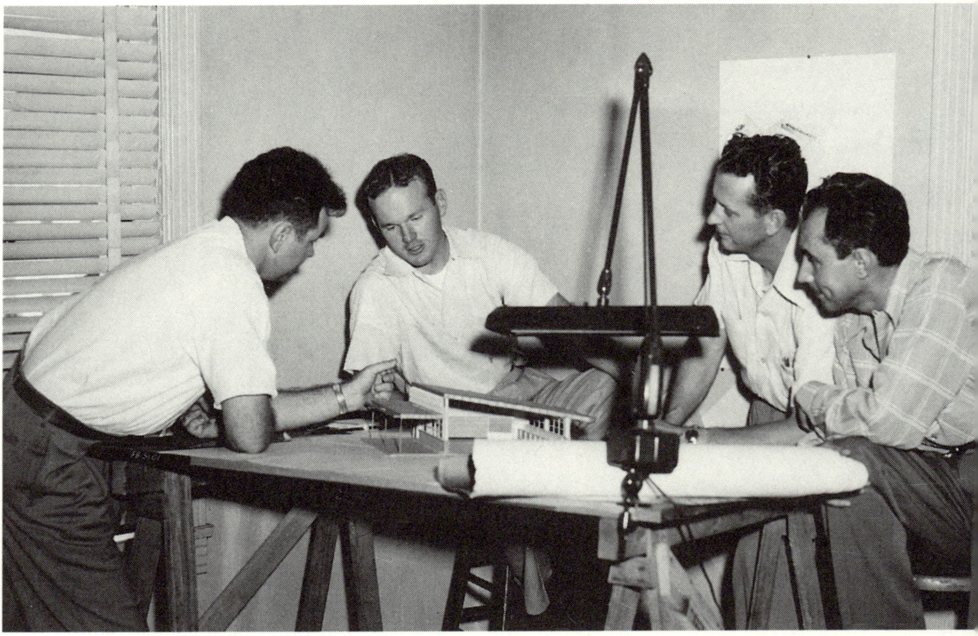

Gathered around a model of a typical classroom for a Blackwell, Oklahoma, elementary school are, *from left,* Bill Caudill, Wallie Scott, John Rowlett, and Willie Peña. This 1948 photo was taken in Caudill and Rowlett's walk-up office over a grocery store in College Station.

in the fall of 1945, nor Rowlett, who left the service early the following year, had any money to speak of when they were discharged. "Our total tackle at that time consisted of our combined mustering-out pay of $1,000," said Rowlett. The new firm, he added, "could not afford both of us, so I stayed in Austin and Bill went back to Texas A&M. . . . It was very rough those first nine months."

"During that time right after the war, the total interest in building had to do with small houses," Rowlett noted. "There were very few commissions available." What tided Rowlett over was a federal stipend for GIs who needed help while finding a place in the civilian economy. A $100 monthly stipend did not go far, even in 1946, but he stood in line to collect it for nine months. Despite the paucity of work, Rowlett's convictions about the right and wrong ways of earning a fee never seemed to waver. In Austin, when an opportunity arose to reap a windfall by drawing very simple plans and sketches of new houses for veterans, he refused to budge from what he saw as the proper, less lucrative way of practicing. "At that time there were thirty-five thousand applications and no one to draw the plans," Rowlett said. "I could draw three or four sketches a day at $50 each. It really made a lot of money. But we held to our ethical practice of a 6 percent fee with complete service. Our purpose was to starve rather than to take advantage of the situation." In retrospect, Rowlett observed, this outlook ultimately helped make CRS successful.

In Austin, Rowlett oversaw construction of the firm's first house, a modern, flat-roofed dwelling Caudill designed for the family of Fred Fenton, a local woodworker. But that job was not enough to keep the firm going, so by the end of the year Rowlett had closed the office and relocated to College Station, where teaching jobs were available at A&M for both himself and Caudill. Their minimal practice diminished to weekend work.

Caudill and Rowlett had taught together at A&M before the war, and they believed that it was better for their students if they were actively practicing their trade. So they never entirely gave up on their practice, and gradually began to get commissions, most of them for residential designs. In 1947, they invited Gordon McCutchan, another A&M instructor, to join them as a partner. Within a few months, McCutchan resigned to teach at Texas Tech University. His departure was, as Tom Bullock said years later, "a peaceful separation. He wasn't interested in business—just wanted to teach and did so for the rest of his life."[2] In 1948, the fledgling firm moved into a pair of second-floor rooms above a grocery store near the university's south gate. There they took in another new partner, Wallie E. Scott Jr., one of their former graduate students, who had just spent a year working in the office of the university architect. It was above the grocery store (since converted into a bookstore at what is now 340 George Bush Drive) that passionate talker Bill Caudill and modest but optimistic listener John Rowlett expanded the name of their firm to Caudill Rowlett and Scott.

Scott had a new car at the time, and it became part of the CRS tribal mythology that he was made a partner so Caudill and Rowlett would have a reliable vehicle for going to job interviews. Actually, Scott put $500 in the firm's coffers to become a partner. William Merriweather Peña, another of Caudill's former students, became the firm's first employee. When he was made a partner in 1949, Peña opposed expanding the firm's name to include his in it. Caudill Rowlett Scott "had a good ring," he said.[3] Besides, if the names of new partners kept being added, the firm's name might eventually be as long as a law firm's. It thus remained Caudill Rowlett Scott until it was abbreviated as CRS in the late 1950s.

A parade of people came into the firm in the 1950s—and in many instances went. Thomas A. Bullock, who had studied under Rowlett and

In 1948, Caudill and Rowlett operated from a pair of rooms in the second floor of this building near Texas A&M's south gate. *Photo courtesy Roland Chatham.*

Caudill at A&M, and Al Martin, a structural engineer, were made partners in 1954. Martin did not fit in well and was soon replaced by Edward F. Nye, also a structural engineer and an old friend of Caudill's from Oklahoma. Charles E. Lawrence became the seventh partner in 1958, followed by C. Herbert Paseur in 1961. Ultimately, eight partners came to be known as the "founders."

At first the architects accepted any commission they could get. They designed a shopping center, a grocery store, and a dental clinic. They drew up plans for tract houses in Oklahoma City. Mostly, they designed custom homes, a common assignment for young architects. (By 1950, Caudill and Rowlett had both turned thirty-five.) The custom homes that CRS created—one in Austin, followed by a series in Bryan and College Station—were distinctly modern.

The Fenton house, with its flat roof and full-height windows, drew from Caudill's knowledge of Frank Lloyd Wright, Richard Neutra, and Marcel Breuer. Some of their houses in Bryan and College Station had shallow pitched roofs suggesting Wright's influence, but the houses' feeling was, in the judgment of Jay Baker and Barrie Scardino, "consistently crisp, lightweight, and tectonic," similar to Neutra and Breuer's.[4] Attentive to sun, wind, and site, and appreciative of regional characteristics such as stone walls while eschewing the reproduction of traditional forms and details, the architects, in Baker and Scardino's judgment, "forged a convergence of modern and rural sensibilities." Drawings of the first two houses by Caudill and Rowlett appeared in an exhibition on contemporary architecture at the Dallas Museum in October, 1946. That same month, a house Caudill built in Bryan for his own family was presented in *Architectural Forum*—his first design to be featured in an architectural journal. Caudill referred to himself as the "Public Relations Department" and constantly sought to put the firm's work in the spotlight.

The firm soon began to emphasize educational facilities. Lack of money for construction during the depression and a shortage of steel during World War II, combined with the postwar baby boom, resulted in a growing demand for new schools. Carving out a specialty in this area amounted to a prescient marketing concept, but Caudill, the firm's intellectual and spiritual leader, needed little economic motivation to focus on that field; he had a deep interest in educational facilities. His *Space for Teaching*, published in 1941, had not brought him design work in the early forties, when money for school construction was scarce, but after the war the booklet found enthusiastic readers among educators.[5] As research architect for the Texas Engineering Experiment Station at A&M and professor in the architectural school, Caudill conducted highly practical investigations of subjects such as ventilation, natural illumination, movable furniture, outdoor circulation, and soundproofing. He produced useful approaches to common problems.

The high regard in which educators held *Space for Teaching* prompted the chairman of the Blackwell, Oklahoma, school board to call Caudill in 1948 and ask if he would be interested in designing a replacement for an

The Fenton House in Austin, Texas, in 1946, was the first Caudill and Rowlett project to be constructed. This elevation reveals a strong modernist influence.

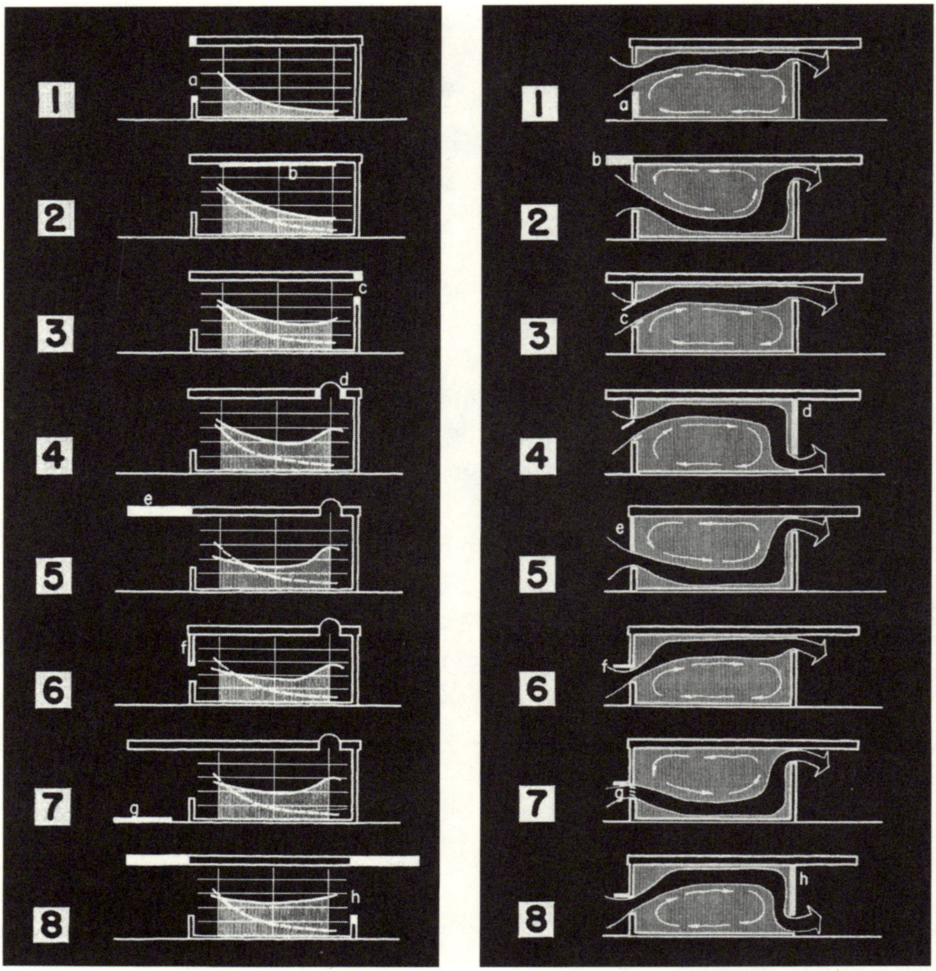

At Texas A&M, Caudill conducted extensive research aimed at more intelligent design of schools. The diagram at left summarizes findings on how light behaves in a classroom. The diagram at right shows circulation of air. Both appeared in Caudill's 1954 book, *Toward Better School Design.*

obsolete elementary school in that town. By the time the project was completed in 1949, a tornado had destroyed another Blackwell elementary school, so Caudill Rowlett Scott ended up designing not one but two schools for that community of ten thousand. The following year, architectural journalist Walter McQuade was looking for innovative new schools to write about for the popular magazine *Collier's*. McQuade knew of the prowess of Perkins and Will, the Chicago architectural firm that had designed the innovative

Crow Island School in Winnetka, Illinois, in association with Eliel and Eero Saarinen a decade earlier. But a feature about a gregarious small-town architect and the pair of modern schools he designed for a town in Oklahoma's wheat belt? That would be an even better story. McQuade's "The Little Red Schoolhouse Goes Modern" gave CRS national exposure.

Modern architecture was being constructed in a number of cities across the country, but it was unusual for modernism to be embraced in remote locales far removed from the nation's cultural and corporate centers. Caudill succeeded in establishing modern architecture in distant places because he was adept at leading rural and small-town school board members through the intimidating process of planning and design. The ranchers, farmers, mechanics, and others who served on school boards knew little about architecture and less about modernism, so Caudill persuaded them to think about what the teachers and students needed: comfortable rooms with breezes dissipating the stuffy air; sunlight tempered by overhangs to keep glare out of children's eyes; movable desks for flexibility; play areas close by. At the outset, many rural school board members "didn't know how to read plans," Peña pointed out. "Bill taught them. He would show them the ductwork, the mechanicals, the electrical on different sheets, in diagram form. Then he would put them all together. And this farmer would say, 'My God, I can read blueprints!'"[6]

"Good communication helped make decisions," Peña noted. In the *Collier's* article, McQuade said of Caudill's tremendous expressiveness: "When he talks, he's very convincing, leaning forward eagerly, waving his hands, rubbing the back of his curly hair, talking fluently about 'logical' schools."[7] Caudill had a strong dislike for monumental old schools, and in rural areas he usually did not have to worry that board members would insist on a look or style that he considered inappropriate. "Our farmers didn't have a tradition," Peña observed. "They wanted a school to work as a school, not as a bank."[8]

The firm's triumphs in places like Blackwell were examples of fresh, functional modern architecture winning acceptance in ordinary places, among unlettered people. If the Blackwell schools lacked the solemnity of early twentieth century schools, if they were short on the dignified civic expression found in the best of the symmetrical old schools with their echoes of classicism, the new schools exuded an informality and functionalism that increasingly appealed to Americans. Caudill said traditional forms lacked logic, a view he shared with many of the architects of his time. Certainly the old forms did not work well for everyday purposes anymore, and they were costly—expensive enough that they could not be built on a mass basis for millions of children crowding into an ever more democratic educational system. The period of the old forms had passed and would not return in a major way until the 1980s, when postmodernists, historic preservationists, and scholars such as Yale's Vincent Scully attempted to bring them back. In the 1930s, forties, and fifties, traditional architecture looked more and more obsolete to people who were in the know. Peña notes that students hated the Beaux Arts mode of design, which continued to be taught at A&M into the 1940s, because it "was like going to a fancy dress ball" instead of tackling real problems.[9] Caudill Rowlett Scott was interested in "real problems," in getting things done, and the firm propagated a cost-effective, functional way of addressing a critical need: more schools. A trade-off—less grandeur, detail, and traditional civic expression but more comfort, economy, and functional performance—was becoming characteristic of postwar life. The firm embraced architecture's and the nation's new priorities and sought to produce buildings that would be as pleasing as the "lean and clean" strictures of modernist esthetics would allow.

Proximity to A&M was helpful to CRS in the early years. The partners who taught got to know talented students, and offered them part-time jobs at CRS while they were in school and full-time positions with the firm after graduation. The principals also gained opportunities to keep up with the academic side of architecture and with research. Caudill held research in high esteem, viewing it as crucial for the field's advancement. However, few architectural commissions were available in A&M's vicinity, so the firm's staff spent a considerable amount of time on the road.

Beginning early in its history, CRS devoted much attention to defining the user's needs, to programming. Caudill and Peña quickly separated programming from design, and swiftly made a distinction between problem seeking and problem solving. Unlike most architects in the late forties and early fifties, they recognized that programming and design were two distinct phases of architecture, one preparing the way for the other. It took a while longer for the concepts of employing specialists and of working through teams to be fully developed, both theoretically and operationally. But those ideas were part of the CRS ethos from day one. The concept of teamwork in architecture was not unique to CRS, but it was practiced more vigorously and preached more ardently there than in any other firm. "Architecture by team" was Caudill's big idea, substituting the team as genius for the mystique of the architect/genius/hero.

The firm's first four partners ***(left to right):*** **Caudill, Rowlett, Scott, and Peña, in 1953.**
Photo courtesy Roland Chatham.

INTERVIEWS

TOM BULLOCK

Wallie and I met in 1942. We played in the Aggieland Orchestra and all that kind of stuff. I came back to A&M after the war and decided I needed a little more income to get through architecture. I had taken civil engineering prior to the war. After the war, I changed over to architecture, and it was taking longer to get out. Also, Jane and I married in May, '47, and our first child, Tom, arrived in December, '48. So I applied for a job. Wallie wouldn't hire me, but John did, and I went to work as a part-timer like so many others did over the grocery store in 1948. In '49, I taught sophomore year in the school. I graduated in '49, but I also taught that year because I had an earlier degree. I went full-time at CRS in 1950. I've been in CRS ever since. . . . [He retired in 1989 as chairman.]

'THE LITTLE RED SCHOOLHOUSE GOES MODERN'

When Bill Caudill produced sketches of the new school he was proposing for the small town of Blackwell, Oklahoma, some of the local people reacted skeptically at first. But they were no match for a genial man who had grown up in surroundings much like their own. According to journalist Walter McQuade, in *Collier's*, this is the scene that ensued when Caudill unrolled the drawings in Blackwell:[1]

One board member gasped : "But Bill, that looks like a cow shed."

"No, it's a chicken coop," another member corrected him.

Caudill smiled. "Well now," he drawled, "it does bear some resemblance to a cow shed, doesn't it? And a chicken house, too. But let's see why."

He and his partners had designed a basic school unit, a long shedlike line of classrooms with windows on both sides. The roof was high on one side and low on the other, with a slanted ceiling inside. There was a substantial overhang on the low side, to shield direct sun, and the sound-absorbing ceiling sloped up to more windows on the high side. Up there was a series of fixed louvers like Venetian blinds to keep the hot bright sun out, but reflect plenty of light inside. The classrooms had areas of bright, warm colors, and there was no ominous blackboard; green chalkboards were used instead. There was no plastering; where brick walls occurred they were left plain.

Caudill lifted the roof off the small model of a classroom he had brought along and showed how the ventilation would work. He had put the model in a wind tunnel, and tested it by blowing smoke through, so he knew. It was designed to move two currents of air through, one across the slope of the ceiling to take out hot air which accumulates there, another current at desk level, to cool the children in hot months. . . .

Caudill was telling them about the radiant heating pipes built into the floor, when there was another gasp. "But where are the halls?"

"There aren't any; this is a hall-less school."

"Well, how do the kids get to the toilet?"

Caudill pointed to the plan. There was an outdoor corridor down the high side of the long shed, sheltered by an overhead canopy. The boys' and girls' toilets were both down at the end of each wing. The first-grade classrooms had toilets attached, and there was a sink in every classroom.

These outdoor corridors were a hard blow for the school board to take.

Of course Caudill had an answer to criticism of the outdoor corridors, just as he had an answer to every other objection his small-town critics could muster. How could you defeat a man who had tested his ventilation theories in a wind tunnel, who had taken the time to reflect on the physiological and psychological needs of children, who had provided a number of unexpected amenities (such as a big covered outdoor area for children's play and community parties), and who had calculated that if you wanted all these good things, you couldn't afford the Classical trappings associated with a thick, monumental, multi-story school?

McQuade concluded the story of how Blackwell reacted to the school by reporting, "When the meeting was over, the Board of Education of Blackwell was not only convinced but enthusiastic. 'You know, it still does look like a cow shed,' the original objector said as they broke up. 'But it sure is a damn-fine-looking cow shed.'"

[1]Walter McQuade, "The Little Red School Goes Modern," *Collier's*

Washington Elementary School in Blackwell, Oklahoma, 1950. *Photo courtesy Julius Shulman.*

Huston Elementary School in Blackwell, Oklahoma, 1950. *Photo courtesy Julius Shulman.*

We can say I was either fifth or sixth [to be elected partner]. I'll take fifth because the other person was Al Martin. Both of us were elected the same year—1954. He was a structural engineer in Bryan. I believe he stayed two years and left in 1956. At that time, Ed Nye was brought in. Now, Ed was a former classmate of Bill Caudill's at Oklahoma A&M. At that time, he was an engineer with Costen Frankford and Short in Oklahoma. That's the firm that Ed Romieniec worked for—again, Ed Romieniec weaves himself in and out of the firm's history.[10] And when Al left, it left us with a void, so Bill called up Ed Nye. I think he made him a partner on the phone. . . . We flew pretty high and fast in those days. That's how Bill managed the firm, but we all became—we were really business partners and business teams and all that; socially, yes, but not so much so. Architecture was our social business, and that's what it was—night and day, the whole thing.

In the beginning, only two people actually operated it [the firm]. There was a third person who was never a partner: John F. Y. Stambaugh, an accountant from Tulsa, Oklahoma. He was a high school classmate of Bill Caudill's and became an adviser to CRS through the '50s, '60s, '70s, and the early '80s. In the very beginning, Bill wanted him to become a partner/business manager, but there just wasn't enough business for that. Correspondence in the files indicates that John helped advise him on even the idea of Bill's going into partnership with John Rowlett. Stambaugh was really there before John Rowlett. I talked with John the other day and said, "John, it dawned on me that this CRSS is not CRS Sirrine—it's Caudill Rowlett Scott and Stambaugh."

[Stambaugh] lives in Tulsa. . . . He would have a completely different point of view on what we're talking about now, but it was all tied together, and I still think he probably made us what we are. He encouraged us to move to Houston, encouraged the business practices—all that kind of stuff. I doubt those two very fine architects would ever have done that on their own. . . .

What Bill and John [Rowlett] were looking for were the different talents that would support their strengths and weaknesses. And by recognizing the weaknesses early, they were lucky. I will say this, though. I think, up to about 1955–56, we really didn't recognize our weaknesses. We all thought we could do design and everything—we were stepping on toes. It was about 1955 that Bill and John Stambaugh recognized there needed to be some management of the company. . . .

I think the important decision was made in '46. The next important one was [in] '48, when they decided to reestablish after going out of business in Austin and reestablished over the Southside Grocery in College

Station—the office that stayed in business until the move to Bryan. When you look at the big picture, the move to Bryan was incidental. [Establishing the] Oklahoma City office [was] incidental. From the business of architecture point of view, going to a corporate form of business that operated for the partnership was a real breakthrough. All of a sudden, we had partners, but we also had two hats; we had vice presidents and the corporate form. It made us more responsible, I think, for the business side as well as the design side. That would have been 1957. . . .

In 1957, two things happened. Caudill decided to move to Corning, New York, to be in charge of the school building program. It was a big one for us then—I believe it was a $10 million program. Half of it was a community college; the rest was high schools. That left openings in the Bryan office because Bill was the head of it all at that time. When he went off, it created some vacancies and allowed more opportunity for others. In 1958, we moved to Houston. It was a big change. There were forty-two people there, including families, overnight.

HERB PASEUR

Okay. In the beginning, I'm a graduate of Oklahoma State University, 1954—a late start. I didn't start until I was twenty-five or twenty-six. In the '50s, CRS started its practice in Oklahoma with schools at Blackwell and Stillwater. As a result of those early schools, they got a lot of publicity. As a young student, I spent a lot of time reading architectural magazines, and it [CRS] was one of the few firms in the Southwest that seemed to be doing things. I also had a prof whose name was Ed Romieniec. I spent two or three years with Ed at OSU, and I think he went on to Illinois before returning to Oklahoma—I know he wasn't there the whole time I was there. Anyway, I got out of school, and I decided to go back home to Memphis. . . . where I worked for Al Aydelott, one of the better architects in that part of the country. Ed Romieniec came back to Oklahoma City. We were good friends (most of Ed's students were); we had stayed in touch. My daughter was having a problem with asthma, and I wanted to get back to a dry climate, so I told Ed I wanted to come back, probably to Oklahoma or Arizona. . . .

I had no intention of going to work for anybody except CRS if I went to Oklahoma. I went to Oklahoma City at my own expense—stayed with Ed and interviewed Costen, then went over to CRS. It was then I met Tom Bullock for the first time, and John Rowlett. It was a small office—probably five or six people. This was in April, '55; the total firm was probably about fifteen then. They had an opening for a designer, so I was very interested in the job—had examples of my work—and I think Tom and John were interested in me, too—that's what they said. They couldn't offer me a job because they didn't have the authority. They had to go back to the board of directors to gain that authority to hire someone.

About a month or so later, I was notified I had been hired and to report to Oklahoma City as soon as possible. I was married—one kid and a pregnant wife—so I loaded up the old U-Haul and came to Oklahoma City. As I remember, I started work on Memorial Day, a holiday. Hasn't changed much since.

Anyway, Tom hired me for the princely sum of $400 a month. He had just written a letter—don't know what he said in it—that prompted John Rowlett to write Caudill regarding Tom's salary. . . . Tom was about to quit because he couldn't live on what he was making. I think he was making like $500 or $600 a month. Anyway, Tom got a raise because of that and then turned around and hired me at $100 *less* than he could live on himself! I still kid him about that.

So that's where it started. At that time in Oklahoma, the firm was getting a lot of small school projects. Tom and John were the partners in charge of the projects. I ended up doing the design on most of them. The first one I did was in Elk City, then a new school in Blackwell. We were successful in growing the office—probably doubled or tripled the size to ten or twelve people. We were working pretty closely with Bryan [then the principal office of CRS] about that time—not everybody in Bryan, but we'd see a lot of Caudill. I was pushing for more integration of design because I really wanted to work with guys like Frank Lawyer and "Tiny" Lawrence and get rub-off from them. It happened very seldom that there was any crosspollination of design between the two offices, and that was a big disappointment to me. All I could think of was "one firm, two locations" instead of separate groups.

Things really began to happen in '57. Bill went to New York, and that created a lot of opportunities in the firm. He took with him two key people, Charlie Estes and Frank Lawyer, and that created more opportunities. Tom started getting involved in the total firm operations then. I guess it was in '58 or so that he moved back to Bryan and became managing partner of the entire firm. The Oklahoma City office continued to expand and was doing very well with new projects in Nebraska and Colorado—first time we had broken out of Oklahoma.

Probably the last project I did on which I was designer of record was the Stillwater High School. It was a unique opportunity because Bill's thesis at MIT had been a Stillwater school, and part of that thesis was side swept into a number of different projects that were to be built in the future. One of them was that high school. Then, in my senior year in school, they had a nine-hour course in design and design development. You took the project through the design phase into design development. The assignment was the Stillwater school—built on the same site Bill had selected in '38.

To make a long story short, in 1957 or '58, they decided to build that school and hired CRS and Phil Wilber, who was the university architect. He was our associate on the Stillwater work. So we designed and built the Stillwater High School, the last design project I did. I had spent time in Bryan and in the New York office and did have an opportunity to work with Lawyer, Bill, and Tiny, and the young hotshots they were hiring at A&M for part-time work, like Paul Kennon and Chartier Newton.

I realized that design came a hell of a lot harder to me than it did to them—that I had to work a lot harder to get a good solution than they did. At the same time, I recognized that I had some organizational talents that didn't seem to be too apparent anywhere else in the firm. I realized I was probably going to be a better manager than designer, so [I] began to position myself that way. When I moved to Houston in '59, we had really just started to get successful in national practice. In the summer of '59 we were successful in getting schools in Saginaw, Michigan, [and] a community college in western Colorado. I was involved in the promotion of all those projects and was presented to the client as "their man"—project manager or project architect, whatever you want to call it.

Q: About the other partners . . . ?

A: Caudill was design, but he was design from more of a research standpoint. He wasn't a pure designer as such; he was a great design leader. He didn't really do very many projects, but he influenced all of them. Rowlett was purely promotion; a job getter, marketer—he developed into that. Scott started out in management, but he gravitated toward job getting, too, and did a tremendous job. Peña, of course, was programming through and through. Tom was management and promotion. Lawrence was strictly design.

Q: What kept it from falling apart?

A: It was joint insecurity: if we didn't have each other, we probably didn't have anybody. That's one of the things that kept us together. We all came up during the depression. Later generations didn't know you could have something and lose it. We *knew* you could lose it because we'd been through that. So that kept us together, too. Also, I think diverse interests kept us together. . . .

I think we had a great leader: Caudill. Without Caudill, I don't think it could have happened. He was the kind of guy who could make things happen and then get out of the way and stay out of the way. That's unusual. He was the great orchestrator—even when he went to Rice [Caudill served as director of the School of Architecture at Rice University from 1961–69 and as William Ward Watkins Professor from 1969–71], we still felt he was involved. That created opportunities that didn't exist before. I really think that's been one of the motivators right there.

ED NYE

I was working in Oklahoma City when Bill Caudill and Willie Peña flew up there in Bill's airplane—landed about two miles from my house northwest of Oklahoma City. They wanted me to come down to Houston—or College Station then—as a partner. I was an associate in my firm in Oklahoma City, so that was a pretty good start as far as I was concerned. They assigned me the structures on the San Angelo High School while I was still up there, so I did most of the structures on that high school before I came to Texas.

Bill Caudill was three years behind me at Oklahoma A&M. I finished in '34, and he finished in '37. We were both working together up there in '37. I went back after being in Texas for a while to Stillwater and worked for Mr. Wilber. Mr. Wilber was head of the Department of Architecture at the college. We did drafting, designing, and inspection for campus buildings. I became the inspector for Gallagher Hall. Bill was a draftsman there, working on the campus, and we played tennis every morning during the summer. [We] had to do it before daylight because [we] couldn't get a court if we didn't—they only had five courts then. We'd meet every morning, play tennis, and then go on to work. We struck up a pretty good friendship while we were there. He was a freshman, and I was a junior, so we knew each other. He had called me a couple of times in about 1952–53, [and said], "Come on to Texas and join us here." But I told him, "I'm satisfied up here and doing fine." But when he and Willie came the fourth time, I couldn't resist them. . . .

When we came down here [to Bryan–College Station], my wife came with me to find a place to live. We couldn't find a place. All the good housing was occupied. She said this seemed like a "jumping off" place. But after living here three years, we went on to Houston, and she said, "You know, I hate to leave this place." . . .

The cooperation between architects and engineers is unusual in this firm. Sometimes [in other firms] when time is running out and we're getting serious and ready to work, they [architects] say, "Hey, hold it up." That's not as satisfactory as working together from the beginning, for that makes for a better solution and better feeling all around—a feeling of participation. . . . That's one of the greatest things I learned. It's glue, you might say, that pulls everyone and the project together. You feel that they are expected to be there for you, and you cooperate with the operation—not like a dictator at the top. I remember very well that some of the engineers felt like we ought to have a separate group; that there ought to be a CRS Engineers, Incorporated. I was against that and felt that we worked closely with architects and ought to stay in the same organization.

We'd research certain types of structures, say domes. We would see what would work: wood arches or steel dome, barrel domes. That was our research: to see what was feasible. I remember one time in San Angelo one of the board members just insisted that we use laminated arches in the gymnasium. He had a friend who had one done that way, and it was successful. We almost came to blows about the fact we didn't want to use wood out there. We used steel instead. Once, he invited Bill Caudill to come outside and settle the matter. At a subsequent meeting, Bill asked me to come with him [because] he thought I could whip the man if it came to that. Actually, I believe I could have whipped him—I was a lot bigger than him.

TOM BULLOCK

So let's start with highs and lows. . . . I tried not to make it personal, but [I] can't help but do that. Mainly, it's what I see as the highs and lows of *my* involvement, which had to do with CRS. One of the very high highs . . . was getting the contract for Norman High School [in] Norman, Oklahoma, which at that time was an exceptional job for a very young firm. The office was probably about two and a half years old—being part-time on the part of Caudill and Rowlett; being full-time on the part of Scott and Peña—over the grocery store. Bill, at that time, was traveling around the country speaking about schools. He was speaking more as the educator to the school administration and teachers than as an architect, and that was the key to marketing in the early days. John was doing some of that, too, and teaching at A&M.

Bill was also spending an awful lot of time with architects who were well known through the history of their practices—either their father's practice or their own startup practice after World War II. We all know there were very few new buildings being built before World War II. Bill and John saw the pent-up demand for schools coming. You remember we talked about *Space for Teaching,* the research booklet published here at A&M that Bill put together. That paved the way for recognition as a school architect without ever building a building. School architects were John Lyon Reid,[11] Larry Perkins of Perkins and Will,[12] Alonzo Harriman[13] of Maine—I'm probably leaving some out. They were the prime ones Bill met with periodically, and he met them through AIA committee activity. I think in that day they called it the School Committee of the AIA (it was really about school design)—a wonderful place for young architects to get together and eliminate competition. They talked really vocally about what they thought school design should be. So Bill got his start there.

He met nonarchitects through that committee like Dr. Walter Cocking, who was the publisher and editor of *The School Executive* magazine, which became a bible for educators and later architects who had their work published in that magazine. So it was an outlet for publications. Bill was strong in his desire to publicize his thoughts and the firm's activity. Through these sorts of relationships, Bill became the young architect with really revolutionary ideas on what school design should be: everything from structure of the actual fabric of the building to the planning of the building. Buildings had been built, more or less, to force programs within them with thick masonry walls—weren't flexible, not expandable. Bill reversed that. He wasn't the only one, but I think Bill became the guy that led in the school business. Light, steel frame buildings that could be expandable—that was unheard of in those days. Partitions that would move, partitions that were teaching walls as well as privacy walls—these things were talked about at these meetings.

JOHN STAMBAUGH

Bill and I went to grade school together in Oklahoma City—fifth, sixth grades—and played on the softball team together. Then we went to junior high and high school together. Our closeness developed around the band/orchestra activities, which were pretty substantial in high school. We played in the band, then the orchestra. We both made all-state orchestra and band. We had a small dance band—actually, six to eight pieces, maybe ten; it varied at times. And we played in the auditorium at noon—all the kids would gather around. We were famous for that.

Dr. Walter Cocking, *third from left,* an influential admirer of CRS's work on schools, presents *The School Executive* Award to CRS for the Will Rogers Elementary School in Stillwater, Oklahoma, about 1951. With Cocking are, *from left,* Bill Caudill, the Stillwater Schools Superintendent, and Willie Peña.

We went to church together every Wednesday night, every Sunday morning, every Sunday night. We skated from Bill's house to the church—four of us. And the four—what we called the "Big Four"—were James McCord, Jay Warner, Bill, and me. We studied together. We would meet on Sunday afternoons and study till we got our work done—principally math, but some others. We did everything together. He [Bill] was a good student; a leader [who was] highly regarded by the student body. One year, all four of us ran for senior class offices—president, vice president; four positions. Bill ran for president. He didn't get elected, but he was very popular, very dynamic—a strong leader. He and I were closer than the other two were.

Q: Tell me about Bill Caudill's speech impediment.

A: When I first knew him, he stammered. I remember in high school, he'd get up and was embarrassed that he couldn't get the words out. But instead of holding him back, it challenged him. He'd get up at the slightest provocation.

He was a man of great courage. He was a speaker without the real ability to speak—a real handicap in most people's eyes, but not for Bill. . . .

He went to OSU and I went to OU, but I went up to OSU at his invitation quite a few times. I'm not sure when he got married to Edith, but I was Bill's best man in that wedding. We kept in constant contact with each other. Then he moved to College Station and prevailed upon me, and the next year, I moved to Houston.

I didn't meet John [Rowlett] until after the war. Bill and I corresponded all through the war on a more or less consistent basis, and I have most of those letters. Bill and I were together when Pearl Harbor came, and we decided we'd go down and join the navy. We both went down, joined the navy, and he was refused because he was color-blind, supposedly. I passed, and I was in the navy. But he joined later as an enlisted man, so we were both in the navy, but not together.

During the latter part of the war, Bill and I corresponded about plans for after the war. We had some plans to join each other. I would practice public accounting and look after the books and records of the architectural firm. Then he mentioned along the way there was a fellow by the name of John Rowlett he had become acquainted with [and] thought highly of, and we talked about how that would work.

I said, "Bill, if you think well of him, I'm sure I will." So we planned to start in Austin initially. I went to Austin, looked over the situation, and they had a little work—which I think John might have developed. I decided a practice in public accounting in Austin was not really my challenge at that point. In effect, I told Bill I would look after things as best I could but that I would probably—and it developed [that] I did—go to Tulsa to go into public accounting. . . . [I] started a firm here; part of a national firm. Bill planned to teach and practice, and he was going to teach in College Station.

Our plan for doing things together was that I would look after things as best I could. I set up the books and records. I told them early I felt they were all like artists—you know, how long does it take to draw a picture? We've got to control our time. When you've got a fixed contract, [the] first thing you do is allocate the profit part of it—25 to 40 percent—take that out, and then determine how many hours are left. We used an overhead rate—not sure what that was, but we estimated high so there would be some safety to it. We developed from the fee minus the profit back to the cost we could have. I really put a lot of effort into trying to get them to conform to that formula.

CRS was incorporated early on. It was strictly for tax [purposes] at that point.... At that time, no architectural firm was incorporated to our knowledge. There was some question as to whether it was ethical to do that.

I believe if I made much of a contribution, it was at the front end, setting up the concept that this is a profitable organization. Time on these jobs was difficult to control. If you didn't give tremendous attention to it on the front end, you would end up not making money. I think that was important. And, of course, saving the tax was important—and being incorporated. The early philosophy—on which I had some influence, I'm sure—was to build the capital of the firm, not pay everything out to the partners. Wallie wanted it all in his hands. He said, "If my share is 20 percent, I want my 20 percent now, not later." But we prevailed, and most of the money stayed in—some bonuses but not much—and we built capital. That was our strength. Not taking the money out [and] letting it stay there was basic, and everybody saw the wisdom of it. I think everybody there wanted to stay with the entity. They had no thoughts of going out on their own. I don't remember anybody ever threatening to go out on their own. They all felt they were part of something that was growing [and] had great opportunity, [as well as a] great leader—Bill at that time, [and] later Tom and Herb.

Q: Discuss the arrangement under which CRS ownership shares would be reexamined and changed annually depending on the partners' evaluations of the value and effectiveness of each other's professional performance during the previous year.

A: The firm changed the share ownership on an annual basis, which is very novel, you know—a unique thing. For these people to speak to each other after those meetings, it was a sensitive thing. Some were constantly moving upward, and some were stagnant. John [Rowlett], for instance, stagnated some—got to a point where he wasn't getting increases in relationship to others....

The corporation was a good vehicle because it was a way to deal out feelings. [It] wasn't just theoretical; it was practical—actually divvying up ownership on an annual basis. The closeness of the individuals and the fact they had no intention of leaving—I never felt anybody was going to leave. We were just trying to get the most out of everybody.

They were also accumulating their estates, which was important to each. I felt it was important for me to not only look at the firm's prosperity, but each of the people's prosperity. One thing I did was to see that they had wills and plans in the event anything happened—life insurance. I reviewed their plans [and] directed them to an attorney. That was way back at the beginning. All that may not have showed in CRS, but it showed in the individuals that were CRS. . . .

We forecast twelve months out front. We may have forecasted beyond that—I don't specifically remember it. I know we were concerned about the future. We talked at some point about computers, and it became an important thing. We were so excited about it, we thought about going public with it. Actually, it [the computer group] wasn't that exciting to the underwriters, but CRS was exciting to the underwriters. Going public was a big step.

Q: Regarding the move to Houston . . . ?

A: In the early days, transportation was by private plane. [That was] dangerous, having the key people fly together—or fly individually, for that matter. Commercial flights came into College Station, but certainly not like they do into Dallas or Houston. The image of the firm as a small-town architect, some felt, might keep them from being considered [for big city jobs]. Also, there were other advantages of location in a larger community. Local business was a consideration. In my mind, the move was a necessity. Tom shared my feeling. Tom and I combined with Bill are more effective than either one of us without him, and we prevailed on him to agree, which he did. He never was against it—just not for it. The question of Houston or Dallas came up. I didn't favor one over the other, except that Houston was a port with international significance.

TOM BULLOCK

The next big change, to me, was all through the '60s: growth. But we decided in '69, '70 to start planning for expansion beyond what we ever expected to do. Our projects were getting larger, more complex, and the idea at that time was to consider becoming a public corporation. That was 1971.

Herb and I were the ones that worked together on that. I give Herb credit, though, for pushing it. All were concerned, because in 1969 there were moves by several businesses—including Westinghouse and several others—to move into the educational facilities business. And we were visited by the president of Westinghouse. It opened our eyes: If they were interested in us—and [they] were at that time—then, my goodness, maybe we could do it ourselves. So we decided to do it ourselves at the end of 1971. Herb took the lead on that. That's when Herb and I separated from the architectural business. As Herb would say today, "Tom and I created our own positions."

Let me tell you about Paseur. My relationship with Paseur started in 1955. He had been a student of Ed Romieniec's at Oklahoma State. At that time, we had about forty-five people in the Oklahoma City office, and I was responsible to John Rowlett for interviewing people to work. Ed told me about this fellow Paseur who was a good designer—in fact, a very good one. And after two interviews—to which he had to drive all the way from Memphis on his own—and after even a partnership meeting to decide if we could hire *anybody,* we hired him as a designer in the Oklahoma City office. He was very good at that, but he was better at client relations. [He] kind of took care of project management and project services in Oklahoma.

Later, he moved to Houston and became a partner in 1961. We were still making associate partners out of key people up to about 1970, I guess, when we turned more and more to the corporate form. And we went public after that—knocked the partnership out for anything but signing contracts. And Herb became so good at what he was doing that in 1965, I believe it was, I had the job of running the company for almost ten years. I think we called it managing director at that time, and we had a separate title of president. I held onto that title. Bill was chairman, and Herb became executive vice president and also managing director. So he ran the company—the partnership—from 1965 to 1971 and became the president of the public corporation in 1971. Architects *can* change from the traditional "design is everything" to "business is everything." He stayed on the job as president of CRS—the public corporation, which we called CRS Design Associates—and retired in 1981. [Herb was] . . . a perfect complementary partner to myself. We worked together the last ten years of his time very close. . . .

Bill Caudill and John [Rowlett] obviously had the same vision. They wanted to do architecture, and to do architecture, they had to find a *way* to do it. Working together, I guess, was the first team—with John teaching to support the office in Austin. He was going out and getting work in Austin while Bill was teaching at A&M. They proved very resourceful in trying to keep the office going.

It wasn't really schools at first. It was anything they could get. Bill was the design concept guy, and John . . . would do the working drawings and supervise the office. Bill was my prof; so was John. I can't say too much about them. They both inspired me greatly in different ways. John was a quiet leader. Bill was a ranting, raving "get-yourself-off-your-butt-and-get-the-job-done" type—and you did. You remember that forever, and you thank him for it.

Let me say this: In the very beginning, CRS started making money, started growing the business on publications—[they were] very conscious of the need to publicize. "Publish or perish," to you people in the educational field. Bill had done *Space for Teaching,* a booklet on schools for the Texas Engineering Experiment Station [TEES], before the war, and he promoted that. So they became known as school specialists through that book. They also did what you might call complimentary sketches. That was really what the book was all about: "Don't build a building and push the program into it—make the building fit the program."

It started at A&M and started with research. There's no question in my mind that, to the very last, Bill was interested in research more than what you would call building design. Bill was a planner—he was a designer; he was a researcher—and that's where it all started.

John was just everybody's friend. [A] great teacher. See, I had a very special relationship with John. He put me to work over the grocery store in June, 1948. I was the one who went to Oklahoma City with him, and we were together for five years. . . .

Bill and John—in the need for capital, in the need for work and talent—brought in Wallie Scott. Wallie used to say, "Yes, because I had $500." They brought Wallie in because Wallie was the outstanding design student. They were looking for quality and [they] were also looking for human beings. They found Willie Peña, too: Another fine student who had come back from the war. From the very beginning, Willie was related to such things as planning prior to design, survey of a school district prior to design. To this day, he gets excited any time a designer comes in and says, "I'm ready to go." He says, "You're not ready to go yet. You can't draw those pictures until *I* say you can because we've got to find some facts about them—the problem areas."

Later, when Bill went to Corning, New York, and left a void in Bryan, all of a sudden there was an opening for a managing partner. I was in Oklahoma, and Willie Peña and Tom Bullock became the nominees. I wasn't at first, and I remember calling Bill and saying, "Put my name on the list, Bill—I'd like to do it." And he said, "You'll have to move to Bryan." I said, "I'll do that, and I'll tell Jane later." I think I won by one vote, so I became the managing partner.

The first partnership meeting I ever went to was in 1954. John and I flew down from Oklahoma to the Bryan office, and they passed out pieces of paper on which you rated everybody but yourself on performance that year. The result would be the amount of ownership you would have for the next year. The ownership was never locked in, never frozen. It allowed opportunity for new people, new blood, to come in and participate and contribute. I think the original partners always felt it would be wrong to keep the pie the same size, for then the pieces would have to remain the same. The pie had to get bigger, so that idea was in their minds from the very beginning. Whether it was something they could define or not, I couldn't say.

I remember in several management meetings through the years I'd use that example with executives in other businesses. They'd say, "What did you say?" Well, we did it, and when they would observe that was rather a hard thing to do, I'd tell them it was traumatic. I remember one year there was almost a tear shed by one partner, but you know, that's what we did.

It was John Stambaugh who collected those pieces of paper and gave us the results. It gave a Herb Paseur a chance to pass up a Tom Bullock. From my perspective, that made the company. For somebody who was there earlier it might not have, but it did. It was John Stambaugh who started this.

Another thing the originals always pushed was growth and profit—business, making money. Bill would say, "We've got to do good architecture and good business at the same time." He'd use the word *good* rather than *great*—"Can't do one without the other."

Including Paseur, we all came out of the depression, and I've said it was the depression boys who felt that way: that we had to grow, had to survive. And to survive, we had to grow. You know, it's got to be bigger. It's got to be bigger because we have forty-five people. It's got to be bigger because we can do more things. It's got to be bigger because we can do more research. If it's just *better*—I can show you a lot of people out there who are better, but they're not doing things.

■ CHAPTER 3

PROGRAMMING AND SQUATTERS

Caudill Rowlett Scott believes that it is important to bring the client in as a member of the team. Then the plans made and the actions taken are more likely to meet all the varied needs of the people involved and to fit the unique features of the situation. Added to this, it should be recognized that when a person plays a part in making decisions, he is more concerned and more interested. People who are actively involved don't need to be "sold." Perhaps here is the real secret to CRS success.

—*"Programming and Squatters," Operations Manual, Section 2.08, ca. 1958, CRS Archives, CRS Center, Texas A&M University*

■ In the early and middle years of the twentieth century, architecture changed in a crucial way. It became more "rational," more tightly focused on the tasks the building's occupants had to perform. Designers had, of course, always cared whether their buildings worked satisfactorily; they were not oblivious to the tasks that went on in them. But often the architects applied historical forms to whatever problem was at hand, manipulating the old forms just enough to accommodate modern activities, and no more. The traditional forms possessed, many architects believed, a time-honored validity that prohibited radical departures. But the results of this mind-set increasingly sparked dissatisfaction. Ancient forms, born long before the skyscraper was devised, long before the assembly line was invented, long before the modern era's most distinctive traits were ushered into existence, seemed to an emerging generation of architects to be anachronistic, out of sync with the huge size and the transforming nature of the twentieth century. How, it was asked, could the old forms supply suitable, believable settings for airports, laboratories, power plants, and a whole panoply of Machine Age activities that were changing the daily life in Western civilization? It was a serious question, and by the 1920s it spurred concerted efforts to topple tradition and create a wholly new architecture.

Modernists who rose to prominence during the 1920s and 1930s—Le Corbusier, Mies van der Rohe, and Walter Gropius among them—rejected the idea of adapting forms that had been passed down through the centuries. Dismissing the old forms as obsolete, the architectural avant-garde set out to devise replacements that would use more advanced methods of construction, employ modern materials like steel, aluminum, and reinforced concrete, and symbolize the spirit of a new and freer era. Modernist buildings, unconstrained by convention, exuded freshness, daring, and novelty.

Yet modern buildings had problems of their own. Sometimes the striking new forms were imposed in a dogmatic fashion, reflecting a contemporary theory of architecture more than they responded to the requirements of the client and the site. Not uncommonly, the brave new buildings functioned worse than the modernist rhetoric suggested would be the case. Thus, although the architectural revolution of the twentieth century massively succeeded in its goal of overturning tradition, it did not necessarily give the buildings' occupants things they needed.

What the architectural profession required was a capacity to assess the users' needs with great care. William Caudill began displaying that capacity at Texas A&M in the 1940s, researching heating, ventilation, and other basic elements of schools. After Caudill Rowlett Scott was formed in 1948, Caudill continued to advocate research—sometimes conducted inside the firm, sometimes at the university—not only for schools, but also for other types of buildings. In November, 1953, CRS landed the job of designing the new Brazos County Courthouse in Bryan, the town next to College Station. This would be the firm's first courthouse, and the architects wanted to discover all they could about planning, designing, maintaining, and administering these government facilities, which, despite their unified image, were odd hybrids: a mix of courtrooms, jail cells, permit offices, registrars, tax counters, public meeting areas, and other miscellaneous functions. Inconceivable as it may seem today, virtually no written material was available at that time to guide a novice courthouse designer. So, CRS embarked on its own study, and consulted a wide range of sources, some of them surprisingly elementary by the standards of our own day. Iron manufacturers, for instance, were asked for advice because those companies built jails and could offer well-informed opinions on matters such as whether to place the jail in the courthouse's basement, on the courthouse's top floor, in a separate building close by, or on a cheaper, more remote site such as a county farm.

In addition, CRS accompanied county representatives on visits to eight other courthouses and jails, and interviewed judges, jailers, clerks, guards—everyone involved in courthouse activities. The firm believed in gathering information from the various kinds of people affected by the architects' decisions. Those visits did not include recent, award-winning recent projects, however. Caudill and Willie Peña worried that if they became overly familiar with a highly praised recent solution, they might end up being too heavily influenced by it, and thus short-circuit their inquiry. They did not want to copy someone else's esthetic response to the problem; they wanted to grapple with the issues open-mindedly.

The result was apparently the first decentralized courthouse facility in the United States. Completed in September, 1956, the Brazos County Courthouse avoided concentrating trials, tax collecting, deed recording, and other disparate activities into a single building. Instead, the facility in Bryan consisted of several elements. The most prominent was a four-story structure containing a jail on the top floor; jury rooms, probation offices, and civil defense on the third floor; two courtrooms and ancillary areas on the second; and a judge's chamber, commissioners' court, and drivers' license bureau on the first. Covered walkways linked that four-story building to five "pods"—one-story structures that handled the county's nonjudicial business and services. People going to or from trials did not have to cross paths with people paying delinquent taxes or applying for welfare or visiting the health department. The courthouse was laid out as a campus on a city block, with offices arranged around courtyards, rather than in the old fashion of a monolithic building standing in the center of its site, dominating its surroundings. A phrase that became current at CRS was "we put the court in courthouses."[1] The courtrooms were air-conditioned and windowless so that noises from outside would not intrude on the judicial proceedings. Landscaped outdoor patios were provided for the public. This courthouse received a good reception and won awards for the firm.[2]

From the earliest days, research was critical to CRS's success in design, but even more important was the process by which the firm worked with clients. An important part of the CRS process was "squatters": an intensive,

The Brazos County Courthouse in Bryan, Texas, shown here in 1954, was CRS's auspicious entry into the field of courthouse design. *Photos courtesy Roland Chatham.*

several-day work session on the client's turf. A team from CRS went to the client's locale and worked there—in the client's offices or in facilities nearby—until the client approved the results of that phase of the project. The term *squatters* is unlovely, but it is concise and memorable, so it was never changed. In fact, some architects who left CRS and founded their own firms, such as Jack DeBartolo at Anderson DeBartolo Pan in Tucson, used squatters—both the technique and the term—in their own practice. Many firms have embraced similar procedures in the past couple of decades, especially for projects located far from the architects' home offices. The Miami architecture and planning firm of Andres Duany and Elizabeth Plater-Zyberk, for instance, has organized on-site collaborative work sessions, often nearly a week long, to hammer out planning and design concepts for hundreds of community and subdivision projects across the country. Many architects, including Duany and Plater-Zyberk, call such sessions *charettes.*[3] Regional Urban Design Assistance Teams (RUDATs) sponsored by the AIA use somewhat similar, if briefer, processes in which the citizenry and professionals work together on urban design problems, often for two to three days.

Squatters became an important tool at CRS, in part because they forged a bond between architect and client, helping the two achieve a close understanding that was hard to acquire in any other way. The firm was first impelled to hold squatters when it had difficulty getting the school board in Blackwell, Oklahoma, to approve a design for an elementary school. Caudill loaded drafting boards into Wallie Scott's car, and then he and Scott drove five hundred miles to that town, stayed there, and worked with school officials until they reached agreement.

By bringing all the participants together at one time and place, squatters forced latent issues to surface. Surprises came to light sooner rather than later. Sources of disagreement were discovered and hashed out. Caught up in focused activity, all sides committed to producing a building everyone could support. In most cases, CRS conducted some preliminary research in advance of the squatters so the architects had a basic understanding of the project and did not arrive entirely cold. Squatters presented financial advantages as well. They reduced the risk of investing too much time in an approach that the client would reject. The sessions concluded with the client approving a preliminary design, so CRS could then collect a portion of the fee, greatly aiding the firm's cash flow.

Even more important than squatters was "programming," a disciplined procedure for identifying problems the designer would be charged with solving. Programming had existed in very elementary form for a long time, going by a variety of names. In Great Britain, architects developed what they called "briefing," which provided a meticulous listing of a project's spaces, arrangements, materials, budgets, and the like. A briefing compiled information that would be used by the designer. In the United States, some aspects of programming were discussed in editions of the AIA manual as early as the 1920s.[4] However, in neither Britain nor the United States was the process of programming fully developed before the 1950s. The briefing, though useful, was, Willie Peña notes, a document "without goals, concepts, and a problem statement."[5]

In the decades after the war, CRS carried out the work of formalizing programming for its own use and ultimately for use by the entire profession. At one time, the firm attempted to name the process "architectural analysis," but that phrase "never caught fire in the profession," says Peña, who became CRS's and American architecture's leading exponent of programming.[6] Peña dubbed the process "problem-seeking" so as to contrast it with the "problem-solving" done later by the designer. The two terms implied an agreed-upon division of labor: programmers (analysts) define problems; designers solve them. The pair of terms favored by Peña neatly indicates the nature of this process. But for an everyday term, architects settled on "programming."

The job of the programmer was to undertake an in-depth study of the problem and to conclude by identifying the salient considerations the designer should address. Then the designer would go about his own work. Programming replaced the old method of trial and error, in which a designer began work frequently with a partial or a skewed understanding of the problem and thus risked producing a design that would fail to address all of the significant objectives.

At first, CRS's projects, such as elementary schools, tended to be simple, so programming activities and design activities both took place during the same squatters week. As projects became larger and more complex, CRS decided to hold two separate squatters: the first for programming and the second for design. A period of time was allowed to elapse between the two squatters sessions so that the client could test the validity of decisions made in programming and so the designer would have the gestation time necessary to the creative process.[7]

Mainly through Peña's work, CRS became the first firm to explain all the components of programming and present them in a detailed matrix that could guide any architect through the process. Because of widespread interest, CRS's presentations of programming appeared in architectural journals over the years, and in 1969 Peña and John Focke, a CRS programmer, wrote the first version of *Problem Seeking*—a booklet intended for clients and for business and facilities planning officials. It summed up the process as it had evolved at CRS since 1948. In 1973, the National Council of Architectural Registration Boards (NCARB) incorporated its contents into the predesign part of the NCARB examination, a qualifying test for an architectural license. In 1977, a second edition was produced as a book for the firm's clients and for architects and students.[8] In 1987, the AIA published a third edition by Peña with Steven Parshall and Kevin Kelly. What had started out as a rough theory, with incomplete procedures, was systematized and institutionalized into a discipline by CRS.

There are still architects who enter the design phase without the systematic evaluation that CRS argued was essential, and even in CRS, designers were sometimes impatient about waiting for the results of the programming before they started sketching solutions. "Peña was always saying, 'You're not ready to design,'" Caudill pointed out. But programming produced more consistent and satisfactory results than could be achieved by diving into the conceptual design phrase prematurely. So it remains in use today, one of CRS's most lasting gifts to the profession.

The first four steps can be carried out in any sequence or simultaneously. But all four must be completed before undertaking the fifth step: stating the problem. Each step takes into account four factors: function, form, economy, and time. The programmer is on the lookout for big planning concepts that can be presented to the designer. A designer receives "little guidance and most certainly no inspiration from a listing of 'spaces required by the program,'" Caudill and Peña once explained.[9] Instead, the information must give the designer a sense of the qualities and concepts the project aims to attain.

There is an art to programming effectively: It requires an ability to distinguish between a client's wants and needs, a talent for formulating concepts, and a capacity for summarizing in simple, clear sentences. Caudill Rowlett Scott found that it was best if someone other than a designer did the programming because it requires an analytical mind, which is not necessarily found in the creative person generating the design.

Programming results in an explicit statement of the architectural problem—a hand-off package from programmer to designer. In this stage, having pondered information derived from the previous four steps, the designer and programmer write down the most salient statements about the problem—statements that can serve as premises for design and later as design criteria with which to evaluate the design solution. "The problem statements must be clear and concise—in the designer's own words so there is no doubt that he understands," according to Peña.[10]

Typically, the salient considerations were narrowed down to no more than ten, so as not to overburden the designer. "More than ten would indicate the problem is too complex or you re using details as premises for design," Peña explained. "The designer wants the essence, and you're not going to get the essence with twenty statements."[11]

INTERVIEWS

WILLIE PEÑA

Bill Caudill was my teacher [in] my fifth year. We had gone to California for a college trip and dropped in on all the architects in California who were doing schools and stopped by to see [Richard] Neutra on the way to see Frank Lloyd Wright. We saw a lot of school architects up and down California. When we came back, we were assigned a problem: the design of a single classroom.

Bill Caudill already had a contract to design the Blackwell schools, and we had seen all kinds of different lighting schemes in California. Now, our class was to do a single classroom. So I did mine, and Bill liked it. He had just hired Wallie Scott, and he said, "Willie, Wallie is coming into our firm. He has a year working for the college architect [at Texas A&M]. He's coming in as a partner. Would you like to come in as our first employee? If you do, we'll build your classroom in the Blackwell schools." Bill was a very caring professor, and he would find jobs for his students. For me, it was the easiest thing—[I] didn't have to move to Dallas, [and] I could just stay in College Station. Sure enough, I came in.

Bill worked my cross section into the plans of the Blackwell school and designed the two [elementary] schools based on that cross section. He took them over to Blackwell, and the clients didn't like it. So he redid them, took them back over there, and they still didn't like them. That's when the [concept of] squatters came up. Bill said, "All right, we're going to come over here, borrow your library classroom, and just squat there and do the job." Bill redesigned the schools in that first squatters. As a result, my original cross section was no longer pure—he transposed it. I had the corridor on the north; he put it on the south. I had the big overhang on the north, and he put it on the south. It became a Caudill design.

Q: Did you go on that first squatters?

A: No, Bill went with Wallie Scott. Wallie had a car—another reason we say he was made a partner. Wallie and Bill went, and I didn't. It leads to something else I think is interesting and which is going to come up later. I came in as a designer/working-drawings person. Wallie had come in as a designer/working-drawings person because he had done the design on the original student center with Brooks Martin at Texas A&M for the college architect. John, of course, was a designer because he was superb, but he was also very proficient in working drawings. We could watch his working drawings develop before our eyes, he would be going so fast—like an abacus, coming out *plip, plip, plip;* just pouring out—beautiful working drawings. Bill was the biggest designer we ever had, but to tell the truth, we were all designers. Wallie was a better draftsman than I was. In fact, I was lousy at it. So it was Wallie who went on the squatters with Bill.

Q: Did Bill and Wallie know they had a good idea when they went up there for that squatters, or did that come later?

A: Bill knew it was a good idea and [that] it was the only recourse to get on with the project. He had previously been working for the Corps of Engineers in Nebraska. At one point, he was the only architect in a group of engineers, and his boss said, "Bill, we're going to Podunk over here and are going to be in the basement of a courthouse and are going to plan this airfield." During World War II, they had to build an airfield just like that—none of that planning for two to three years. So this engineer had organized a team of engineers, and Bill was going to be the architect on that team of specialists. They went to this town in Nebraska for two weeks—or something like that. Bill was amazed how much work they were able to do as a team under pressure and with the shortcut in communications. There they were, six or eight of them, working on this project, and the project went fast. So Bill knew it could be effective, and he was applying it.

The word *squatters* is a Southern expression and pertinent to Oklahoma. Later on, the *Architectural Forum* didn't like the term, and their writer, Walter McQuade, didn't like it either. So we began to call it "on-the-spot design"—terrible! Nobody bought that one. So it remained squatters, an ugly term.

First one I got involved in turned out to be a programming squatters. Before then, Bill Caudill had sent me to Elk City, which was his wife's hometown, and we had a project to do there—the Fairfield School. Bill said, "Willie,

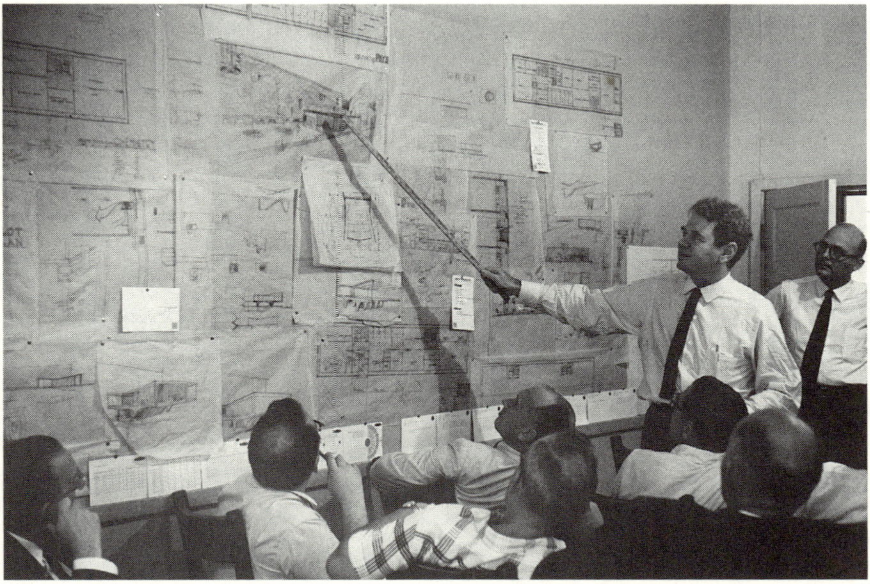

Caudill leading a squatters session in 1960 for the design of the Olin Hall of Science at Colorado College in Colorado Springs, Colorado. *Photo courtesy Myron Wood.*

I want you to go to Elk City and come back with a program." By this time, I had been made a partner, so I felt it was my responsibility. But I really didn't know what I was going to have to do to come back with a program. There were no rules, no criteria. But he said, "You know: How many classrooms? How much money? Site survey, et cetera." So I went, [and] sure enough, I enjoyed the hell out of it. I interviewed the teachers, superintendent, and some of the school board members. I got the information I needed, came back, and gave the information to Bill. Two or three weeks later, he went up there to design the school.

So right then and there, Bill was separating programming from design. One of the reasons was that he felt secure as a designer. There are a lot of insecure designers, and therefore, they want to hog it all. Not Bill, he was very secure in his ability to design. But, "Give me a program," [he said.] So we separated it. We didn't know that what he was really doing at the time was separating analysis from synthesis.

Thereafter, I was known as a programmer. Bill already knew the term. He didn't like it and wanted to change it, but he had already used the word *programmer*. That was probably September [1950], and in December, we had the job to do the Norman High School. In those days, he was teaching and couldn't just take off and go to Norman. So we went during the Christmas holiday. Luckily, we found enough teachers in town to interview. The superintendent got them for us.

We were staying at a motel: Cleon Bellomy and I in one room, Bill in the other. In his room, Bill began to put things on the wall. Some were these big sketchbook sheets. He asked me to put the information from my interviews on the wall. There was no organization to it like we have now. Now we have categories. But it was a wall display—Caudill had analysis cards, tracing paper with something of the site, something about the budget.

Toward the end of the week, he woke us up very early one morning and told us to come over to his room. So Cleon and I went over bleary-eyed. "Look what I've got," [he said]. He had six salient considerations for the design of the Norman High School. We didn't recognize it at the time, but it was a statement of the problem. He asked, "What do you think of this?" He had these six statements not related to the solution, not design solutions. They stated a condition. For example: "Since the students in a high school spend a lot more time in the halls than they do in an elementary school, if you spend ten minutes of every period there and have six periods, you have sixty minutes in the halls. Therefore, the halls should be made part of the teaching process and exciting."

Here he was, saying that the difference between an elementary school and a high school is the *hall*—what do you do with the halls? "In an elementary school, it's a self-contained classroom"—he said it very simply, and I'm elaborating. He had six of this kind of statements. Later—much later—we looked back on them and said, "That was the first statement of the problem; Bill had avoided the solution." When we came back, we put it into a published report.

We did something else important: a survey of the Norman school needs. Everybody seems to give Bill credit for writing *Space for Teaching.* This was a big impetus for the firm—just shot the firm into national prominence after the war when the educators discovered it. But I credit another little publication in 1950. You remember we went to Blackwell in December, 1950. Sometime earlier in 1950, he published for the Texas Engineering Experiment Station the little booklet called *Take a Good Look at Your Schools.* It was an approach to long-range planning. In that report, we had our enrollment projections—which I did as programmer—the map of where the students lived, and where they were likely to live in the future. This report then became our long-range plan for Norman, as well as the programming for the high school itself.

In it, Bill had some sketches because at that time we were alluding to a method of programming but didn't know the difference between design concepts and programmatic concepts. Bill had some design ideas he threw out—not solutions, just ideas. So that report became very important to us, for in the introduction he spells out the idea that programming is problem seeking, and design is problem solving. Right there.

One of the things I think we need to look at is the fact that architecture itself was to the point at which Walter Gropius said the approach would be the design of the building according to certain circumstances.[12] In other words, it wasn't just designing a building then putting something in it like it had been done previously. If you remember design school, you saw a lot of classical buildings with columns on the outside, and then they poured education into it. Modern architecture was looking at some other approaches to design of a building. Bill had written *Space for Teaching,* saying the traditional method is wrong: We have no good light, circulation, ventilation—we need to bring up the comfort level of schools. We had to design them according to new teaching programs because the old classrooms were built twenty-eight feet by thirty-two feet—standard size—with windows on one side, and that was it. Then you screwed thirty desks to the floor. The traditional design was not adequate for the new teaching programs in which students might be in a circle at one time and several groups at another time and one group at another time. So the traditionally designed schools were not working—neither for comfort nor for new teaching methods.

Now you start with what you might call a program with new ideas for comfort and function—which didn't come up with traditional buildings but did come up with modern architecture, which said you really should design to circumstances surrounding the job.

The schools needed new programs, new teaching methods, new standards of comfort because the old standards were lousy. Bill's *Space for Teaching* shows that the typical classroom had one light bulb, and there was no cross ventilation because the windows were only on one side and the corridor on the other. They were hot and poorly lighted. The traditional schools were not doing the job. We had new standards, and he pointed that out in *Space for Teaching.*

Functionalism was a strong philosophic strain in early CRS thinking. In a dedication brochure prepared for the opening of the new school in Blackwell, Oklahoma, in the spring of 1950, the firm made manifest its views regarding the relationship between architecture and functionalism:

> Architecture in the United States for a quarter of a century has felt the influence of many designers seeking radical changes. The situation today is the same as in the beginning. It has been a struggle between those adhering to traditions and old antiquated customs and those advocating reforms and initiating change just to be different. However, even the conservative designer has come to realize that since the activity inside the schoolroom differs so greatly from that of olden times, the design and the facilities of the present-day classroom must of necessity be changed.
>
> Although the architecture of the new schools in Blackwell is a radical departure from the old traditional school buildings, every feature has a positive and definite purpose in providing comfort, health, and safety for the child. We urge you to study the merits of these buildings and to learn from the students and teachers who use them how they fulfill the needs of a present-day program. Many people have come to realize that a beautiful school building does not necessarily mean a three- or four-story brick structure topped by a magnificent and expensive tower. Beauty today requires that a building be practical and economical and that it provide a real learning environment.
>
> The interior of each classroom has been carefully designed. All the elementary principals in the city of Blackwell were frequently consulted in the designing of the classroom. The entire building is a result of cooperative planning on the part of the architect, the teachers, the patrons, the Board of Education, and the Superintendent of Schools.
>
> We must withhold final judgment regarding the value of these buildings until use by the students, teachers, and parents affords an opportunity to test and to prove their real worth. If the Huston and Washington Buildings provide maximum light, heat, and ventilation and enable the child to attain maximum mental and physical growth and development, the purpose and ambition of the planning group will have been realized.[13]

The squatters process played an important part in the way CRS organized and managed projects. Whether the projects were large or small, foreign or domestic, old or recent, the CRS team went to the client's home base to work. As projects became more complex and larger, more squatters and more specialized squatters were held, but the concept continued to be a significant operational factor in CRS—and one that always included substantial client input.

FRANK LAWYER

I had been on my one hundredth squatters, and the firm had a gathering in the drafting room of everybody in the office and presented me with this beautiful wooden bowl. It was a milestone for the firm and for me. That was in '68, and I retired in '83, so there were close to another hundred squatters after that. I did a lot of work and had a lot of great experiences. I'm thankful I got to join the firm.

I feel fortunate to have been in a firm that really believed—not [just] lip service—in the team concept. It allowed me to operate in a way I liked because I need a team. I'm not a complete designer, a complete architect in any sense of the word—I needed all these people to help me out. I think it was great to be with a firm that believed in team and not in developing individual talents and exploiting those or trying to give a lot of publicity to certain high-falutin' designers. That's why I enjoyed working with the people on all those squatters and working with Bill. I probably would not have been successful in another firm where I had to work alone or feel I was carrying the load for the whole project myself. . . .

Of course, the squatters was the great invention, too. I feel like I contributed something to the firm's squatters. My strong point was that I could come up with some pretty good ideas for buildings on squatters and could get those generated and down on paper in a week's time—seems like every squatters was a week.

I designed a lot of buildings here, and I don't think any of them was great, but I'm still proud of the things I did. I developed ways of working, sketching, et cetera that made the squatters work pretty well. The squatters concept was good for us to establish some direction—nothing finished, just some ideas, direction—then get them into some kind of form that can be presented so the client can have some idea of how the architecture might be. Then changes could always be made, but if the client felt comfortable with that direction, you could develop it further. It suited my way of working very well, or maybe my way of working suited the squatters. . . . We did a lot of long days and nights on those squatters. They were successful and made the firm a heck of a lot of money.

Clients loved them, for the most part. The only client I know of who maybe didn't was Aramco, for some reason. I remember one time after we had been in the Middle East for a while and came back, one guy running that particular show said, "If you show us any more of those damned snow cards,

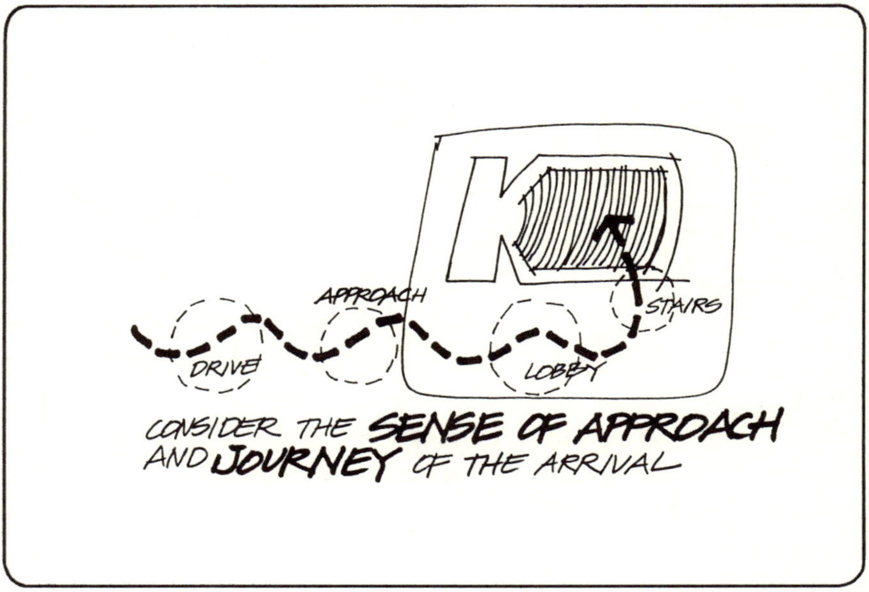

An analysis card or "snow card" used in designing the Jesse H. Jones Hall for the Performing Arts in Houston. *Illustration courtesy CRS Center Archives.*

I'm going to walk out of here right now." Our whole presentation was going to be more snow cards! That was the only time I recall somebody who didn't like that approach.

Snow cards, or more properly, concept cards, were 5½ inches high by 8¼ inches wide. They were developed as part of the programming process and became an important, characteristic part of CRS communication. Using a wide felt-tip marker, it was possible to express one idea and a visual key or sketch on each concept card. Brevity was a required discipline in using concept cards.

The whole program, or presentation, was put on the wall and could be grasped in ten or twenty minutes at most. No hidden messages; it was all out in the open. Clients could amend them or make up their own concept cards, whereas, they would not join so easily in amending a prose program or a drawing.

Two concept cards could be photocopied on a standard 8½-by-11-inch sheet of paper for a permanent record, and a programming or planning document could be put into a standard notebook with a minimum of additional effort. In short, the concept card became an integral part of the CRS communication style.

JIM HUGHES

In the first twenty years or so, most of the projects were fairly small and were all over the country. We did those jobs long-distance. We worked with clients in other states, and we handled those projects within the same fee structure they would pay a local architect. Only in rare cases were we paid for travel, which meant the firm had to develop some unique processes in order to make a profit in spite of the extraordinary expenses involved in doing a project in Michigan, for example.

One of the ways this was done was the squatters concept. When the team gathers to design, let's say, a school project in Michigan, they go with full knowledge of that project before they leave. They have probably spent a week working—not designing, but maybe coming up with two or three concepts of how the site might be utilized for whatever the program intent was. On the team would be a lead designer, obviously, with whatever assistance necessary. There would always be a manager, and usually a technologist as well. So you would have from four to six people on a squatters depending on the size of the project. The smaller the job, the smaller the team.

The wonderful thing about a squatters is [that] the team could travel on Sunday, start work early Monday morning, and usually work till midnight every night. On Friday afternoon, we would present a design concept to the client. Throughout that week, the client was involved daily in everything that was developing.

We worked in all sorts of crazy places: hotel rooms, school buildings, classrooms—in any place available to set up shop. Usually, we brought our own parallel bars, T-squares—whatever we had to have to do the work. With client involvement, it worked almost without exception in my experience, and I was involved in an awful lot of squatters. I don't ever remember a failure where we went home without an approved design. It's bound to have happened, but the exception is so rare [that] it's unimportant to the overall success of the concept. There's an enormous efficiency in that, with about two weeks of concentrated effort, we would have an approved schematic design. Other firms might spend six to eight weeks or longer and might go through two or three different processes. Traditional practice is to design a facility in the office, take it to the client, and hope the client would approve it. Often they do not, so it was a back and forth proposition. But we were with the client daily, so the concept we came up with by Friday afternoon was not just ours, it was the client's as well. It was almost a foolproof process.

Q: The programmers had been there before the design squatters?

A: Programmers had always been there before. Everybody played a role. When you came back with an approved design, it still needed a lot of work to refine it, but it was a basic concept of space, relationships, architecture, [and] function within the area parameters of the project and hopefully within budget. An approved design isn't worth a damn if it's way over the area or way over budget. By and large, these things worked out very well. That's where the team concept came into play: through the specialization of the individual, the organization of the team, and the squatters concept. There's a special way a squatters works. It sort of evolves during the week's activities. After you've been through a bunch of them, you begin to know what takes place—or what *should* take place—by Tuesday, by Wednesday, by Thursday. . . .

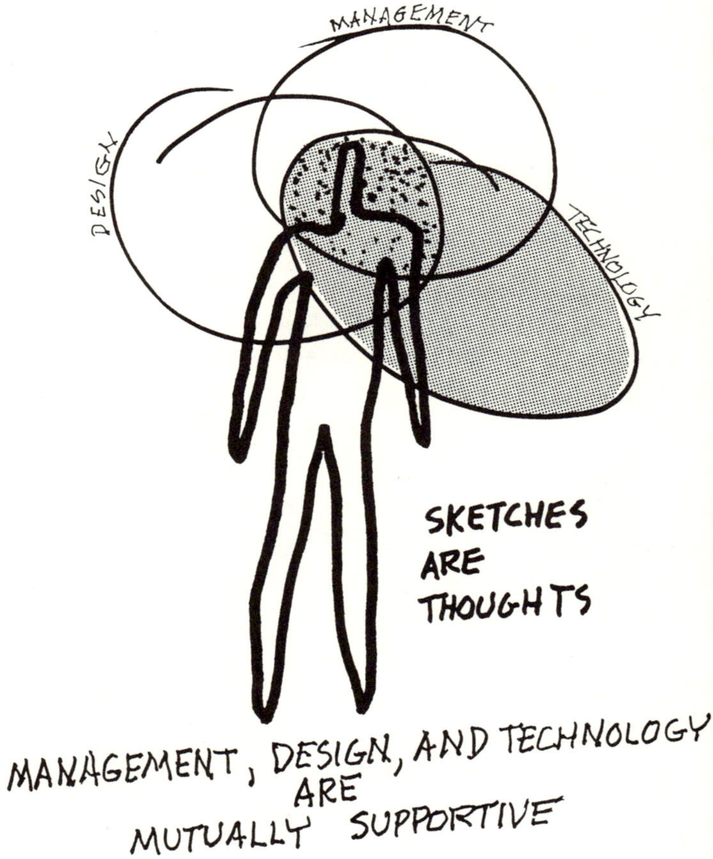

A Bill Caudill diagram indicating the interrelation of management, design, and technology.

Usually the manager, the designers, and probably the technologist are experienced squatters. Having been through it two to three times, you begin to sense the cadence. You know how to move the thinking process along and keep the thing moving. Of course, every designer has his own way of doing things. Norman Hoover was a fairly new designer at CRS, and we had an elementary school project in Aurora, Colorado. I was the project manager, and he was the lead designer. It was the first time I had been on a squatters with Norman, who hadn't actually been on that many squatters with anybody. Norman had a rapidograph pen with a very fine point and a roll of butter paper [yellow tracing paper]. He sat and did little black line squibbles about the size of a large postage stamp. He sat for two, three, four days doing these.

Occasionally, I'd go over and say, "Norman, how are you coming along?" He'd reply, "Oh, just fine; just fine." About Thursday, I was ready to panic—no design, nothing! Sometime Thursday afternoon, he stood up; stretched. He had this whole thing in his mind, and in just a few hours' time, he laid out the whole project. It was beautiful and worked perfectly. It was his unique way of designing. He didn't do elaborate sketches and throw paper around like a lot of designers do. He had it all in his mind and knew exactly what he was doing.

RALPH CARROLL

Frank [Lawyer] would shoot me for telling this story, but I'm going to tell it anyway. It was a junior college we were working on. Frank was designer [and] I was project manager. We had started building models on the squatters, and that really got tough when you had to produce a mass model along with the drawings and everything else. Usually, those models would be built Thursday night for our Friday noontime presentation. A young fellow—[I] believe it was Rick Zieve—was cutting chipboard, piecing this model together. I was doing snow cards, and Frank was sketching. Unbeknownst to anybody, Rick [had] cut a piece of chipboard, [and] it flew up into his mouth and lodged in his throat. Rick started coughing, clutching his throat, [and] getting a little red in the face. We had been up for two or three nights in a row. Frank looked at him and said, "Catch him—don't let him fall on the model!" But he spit out the chipboard and didn't fall on the model.

It's true [that] you got to know people very well on squatters—and clients, too. It was a good experience all the way around. There were always humorous things that happened on squatters. One time, we were on [a] squatters—Frank and I—for the Corpus Christi Auditorium and Convention Center, which took *years* to get off the ground. Like, seven years. I think this was about the third year. The bond issue had passed, and they asked us to proceed with the design work. On Thursday evening of the squatters, very late—we were set up in a hotel suite—the city manager came around and said, "Throw your pencils down. It's all off. The City Council won't be able to meet tomorrow." Some emergency had come up along the Gulf Coast. "They won't be able to see your presentation tomorrow." We didn't stay up late that night and in fact went out and had a leisurely dinner. But we did put it together, and [we] made the presentation to the hotel staff. They enjoyed it, for they had been interested in watching us.

JOHN FOCKE

I joined CRS in the summer of 1968. I had just finished graduate studies at MIT and was at that time very systems oriented, process oriented. During the course of those early weeks and months, I met Willie Peña and learned for the first time about programming, which was really pioneering at that time.

Programming certainly had come up during my professional education—but never to the point that it had reached a discipline itself or a process. CRS had the framework of a process that, for me, had a lot of intellectual content, and I just became very interested. At the time, to even be considered to become a programmer at CRS, you had to pass an IBM numerical exam that Willie administered. I did and expressed an interest in getting involved. He immediately put me to work on area takeoffs on buildings. My first project at CRS was with Jim Gatton, working on the programming for the Corpus Christi Convention Center. My first squatters there happened to be Frank Lawyer's one-hundredth squatters—the Corpus project. I was very impressed.

My second project was to undertake some research, initially with Willie, in the area of programming and building type research. Later, [I worked] with Tom Bullock on a project I think Jonathan King probably initiated in New York having to do with the application of fast-track scheduling and systems building. Tom initiated an in-house study, [but] there were others involved in it. That was my first encounter with leading edge research at CRS—or in the profession, really. It led to great things for me and for CRS later as I began to develop the concepts and market the notion of fast track and systems building. This was coming at a time when we were seeing double-digit inflation. Time was knowledge, and the market was just starving for this kind of process.

That was a situation where the seed of an idea went directly to the marketplace. It was very successful because there were a lot of smart people out there who understood what had to be done and [who] were willing to work as a team to make those things happen. You cannot fast track or do systems construction without the team. So that was really a kick start for me at CRS: To have both the incredible project experience with Jim Gatton and Frank Lawyer, and then to work with Willie Peña and Tom Bullock on research. As things developed over the next few years, Willie involved me in further documenting the programming process, and we did a first "primer"—a paperback CRS publication. It seemed at the time that CRS was publishing leading edge pieces annually. Not just by Willie, but [by] others, [too]. They were very exciting times for me, and I think [they] sort of welded me into a career in the specialty of programming and analysis in architecture.

I had an opportunity to apply some of the management techniques and skills I had learned to what had grown into the Programming and Planning Division of CRS. That eventually grew to about thirty-five people and furthered the specialization of CRS in the predesign phase of projects—programming and planning in several building types: health care, educational facilities, and college/university planning. At the time, there were a lot of young people at CRS just out of graduate school with four or five years' experience. CRS had us on airplanes all over the country. It really accelerated our learning curve in the profession, for we were exposed to clients, to boards of directors, building committees, and the public. We all felt we were on the leading edge of what was happening in architecture because we were out there with clients who were doing things, and we had a company behind us [that was] pushing us and providing the resources we needed to advance the state of the art.

Programming gives the owner or client a voice and control of the decision making that precedes design. As I think back to the days when Willie fought to keep design ideas out of programming, what he was trying to do was keep the process open to the client and not trap him into something he would regret later.

That sort of triggers a thought I've had on the whole process of programming [that] I'd like to get on the record here: The CRS technique was to graphically document information and present it open[ly] to everybody—attested by everybody. As the practice of programming became more sophisticated on bigger projects, in some areas, it's become a process of who can document the most information. Once it gets into a report, I guess it's accessible to everybody, theoretically. But there are not many people who

Even children were allowed a voice in the design process during a squatters session for Fodrea Community School in Columbus, Indiana, in 1971.

are going to dig it out. I guess that's why even with today's computers, word processing, and reams of paper that the old CRS snow card is still probably the most powerful communication tool because it's so user friendly and accessible. We have tried to get clients to work with us on the computer, but the computer limits the participation to one or two people. With the simple snow card, you can deal with a roomful of people all day and communicate. I think that whole subject of communication at CRS was something practiced inside and outside the firm. In those days—before CRS became so structured corporately—communication inside the firm was as open as it was with our clients. It was very easy to access people and share ideas. Without that communication, the ideas really never go anywhere.

CRS was like this huge vacuum that just pulled ideas to it. I think the reputation the company had in schools and the profession drew bright people to the firm. They felt [that] if they had an idea there would be an ear to listen and a chance to pursue it. We also found that, because of the position the firm had, a number of us were getting invitations to lecture at Princeton, Berkeley, and all over the country. It was very exciting for young architects to go back to such prestigious institutions and talk about "the leading edge." We all felt we were pretty special.

BOB DOUGLASS

Q: Did the CRS programming techniques, which had grown up in school design, work pretty well in hospital design?

A: In a way, they did. They worked theatrically very well in hospital design. They worked to help the user groups visualize what was happening and the point of it. They worked to make users feel involved. They didn't work at all from a quantitative standpoint. They were very inadequate from the standpoint of defining functionally and quantitatively what really needed to happen. This is why [there were] the early conflicts that Jim [Falick], particularly, had with Willie Peña. We simply had to do the programming more rigorously from a quantitative standpoint than Willie's traditional way of working with school groups would allow. But we worked it out, and that was one aspect of the programming story.

The other aspect of the programming story was the conflict Jim and I had early on where I tried to explain to him [that] the best way for us to get referrals was through the hospital consultants because they were in touch with a dozen or twenty opportunities, whereas a specific hospital administrator would represent one opportunity—that the hospital consultants' whole business was to do programming, and if we tried to do the programming, we would antagonize these people and wouldn't get the referrals. I won that argument eventually, and Jim agreed we would sort of back away from the quantitative programming work and encourage the consultants to do that. But we would do the theatrical side of programming much in the style of Willie—snow cards, et cetera. So that was the first couple of projects.

Q: You were involved in developing a gaming technique that supplemented the traditional CRS snow-card business. Tell us about that.

A: I'll tell you my story. When I came to CRS, I had been working with Dick Johnson, who was also a community college trustee. His community college had hired CRS to do a campus for them. He liked the firm but knew CRS didn't know anything about hospitals—at least that was his story. He was convinced that I did. So when I went there, Dick and I put together a proposal to do a so-called system study of hospital design for the U.S. Public Health Service. The setting for this experimental project was the Galveston Public Health Service Hospital.

We got the contract, and Bill Cannady and his design team were assigned to it. I was assigned as a kind of lead planner, and we had to work with a group of consultants from A. T. Kearney that included hospital administrators, economists, sociologists, and industrial engineers. The idea was that the Public Health Service, in bringing all these disciplines together, would get a far more rational, scientifically dependable result.

In fact, we got chaos. Nobody knew how to talk to anybody else. We thrashed around in increasing frustration and hostility for at least a full day. That night, Bill Cannady and I were having a drink at the hotel [and] wondering what we could do about it. I told him I had just finished reading this book *The Double Helix* [1968], by James Watson, who discovered the structure of the DNA molecule, the double helix. In that book, Watson had described the rather primitive method they used to model it and discover the complex form that defied the usual ways of X-ray examination by actually trying to model it in space—physically model it and connect it like tinker toys. I said, "Why don't we try to follow these rules the industrial engineers are coming up with about proximities, relationships, and affinities—forget about this as a building, and try to figure out some way to model it in space? Once we get the ideal set of relationships among the pieces, then [we'll] take the next step and figure out how to make it architecture—figure out where it needs a front door, where it has to touch the ground, et cetera."

Bill was intrigued [and] excited and started tearing pieces of paper from the napkins, moving them around. [The] next morning, we went back to the hospital, and one of the guys on the team found some storm windows in a storage shed on the grounds of the U.S. Public Health Service Hospital—found these layers of glass. In a cleaning cabinet, we found some GI cleanser cans we used to separate the layers of glass vertically. We started doing some colored paper—cutting out blocks of space, arrows to show movement, black bars to show where connections should not occur. We started messing around with this.

There had been a blowup at the end of the previous day where the A. T. Kearney people said in effect: "You guys are nuts and are not cooperating, and you don't understand—you're just architects." They had gone off to their end of the room to do their thing: industrial engineering diagrams. It got so complicated, they had to give up on them—they couldn't make it work. One by one, they eventually started coming over. They'd look and say, "Why did you put that there?" We'd say, "We thought pharmacies should be next to . . ." They'd say, "No, no—that's not the way it works. You should

A 3-D game board is created during a U.S. Public Health Service Hospital squatters session in Galveston, Texas, in 1969. Members of Bill Cannady's design team included Bob Ambrose, Ray Bailey, Bob Douglass, Bill Merriman, and Guy Jackson.

put the pharmacy here, because it serves this way and needs to connect that way." Before long, this little game business had attracted the crowd and had, honest to God, welded the team back together. To my knowledge, that's how all that started. Bill was such a craftsman—he visualized the final product of this so completely that we finally sent out for layers of Plexiglas; the best, most intense, pure colored paper; tape to mark the separate means of movement. So when we finally built a model of the real proposal, it was a beautiful work of sculpture that belonged in a museum. It knocked everybody for a loop.

Q: Did it work as well as the storm windows and the industrial cleanser cans?

A: No, but it was the presentation model. It was around for years because it was such a grand piece of work. You know how it was before CAD [Computer-Aided Design]—every layer of Plexiglas had a separate message. This layer was the nursing movement, another was the logistic and materials movement, another was the public. These were all built up, spaced nicely so that it was a fabulous piece of sculpture visually.

Forrest Wilson or somebody from *P/A* [*Progressive Architecture* magazine] was visiting CRS and asked me to write this up. So it was in *P/A*, and then what I described to you is in Bill's book.[14]

Anyway, it was a great adventure and a wonderful memory. One of my favorite things about Bill Cannady and his team was that they always packed a Frisbee and a football in their squatters kit. It was really a godsend on that project because after we started the gaming idea, we started to formalize. We could see that it worked, so we brought the users in.

The Public Health Service is very hierarchical, like the military. You had to make sure you got the right people in the right order and served their sense of rank properly. But Bill would say, "Come on; let's go out and play catch," and a Health Service officer would say, "Let's toss the Frisbee back and forth." So they did that. Occasionally, Jim was there, and he'd take them out for coffee and sort of smooth their feathers. So we had this wonderful game working. It was really the big breakthrough on the project.

Personally, my version of that history goes back to the fact that I had to stand in the "Renew Your License Plate" line for half a day in Houston. It was during that half day that I read this whole James Watson book and started to think, "Wouldn't that be an interesting way to try to define architecture functionally—without its having to be constrained initially by foundation, front door, et cetera?"

Squatters was a real experience for me. The first one I went on was with [Paul] Kennon and Jim to the University of Maryland. We did a mental health/retardation hospital there. It was kind of the prototypical squatters because Kennon had a model about the size of a car that we'd built ahead of time. He demanded that nothing begin until that model arrived. The model got lost, and the whole team went off in all directions to try and track it down. Jim was in a flurry of activity—making snow cards and performing for different groups that would come in. I was the new kid—it was about the first thing I had ever done at CRS—and [I] wondered what the hell all this chaos was about and [asked myself], "Is this really the way it happens?" Amazingly, a wonderful piece of architecture came out of it; the client adored everything about it. Jim and Paul presented the scheme on the final morning [with] the room full. Thirty-five to fifty different kinds of client representatives stood up and applauded. I'd never seen anything like it in my life—absolutely breathtaking.

■ CHAPTER 4

"LEAN, CLEAN, LOGICAL"

■ TIB: 21 JUNE 1967

We seek an architecture of probity. We want no flippant forms, forms that do nothing, mean nothing.

We want a certain seriousness in our architecture in which forms and their spaces adhere to the highest principles and ideals.

We want not only a rightness but we want one step farther up: uprightness.

■ "Lean and clean" was the phrase Bill Caudill often used to describe CRS's buildings, especially in the early years when schools were the firm's specialty. The partners wanted their architecture to be fresh, functional, and unfussy—a Texas version of Mies van der Rohe's famous aphorism "Less is more."

Within the lean-and-clean mode, CRS had plenty of room for maneuvering. At first, the firm's schools tended to be relatively simple, mostly horizontal buildings. Avoiding applied decoration, CRS produced a planar architecture that reflected the influence of Bauhaus and other modern design sources. The extraneous was pared away. In the 1950s, CRS schools often featured simple shed roofs, with windows placed to obtain maximum benefit from natural ventilation and natural illumination. All the early schools were one-story, and some had their classrooms in a single line with a corridor running along the side, rather than having rows of classrooms on both sides of the corridor. The long, narrow arrangement allowed light to enter both sides of the classroom, and it let breezes waft through and expel the heat, which was almost always a bigger concern than cold in the Texas and Oklahoma communities where CRS got its start.

The firm's designers concentrated on making the space, as well as the air, flow. Rather than have walls meet to form a tightly enclosed room—a traditional box—they frequently postponed the intersection of walls, and designed as Mies did, with planes that accentuated continuity, openness, and generosity of space. As time went on, the firm increasingly used gabled roofs. These, too, emphasized continuity. The triangular gable-ends, when filled with glass, allowed light to come in and space to extend out. They realized that classrooms did not require horizontal ceilings: The top of the classroom could be the sloping underside of the roof, fully visible from below. Some interior walls rose to standard height and then had a transparent partition of glass extend the rest of the way, from the top of the wall to the roof. The occupants enjoyed an expansive, unconfined space, spilling beyond the room's boundaries.

Bellaire Elementary School, built in San Angelo, Texas, in 1955, featured a circle of classrooms beneath a rectangular roof. *Photo courtesy Mears Photography.*

The extrawide corridors in the Norman (Oklahoma) High School functioned as a social center. Built in 1951, the school received a First Honor Award from the AIA in 1954.

Flat roofs were chosen for other CRS schools, with big overhangs to deflect sun and rain. A notable example was the Belaire Elementary School in San Angelo, Texas, which had a circle of classrooms beneath a deeply overhanging rectangular roof. At its outer edge, the roof was supported by the slimmest of metal columns, accentuating the feeling of lightness.[1] When the firm eventually started building two-story schools, part of a second-floor block of classrooms might float above an outdoor area where youngsters played.

Corridors became places for student activities. Study carrels were sometimes placed along a corridor's edge. Open storage units for books and other articles served to separate the corridor from an adjacent gathering area. If the corridor were made extrawide, as in Norman (Oklahoma) High School in 1951, it became a social center. In warm climates, the corridors might be out-of-doors under a simple roof—an economical solution that allowed designers to allocate more of the budget to purposes more critical than

Central High School in San Angelo, Texas was designed as a campus consisting of thirteen separate buildings. Constructed in 1955, it was Texas's first fully air-conditioned public school. *Photo courtesy Ulric Meisel.*

circulation. One of the firm's influential early projects—Central High School in San Angelo, Texas, in 1955—took openness at the high school level to new lengths. Instead of gathering all the activities into a single structure, Central High spread out to form a campus with thirteen buildings in all.[2]

In Tyler, Texas, a member of the faculty committee considering a new gymnasium remarked, "Wouldn't it be nice if we could have an indoor play court as nice as an outdoor one?" From that suggestion sprang an entirely open gym under a ridged steel frame in Tyler in 1954 and, a year later, a domed, glass-walled gym for St. Joseph's Academy in Brownsville, Texas. The domed gymnasium obtained an abundance of natural light while forming a simple and graceful silhouette.[3] In 1962, CRS designed Public School 219 in New York's Borough of Queens—a demonstration school for Queens College and showpiece for the 1964 World's Fair. Structural engineer Ed Nye gave it a domed roof and left its ribbed structure exposed on the interior, resulting in an airy, flexible open-plan school where as many as four classrooms could be combined into a large, loftlike space for team teaching.[4]

Natural lighting was the big design idea for the glass-walled gymnasium at St. Joseph's Academy in Brownsville, Texas. *Photo courtesy Roland Chatham.*

Public School 219, the "dome school" in Flushing Queens, New York, was an open-plan facility designed for maximum flexibility.

The firm was not averse to changing course when conditions changed or new possibilities appeared. After mastering cross ventilation and natural lighting in the late 1940s and 1950s, CRS made Central High in San Angelo Texas' first fully air-conditioned public school—a building whose sealed exterior pushed school design in a new direction. As mechanical air-conditioning became standard, as schools became bigger, and as CRS moved to the high school and then the college level, the buildings shifted from being light and sometimes playful to being more formal and sculptural. Frank Lawyer, in particular, was known for the sculptural approach he brought to institutions like Cypress Junior College in 1970 in southern California. Administrators wanted a campus that would be economical yet permanent, so Lawyer chose concrete as the predominant material, and shaped the buildings with deep recesses to invest the concrete with character. In contrast to some of CRS's early work, Cypress hewed closer to Eero Saarinen, who was then the reigning master of expressive, uniquely shaped buildings. A commuter school, Cypress needed plenty of parking, so the campus was bi-level, with vehicular traffic at ground level and with pedestrians using a raised plaza that connected all the buildings.

CRS had no interest in developing a homogeneous style for its work. "We didn't sit down and say we want to out-Wright Wright or we want to do Neutra in spades," Charles Lawrence noted.[5] The esthetic chosen for a project varied with the team, the assignment, the place, and the climate. Lawyer called it "just logical architecture," rooted in the project's needs.[6] Olin Hall, a science building designed in 1960 for Colorado College in Colorado Springs, had what the architects termed an "exoskeleton." The utilities were stuffed into thick outer walls largely devoid of windows, and the four-foot-deep utility chase along the perimeter gave the college the utmost flexibility for positioning and repositioning laboratories within the interior. Three years later, the firm designed Larsen Hall for Harvard's Graduate School of Education. It was a tall building featuring a continuous brick skin with irregularly placed windows—some protruding, some deeply recessed—as in Marcel Breuer's Whitney Museum of Art in New York, which was built not long afterward. The architects described their design partly as a quest for a "feeling of permanence" and a reaction against curtain walls, which they then saw as being "dated circa 1945–1960."[7] Flow of space was less important than a strong enveloping form—the monumental object.

A building in which CRS took great pride was the headquarters the firm designed for itself in 1968 along Houston's West Loop 610. The "White House," as it was called because of its white-painted concrete exterior, was

Cypress Junior College in Cypress, California, in 1970 reflected the influence of Frank Lawyer.

The laboratory wing of Colorado College's Olin Hall of Science, built in 1961. A four-foot-deep utility chase along the perimeter maximized the flexibility of laboratory locations. *Photo courtesy Rondal Partridge.*

The Roy E. Larsen Hall, built in 1965 for Harvard University's Graduate School of Education in Cambridge, Massachusetts, featured sculptured brick walls to complement the old brick prevalent on campus.

reclusive at first glance. People entered through a small elevator lobby on a rooftop parking deck. When they emerged below, they found a wide-open interior—essentially a glass box with a reinforced concrete structure—filled with light and views. The ceiling's illuminated concrete "double-tees" and glass-walled conference rooms placed at intervals throughout the building made for a spacious workplace, rimmed by views of the surrounding bayou. The building reflected two principal aims: preserving a sense of communion with nature (with as little intrusion on the site as possible) and encouraging the firm's participatory, nonhierarchical style of management. At the time of its construction, the CRS headquarters was one of America's largest demonstrations of the "office landscape" concept. The building's openness made it easy for employees of every rank to see one another.

Probably the most challenging buildings to design were hospitals. The users' needs were paramount—literally a matter of life and death—yet esthetics mattered. Though some of CRS's health care facilities were accused of being too much "a diagram, clothed in materials and structure," the best hospital projects possessed zest.[8] Desert Samaritan Hospital in Mesa, Arizona, one of CRS's early health care projects, designed about 1970, broke with the convention of concentrating all of a hospital's departments into a big, predominantly vertical building. Attempting to create nursing areas more attuned to patients' needs and to accommodate outpatient procedures better than could be done in a centralized structure, Desert Samaritan offered one of the first ambulatory care centers designed as a hospital extension—connected to the hospital rather than embedded in it. The ambulatory care

The approach to the CRS office building in Houston, known as the "White House." It was completed in 1968. As one visitor said, "Architects who'd let people drive on top of their building and drip oil couldn't be all bad." *Photo courtesy Ben Schnall.*

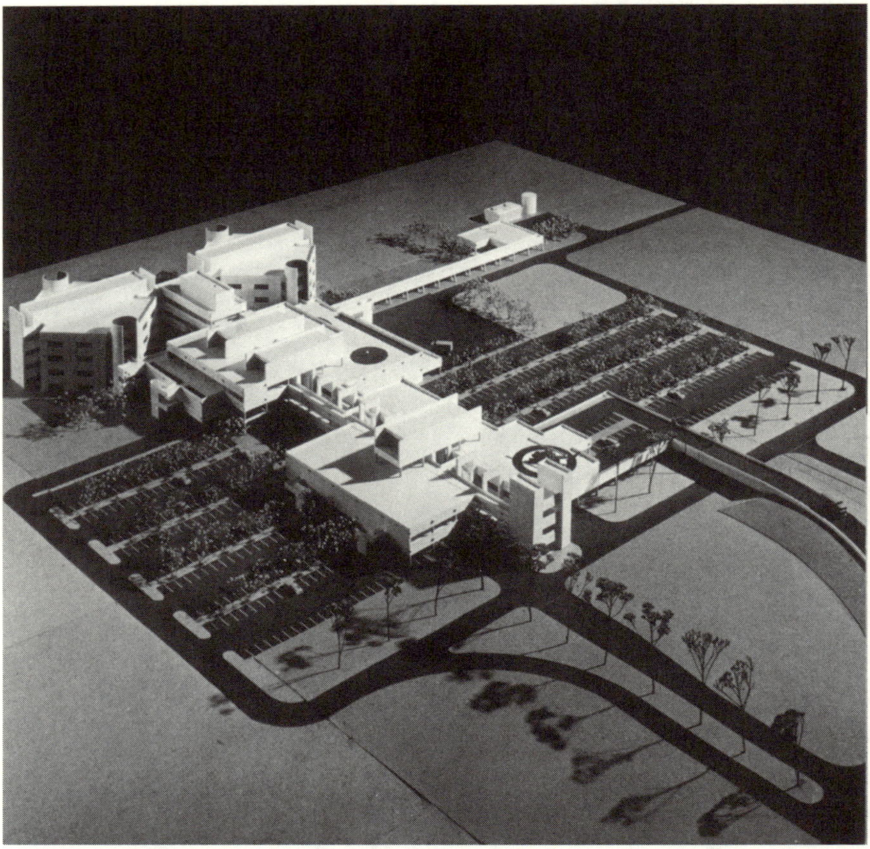

A 1970 model of Desert Samaritan Hospital in Mesa, Arizona.

center was composed of curving and rectangular segments that spread, no more than four stories high, across the desert landscape, bringing patients close to a natural setting. Individuals arriving for outpatient treatment did not have to go into the hospital lobby and confront a maze of confusing corridors and elevators. They entered the ambulatory care center itself. The windows in the patients' rooms were deeply recessed, and every bedroom had a shaded balcony. Bathrooms were positioned against the exterior wall so as not to place an obstacle in the way of communication between patients and staff. In general, CRS's hospital designs explored emerging concepts of how to serve patients and provide a less anxiety-provoking environment. Texas Children's Hospital in Houston, which CRS started work on about 1965, provided all private rooms and made the accommodations large enough so that parents could stay with their children. The hospital also offered play-rooms, as well as break rooms where parents could get relief from the stress.

Jesse H. Jones Hall for the Performing Arts has a luminous effect on downtown Houston at night. The multipurpose hall was built in 1966 to accommodate opera, drama, and music recitals.

The main entrance lobby of Jones Hall features Richard Lippold's "Gemini II" sculpture.

The firm achieved some of its greatest distinction designing concert halls. Jesse H. Jones Hall, occupying a block in downtown Houston, was CRS's first performing arts center and an auspicious start. Designed in 1963, Jones Hall housed the Houston Symphony, but the hall was also intended to be flexible enough for opera, ballet, and theater. This meant that the size and acoustics of the three-thousand-seat hall must be capable of being altered for different performances. Charles Lawrence led the design team, and theater specialist George Izenour provided hands-on guidance as the team devised a counterweighted ceiling that moved up and down, shutting off the third-level balcony and reducing the seating capacity to eighteen hundred for Broadway-style productions.

The hall was shaped like an egg. The lobby, where receptions and public mixing took place, was wrapped around the hall, and an arcade surrounded the lobby. This unique form provided a lively yet formal exterior that put the lobby's activity on display to the city through an abundance of glass, while at the same time setting up a much-loved procession into the performance hall. Jones Hall, through its suave marriage of technical and esthetic demands, paved the way for CRS to get assignments to design performing arts halls in Akron, Ohio; Louisville, Kentucky; Orange County, California; and elsewhere.

The Edwin J. Thomas Performing Arts Hall, completed a decade later at the University of Akron, featured huge, angled segments of poured concrete. Although it bore little outward resemblance to Jones Hall, it carried on and refined the Houston hall's ideas. Whereas the counterweights at Jones Hall were hidden in hexagonal walls, in Akron the pulleys and cables were celebrated: made into a striking sculpture that enlivened the lobby, their positions changing when the ceiling descended to reduce the hall from 3,000 to 2,400 or 900 seats. The forty-four-ton hung ceiling made of metal sections was balanced by forty-seven tons of weights that were suspended as twenty-seven chrome-plated steel cylinders in the ninety-foot-high lobby. *New York Times* architecture critic Ada Louise Huxtable praised the Edwin Thomas Hall's combination of drama, sensuousness, and avoidance of glamour clichés, and pronounced the Akron building "a splendid performing arts center, synthesizing all that has gone before it."[9]

In the three-thousand-seat Orange County Performing Arts Center, which opened in Costa Mesa in 1986, the challenge once again was how to accommodate different kinds of performances. Three acousticians—Jerald Hyde, Dennis Paoletti, and Harold Marshall—suggested to Charles Lawrence that the hall be designed with sidewalls that would bounce sound back toward the audience, a process that enhances the sound. Optimal reverbera-

The Edwin J. Thomas Performing Arts Hall at the University of Akron in Ohio, built in 1973. *Photo courtesy Bruce Kiefer.*

The counterweights and pulleys that help reconfigure the ceiling in the Edwin J. Thomas Performing Arts Hall also function as pieces of sculpture in the lobby. *Photo courtesy Bruce Kiefer.*

tion, with angular walls and jutting balconies that act as acoustic reflectors in an asymmetrical interior, dictated the building's overall shape.[10]

Each major concert hall designed by CRS used a glass-walled lobby to put the public on display and generate excitement on performance nights. By the 1980s, when the Orange County center was being designed, the technology of glazing had evolved, so the lobby's iridescent stainless steel and aluminum sculpture, Richard Lippold's "Fire Bird," not only soars 120 feet skyward but also extends through the glass wall, its bolts polished like jewels.

The invitation that CRS received in 1964 to recommend a site for a campus in Saudi Arabia (ultimately known as the King Fahd University of Petroleum and Minerals, or UPM) ratcheted the firm's work to a far greater size. It joined the tiny proportion of architectural firms capable of designing and overseeing construction of megaprojects. Just as it did on native soil, CRS sought to design buildings and complexes overseas that would fit the site, the climate, the culture, and the buildings' functions. The university was built in Dhahran on a *jebel,* a rocky plateau that enhanced the campus's prominence. Lawrence led a search for forms and materials that would work well in the desert and express a sense that they were Saudi, not imported. The result, built over many years, was a concrete campus with a pointed-arch colonnade and pools, fountains, and plantings that gave it the atmosphere of an oasis.[11]

The Carver-Hawkeye Arena at the University of Iowa was a design response to the desire for energy conservation and the need for column-free space. It was built in Iowa City in 1981. *Photo courtesy Balthazar Korab.*

In the 1980s, CRS's most notable designs reflected the influence of Paul Kennon. He was especially interested in air-supported structures, and led the firm's forays into designing them for gymnasiums and other athletic uses, where the aim was to enclose a large space economically, without columns and other obstructions. Positive air pressure generated by the mechanical air handling system reduced the need for a heavy structural system. Kennon was design principal for the Carver-Hawkeye Arena at the University of Iowa. The fifteen-thousand-seat facility was built into a natural ravine, reducing the exterior wall exposure by 75 percent. The roof was suspended from the bottom of a lightweight steel, skew-chord truss that further conserved energy by reducing the interior volume of conditioned air. A large, Teflon-coated fabric lantern was centered on the roof of the structure, providing natural illumination for the playing floor. Kennon was also responsible for the Chrysler Technology Center in Auburn Hills, Michigan, a 3.3-million-square-foot megastructure for some seven thousand employees involved in hundreds of tasks related to vehicle design and engineering, testing, lab work, training, pilot manufacturing, and support activities. The Tech Center was designed so that vehicles could be driven under their own power on "streets" shared by pedestrians throughout much of the complex's first floor.[12]

A 1992 model of the Chrysler Technology Center in Auburn Hill, Michigan, a 3.3-million-square-foot megastructure designed to integrate all disciplines under one roof.

The firm's final important building was the George Bush Presidential Library at Texas A&M, whose design was begun in 1989 under Paul Kennon.[13] The bidding and construction were completed by Hellmuth Obata Kassabaum, the big St. Louis firm that absorbed the CRS design group in 1994.

During its more than four decades of existence, CRS won over three hundred design awards. The firm pushed for quality designs from the very beginning, and if not every building achieved exceptional artistry, there nonetheless was a persistent ambition to do high-quality work. In periods when too many undistinguished buildings seemed to be coming off the CRS drawing boards, Caudill would sound an alarm and try to make design a high priority again. It was a balancing act, because although design mattered, it was not the sole criterion for success. Caudill and the firm as a whole believed in measuring the quest for outstanding design against a concern for economy and technology. The objective was not to produce "great" architecture; it was to produce good architecture consistently.

"We didn't have shockers, like Bela Bartok didn't have shockers," Willie Peña observed. "We didn't have a house like Mies or Philip Johnson had that was a jewel that made their reputation."[14] But the firm did design many high-quality buildings that have stood the test of time.

INTERVIEWS

FRANK LAWYER

If you are going to have an architectural firm, I think design ought to be the top priority, given the most emphasis. Design is not everything, but [it is] high on the list of being necessary if you are going to have a successful architectural practice. I measure success on how well the building is designed and how well it works. If it's poorly designed and works great, it's just going to be a good building. If it's well designed and works, it's going to be a great building. If you are a top quality firm, you should be able to have both. There ought to be room for good design, good technology, good management. . . .

Most of the time, I think we had it. I don't think we ever had a project where . . . design, technology, and function got out of balance. Those things were equally important. The old tripod Bill used to talk about—form, function, economy—most of our projects had those three qualities. Sometimes one would get a little out of kilter, but it was a goal for all of us to aim for, and most of the time, I think we hit it. Gosh, the firm has done some really great architecture—and not necessarily projects I've worked on at all. I feel very good that I had the opportunity to work for this firm. They were perfect for me. I need a lot of help when I design. [I'm] not a very good technologist or engineer. I'm a pretty good designer, but I need those other guys to help my project.

Q: Did you feel when you were at CRS that the style with which the work was approached—in other words, the separate programming by a different group before you began design—inhibited creativity in any way?
A: I always thought I needed all that kind of help I could get. I didn't mind at all not getting into the nitty-gritty of programming. I loved the approach of the programming team working with the client and getting a lot of things settled—out of the way, in the wastebasket—and the important things brought forward. It made our job simpler. . . .

I could accept the program [already] developed and enjoyed working with the boiled-down version of the budget, room requirements, and all the various things—the goals they always brought out as very important to us from the client's standpoint.

Q: But you didn't feel that being detached from the give and take of the programming process was a disadvantage?

A: No, I didn't.

Q: CRS had a mentor system in which people like you and Bill took incoming people under their arm. Do you feel that worked well?

A: Yes. I feel it was another thing Bill inspired. You trained the people under you to become better than you. We had some wonderful young people come up through the firm [who] went beyond our expectations. I can recall several: James Wright, Jay Bauer, John Focke was another . . . [they all] had the intelligence and the soft approach with people that I liked.

Q: Can you think of other significant designers who got their "graduate degrees" at CRS?

A: Rick Zieve. Jim Gatton started out in design—did a fine job—and then got into management and [did] a great job there, too. John Powell, but he started with Perkins and Will, I think. Chuck Thomsen started in design, too, and worked on my team for a while, but I had very little to do with his growth.

Q: There are lots around town like Bill Merriman and Ray Bailey.

A: Oh, yes, yes, yes—two of my favorite guys who went off on their own.

Q: Tell me about Tiny Lawrence.

A: Tiny is so creative and a delightful person to be with and work with. I feel he had more creative ability to do a beautiful job than anybody in the firm, including Bill. I think Bill was very inventive and very dynamic with great ideas, but Tiny could make it beautiful. Everything he touched had great architectural sense. He always managed to integrate the necessary parts of the building in a way that I never did. The structure, mechanical, and architecture all seemed to come together in a beautiful way. He's the most complete architect I've ever worked with or has ever been at CRS. I would rate him one of the best in the country. Every building had so many exquisite details that separated him from most of us. He concentrated on the total building from the landscaping all the way through the building into the details: the furniture selection, the color selection. He was a master at coordinating all this work and being responsible for it in most cases—the absolute designer on all his projects.

Of course, Paul Kennon was another marvelous, creative architect. I think Tiny had more natural ability, but Paul got so successful. . . . He [Kennon] put in more hours than anybody I know of in the firm. He also had great ability. I'm not saying hard work was all of it, but he put so much time on everything he touched, he *made* it work. He made architecture out of it. So those were the two creative geniuses in our firm, and their architecture stands right up to the best in the country.

Q: Tiny likes to make architecture out of structure, partitions, and the essentials of building.

A: Yes, and he always tried to make the mechanical and structure part of the expression of the architecture. I too often would get in too big a hurry or [not] have the ability to take enough time to integrate them, so I would more often than not put in a false ceiling, and all that junk in there was hidden. Consequently, my buildings never had the depth, character, or sense of unity that Tiny's or Paul's buildings did. I learned a lot from those guys but was never on their level.

Designer Charles E. Lawrence explains the architectural concept of Jones Hall.

Q: Who do you think made CRS different from all those other post–World War II firms formed with a couple of ex-servicemen that prospered locally but didn't become national? I mean, if you're thinking of a place to start a famous national firm, I don't think College Station would be your first choice.

A: I don't think so either. I don't know that it was their intent to become a national firm. I don't believe that was their goal. I believe they were just two guys who wanted to do good schools and were the kind of guys who hired the right people and could instill the desire in them to work hard and do good work. They were just down home kind of guys themselves, and those were the kind of people they hired.

I always thought it was amazing, particularly after the firm became very well known and successful, that none of the partners were country club members. There's nothing wrong with that, but that wasn't something they thought was important. The important things to them were getting good clients and doing good work for those clients.

I've always admired the partnership for what they stood for. I felt they thought a lot of their employees, treated them well. I'm speaking of Bill, Tom, Wallie, Willie, Herb—they seemed to know how to hire the right kind of people. Once in a while, when they hired someone not right, somehow he didn't last long. I thought those who stayed on and were loyal to the firm were also loyal to the ideals of the firm. They thought the direction the firm was going was right.

Q: The designers at CRS started out mostly doing little western schoolhouses and a few years later there was the same group of designers, mostly, doing projects in Saudi Arabia that were immense beyond any of our imaginations at the time. How did you make these jumps in scale?

A: It wasn't a jump. It was a slow train to China. We went from little kindergartens to elementary schools into junior highs. I remember when we got our first high school. I think there were about twenty-five guys in the firm, and Wallie came saying, "We got Port Arthur High School! Yea!" We practically had a party right then because it was a big jump, the biggest job . . . . . We just kept getting more and bigger schools, then [we] got off into other kinds of buildings. It was a continuous growth. It wasn't difficult to make the move into university work and bigger buildings. [It was] a kind of natural progression. Honestly, a bigger building is no more difficult to design than a house if you do it right.

JAMES THOMAS

When I was at CRS, architecture was fairly serious, and Caudill had it categorized into planar, plastic, and structural. We always joked that everything with Caudill came in threes.

Q: The influence of Christianity in his early life?

A: We got a huge bang when he discovered the word "troika," which is Russian for "a group of three who led." He was a wonderful man, and he really changed architecture. . . . He had tremendous insight. I think he was frustrated in some respects because he would have liked to be intimately involved with every project and could not be.

The one thing you dreaded when you arrived in the morning was a big piece of tracing paper on your desk with a big note from him. He had been there at four o'clock in the morning looking at your drawings! There was this oft-repeated, "Where is the concept?" or "What happened to the concept?" It may be five months after the squatters, and you'd had five months of negotiation on the contract with the client and the code people, the contractor—and you had lost the concept somewhere in all of this. Caudill was typically right that you had not kept a real goal in mind. You had been working on the details trying to satisfy a bunch of people, and you had lost the concept. But it was the way things worked, and it was almost always too late.

Q: He kept the big picture pretty well.

A: That's right. . . . I always felt I was in the presence of greatness on a level with some of the architects who have many, many monographs published about them. He simply had a different emphasis in his practice.

I think something ought to be put in here for posterity on the design of the CRS office building, which is now referred to as the White House. I was very busy when this all started. . . . Caudill and [Jack] DeBartolo figured out the right plan. . . . I think the results were wonderful, and when I left CRS to go to [S. I.] Morris, as much as the people, I missed the space. As an old Boy Scout, I was sort of a nature freak, and you were really sort of in communion with nature. We used to watch the bayou at lunch . . . the gars frolicking in the bayou.

The office area of CRS's Houston headquarters opened on all four sides onto a natural environment. *Photo courtesy Rondal Partridge.*

Q: Well, it was pretty exciting being in the middle of the jungle.

A: Yes, right in the middle of the city. I was very busy, and they assigned Stuart Nimmons to do the interiors. I was sort of ticked off, but I understood because that was his full-time business: to do the interiors. Caudill had laid out the scheme where you had big bays, then you had low ceiling circulation areas. . . . They had all kinds of problems with walls and circulation and communication and acoustics. . . .

About this same time, Herman Miller announced that they were having this big time development in office planning. I was invited up there to the presentation—which was called "Action Office 2"—because we had done a lot of work with Herman Miller at that point. It was basically the first of the open-plan office systems, and I came back very enthused about it. About that same time, Stuart Nimmons and a couple of the other partners were not doing too well on the planning of the [CRS] building, so I ended up with the responsibility for the planning. I think my main contribution was to figure out that the needed conference rooms, which were programmed as very small conference rooms to accommodate six to eight people, were not going to fit in the big, tall bay spaces. So I made a plan where all the low-ceiling circulation spaces that Caudill had designated became conference rooms.

Q: Those spaces were originally designed as hallways?

A: Hallways. . . . They would be walled, and there would be a lot of display space along those walls. But nothing was happening. You would go down that long hallway and on either side, there would be these tall, blank spaces.

We had terrible acoustical problems in the old building because there was a hard floor, so the idea was to put everyone in separate big rooms connected by these long hallways. So I suggested that we just go with the open plan [and] carpet the space—which Caudill did not want. He wanted a concrete floor everywhere because his concept was that you would have what he called "islands of design"—which were the lobby, the conference rooms—and that everything else would be built and finished like a garage: raw concrete floor, raw concrete columns, and a raw concrete ceiling. It was to be a contrast of highly finished versus virtually unfinished. The contractor did such a lousy job on the concrete that we ended up having to paint it. The acoustics became such an issue, and cost became such an issue that my suggestion of opening it up and having these small, individual conference rooms as sort of buffers saved a lot of money and worked out fine. That was an incredibly exciting project, but I had to do it with carpet.

Q: Carpet was an important addition, too, because it not only kept noise down, but nobody had to fiddle around acoustic tile on the bottoms of the double Ts.

A: That's right. I'll never forget the first time I walked into the space after the painting had been done and the lights were turned on. The place was still locked up for construction, and I came in through a back door. We had bright white paint on the Ts and the floor was empty, but the carpet was down, the walls were painted, and the lights were on. They were brand-new fluorescent lights, [and] it was a lovely shaded day outside in the woods. Coming in from that area by the library from the back, it was suddenly like you were in a space that was skylit. The light was so bright and evenly diffused. It was really exhilarating. . . .

Another interesting thing is that we forced everyone into this open plan. They had been working in a space that was simply open with an asphalt tile floor. The acoustics were awful. The phones were ringing all the time, and it had become very crowded. It was really an unpleasant and sort of inefficient place to work. At the same time, nobody was given an opportunity to say they wanted a private office, so we anticipated a lot of difficulty in moving.

We had a huge "throw away and file" session before we moved. We made everybody throw everything away that had no value and take everything else home. The truck arrived, and all they took from the old office was paper, files. You brought your desk stuff in your own box. . . .

We opened the building on Monday morning at eight, and at ten o'clock Trammel Crow arrived for the biggest interview that we ever had. We were trying to get the Allen Center. By nine o'clock, everything had been put away. The system worked so well, and the people worked so well that everything simply was absorbed, and the place looked like we had been there for weeks working happily.

We had a meeting at the beginning of the day before [we moved], . . . and I said: "Please get your stuff put away. At lunch, tour the building, but be at your desks when the Crow people come. And if you have any complaints, have any problems, need anything else—don't tell me [now]. Put it in writing next Monday."

So I thought, "Oh, shit. Next Monday is just going to be hellacious!" Next Monday, I got this stack of "thank you" notes and one request from

Brawley King for one more file drawer. That was the only thing. So it was probably the most successful of the projects I've ever had in that respect. It was also the most time consuming and backbreaking. That was a project where all the partners were involved in making decisions. I remember at that point the computer was involved and had been brought in to keep budgets and man-hours and that sort of thing. [Herb] Paseur early in the project had directed—that was my recollection—that all those man-hours be suppressed, that no one was to know how many hours had gone into planning our own office building. It was a fantastic opportunity, which I look back on with a great deal of pleasure.

CHARLES LAWRENCE

The way I read it, the whole idea of specialization sort of took form before I joined in '51. . . . I came into the firm actually asking to do what we then called working copies, which are now construction documents. [I] got a lot of help. I really needed to get into the guts of how you put something together to be a good designer. They kept throwing me back into the design pit. . . . I think probably because I was so damn slow. Fortunately, I stayed in design and kept going.

As it relates to growth, there was another statement that stuck with me from that first year, and that's: "The firm always wanted to do good architecture and make money and have fun doing it." And I think that's a pretty good trio of goals that are not necessarily sympathetic to one another, but there was a dedication to saying, "We can do all of it if we just set our minds to it and think about it." And I think that's pretty much what everyone kept in front of themselves as we continued to grow.

There was also the belief—and I think it was an honest one and an accurate one—[that, in order] to continue to offer growing opportunities for the talent that came into the firm, you have to grow. If you had a ten-man firm and you never got any more business than a ten-man firm could handle, and somebody came in and developed skills, the only place he could go is out. So growth was seen as a vehicle to offer opportunities for people who came in and were honing new skills and growing professionally to continue to grow and [have] some place to grow into. And it seemed to be one of the driving forces to opening up offices in other areas. . . . When you uproot some leadership and put it over there . . . there's a vacuum here, and some leadership has to step in, or someone has to step in and assume leadership and see if it works, and then there's an opportunity here. And that was very much an integral part of the philosophy of opening up other offices. . . .

I was the first non-Aggie to join the group. I was the first one . . . who was not taught by Bill Caudill. Everyone then in the firm either taught with Bill, as John [Rowlett] did, or was one of his students who was very bright. . . . Then [he'd say], "Hey, we've got to get this guy in." And I think I was not a troublemaker, but I was probably the first person who disagreed with Bill on things and sort of hassled him about design. And he was—thinking back on it, I think he was very gracious about all of that. . . .

He had depth of understanding, concern for all aspects of architecture, and the vision to look ahead and think about where we might need to go based on where we were and what he conceived it [to be]. And, of course, not the least of these facets was design. . . . I don't know what Bill's strongest asset was, but it certainly could be design. But he was not just a designer—he had this wonderful range of perception. . . . I think that's what made him a great teacher. . . . The way I remember it, we were really getting into schools very big at the time I joined the firm . . . . We had just been given the million-dollar Norman High School. Now, that was a million-dollar construction. There was really a celebration going on as I came into the firm. . . . We worked in association with Perkins and Will on that [project]. . . .

As I read it, the firm had already decided that we really needed to hit this school facilities [idea] and run with it. And it was all very natural, 'cause Bill had written his thesis on the relation between teaching methods and school facilities and had preached on that. . . . When I joined, they had already built a number of elementary schools and maybe a junior high school and had gotten the high school in Norman, Oklahoma; which was really a big job for us at that time. As I see it, it was just snowballing at that time, and we just took it and ran with it. . . .

I think what made it work is that Bill was totally dedicated to quality. Everyone was. And Tom was, and Wallie was, and so they were all watch-dogs watching us grow—making us grow. But at the same time, [they were] keeping a tight rein on where it was taking us. . . . "Are we getting a little out of line here, out of line there? Let's get back—we need to be doing *this,*" or "Watch out for this because it's diluting our quality." There was always a rein being held on slipping quality or doing things that we thought might make quality slip. . . . You know, you just don't hit it all the time. But I don't ever remember a time when the firm's . . . leadership . . . took an attitude [of,] "Well, we may be slipping in quality, but what the heck?" . . . That never happened. . . .

We moved to Houston in the teeth of the downturn of the recession. Our work had dropped off; we had to let some people go. . . . It [relocation] was a gutsy move. Again, I was not involved in it. Tom and Bill decided—well, they had talked for years about . . . moving to a metropolitan area where we could begin to get work at home 'cause all our work was really out of Bryan; virtually all of it. We were always getting something out of city, out of state. We felt . . . that to really continue to grow and develop, we needed to be in some big area or a city, and it seemed to boil down to a choice between Dallas and Houston. Tom, I think, did a study. . . . I was the oddball saying, "Why in the hell don't we move to Austin because all of our work is out of town anyway? We've proven that we can work and do good work and make money outside of our home office, and the quality of life"—we didn't have the expression then, but living in Austin would be so much superior, I thought, because I went to school [at the University of Texas] there—"would be so much better than Houston or Dallas. Let's go there and really live in the best environment we can and continue to work."

All I could hear was those Aggies boo and hiss! I really have a hunch—and I'd like to ask Tom sometime how many times I came close to being fired because I'm sure there were at least two or three, and that might have been one of them. I was already a partner at that time. Anyway, the decision was made to move to Houston, and Tom—he was either here as we moved or slightly after then because it was rationalized that: "This is not a bad time to move because we'll have fewer families to move. The expense is less, and you know we're not getting work here anyway, so let's just go ahead and do it." And we came here on a shoestring and just barely stayed alive until we got a few jobs. . . .

Willie probably told you that he and I had a longstanding, unresolved conflict about programming and its relationship to design. . . . Willie thoroughly believes, and I think always will, that programming should be carried out in complete isolation from designers . . . [to avoid the possibility of] programming with prejudice, which I think [there] is a very strong tendency for a designer to do. And so, in theory, I think he's absolutely right. But on the other hand, I'm absolutely convinced that the strongest architecture is developed when a conceptual design mind is involved in programming, at least as a sit-in and observer to the process because there's always a difference between listening to someone firsthand and [reading what they've said later. By listening to] what they say and the inflection they give, you get an interpretation. If someone writes that up and you read it, you might miss things. I think you get a different interpretation. There is a very real danger of a designer involved in programming prejudicing the program, but my contention [is]—and I don't know whether Willie's ever denied this or not, but I've told him before—that Bill Caudill *always* programmed with prejudice. He went into it [a project] wanting to accomplish a certain thing, and thoughts and decisions and questions and answers were manipulated to a certain direction. . . . I think that's perfectly all right if there's a skill there to help or have that process lead to a stronger design solution in that building. In practice, and in real life, I think it can be a strengthening of the design of the product. In theory, there's always the chance it could work against that or give some sort of an odd bent to the design. So I don't think there's an answer there except that with a good, strong designer who has his head on right, I think to sit in on the programming and observe and hear things firsthand is helpful. . . .

Willie fought very hard to keep me off of programming, and I fought hard enough in the last three or four years that I was active to always be able to go into the programming team and sit silently and observe and take my own ways. And I didn't try to write the program. I just had to be there. . . .

I've always been very dedicated to design, although I don't think it's everything. I think it should be the reason why we are in architecture. I wouldn't be interested in architecture if it was just to do buildings. I don't care what they look like. So for that reason, I think it should be the most important aspect of why and what we do. I'll give you a little of my prejudice if it means anything or not. There were several reasons why I took early retirement. One was health and the wonderful pressures of running hard and fast like we did at CRS. . . . The other was I'd become so disenchanted with architecture as it was spilling out and being published in the media. . . . I'll tell you another thing that I believe very strongly and I always will, I guess. . . . I was able to influence this in my last eight or ten years at CRS. I think that the potential for a good piece of architecture is formed and set—the degree of possibility for your architecture is set—at the interview. And when you think about that, it's just simple fact. You're meeting with a group or person who is a prospective client—they're asking questions, you're telling, you're asking questions. If you come across as sort of "whatever they want you're going to give them," then you're never going to be able to drive something through that you know is right or good for them. On the other hand, you let them know—or get them to feed back to you—that quality is very important. You want the absolute best quality you can for the dollar [figure] you get. That . . . [might] be a very low dollar [figure], but you could still produce the best quality for them. [You also want to get them to feed back] that they do want something that transcends being just a building. . . .

A lot of clients really wanted their building to be important. God, the jobs we did in Saudi Arabia were very important to every Arab client I dealt with. . . . [They were] impacted by what . . . [they] saw as . . . [they] approached them [our buildings]. Just visually, you influence people when you expose them to your building. That's wonderful . . . because then you have all sorts of opportunities to feed concepts into the goal that is . . . agreed to, and if none of that ever arises at an interview, then you have a hard time climbing out of the hole, I think, when you start designing. So I have worked hard to get a policy set up where the design group leader was part of the team that went for an interview for prospective jobs. And we actually had to go to squatters prior to the interview to determine exactly how we were going to present ourselves, and what kind of material and what pitch we were going to give. So we went in having some sort of direction to what we were going to lay before them in that prospective plan. I think that's very important. If you don't do that at the very beginning, you set the genesis for the whole potential at that interview. . . .

I came to a vision of architecture about fifteen years ago that I think is still valid. In the end of *The Ed Sullivan Show* era, periodically the juggler would show up, and his act was to take about ten plates and ten cue sticks, and he would put the plate on the table—spinning—and he'd just sit there. And then he'd go over and get another one started. . . . His trick—of course, he played the audience beautifully—was to have all ten spinning at one time. But the first one he spun—the one he spun the last or the first—was beginning to lose its momentum, and it would start wobbling and everything. And the audience would go, "Ohhh!" and he would run over and give it another spin. I think that's what architecture is. You have all these facets that you need to spin and give attention to, and if you just sit there spinning one of them, the other plates never get off the table. But you get them all going, and you have to kind of move from one to . . . . [another] as they lose momentum. And I think that's the way it is naturally.

■ CHAPTER 5

COMMUNICATIONS

■ TIB: 31 OCTOBER 1968

"GET TO THE POINT!" That's a tired old expression, yet still most expressively appropriate for a person who has to listen to talk that goes on and on.

In this day, much of our time is involved in conference and committee action, talk is not cheap. It costs all of us precious time. We need more of (B) and less of (A).

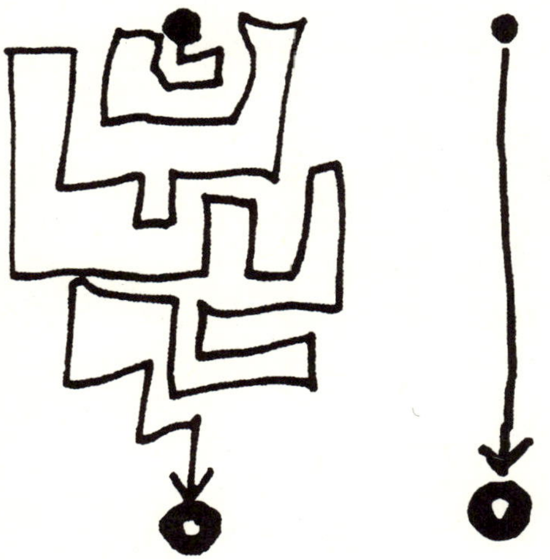

(A) (B)

■ Ambitious architects have to do more than create buildings. They must communicate—with colleagues, clients, the public, and others. During the twentieth century, successful American architects learned to discuss ideas and exchange information in remarkably diverse ways: not only through conversation, correspondence, speeches, and books, but also through research reports, presentations to professional organizations, publicity in specialized and mass media, and new forms of interoffice communication.

No firm surpassed CRS at finding ways to disseminate its messages and take in new information. All at CRS believed in communication. Very early, the firm recognized that the only cost-effective way to obtain commissions far from its home base was to reach people by a variety of methods: writing compellingly for specialized audiences, winning recognition in magazines and other printed media, giving speeches, leading discussions, participating in programs. There was a rule that if a staff member was involved in an innovative process or building design, he or she was expected to publish an article on it. The firm's members quickly learned to write for all sorts of publications. Although CRS extensively self-published, even more information about the firm's work was disseminated in architectural, education, and medical journals. No outlet went unexplored.

Much of the leadership in this realm came from Bill Caudill, who was an almost compulsive communicator. Caudill employed a charming combination of content, humor, and self-deprecation that made him much in demand as a public speaker. His writing—informal, idiosyncratic, and highly articulate—exuded an individuality and style that appealed to architects and nonarchitects alike. The 120-page booklet *Space for Teaching*, published in 1941, was Caudill's first major writing effort to attract the attention of architects and educators, but he also scored heavily with *Your Schools*, a shorter booklet that appeared in 1950, when the nation's schools were about to be inundated by the first wave of the Baby Boom. A good deal of CRS's early recognition came from articles, reports, pamphlets, and books—some of them produced by Caudill and the rest of the firm, some of them generated by the press.

The hallmark of CRS's communication was its directness and clarity. "If they don't understand you, you haven't said anything." Caudill once quoted an air traffic controller as saying. "That's the essence of communication."[1]

Good communication helped the firm team up successfully with companies that were hundreds or thousands of miles away. As CRS established a shifting succession of branch offices around the country, and as the firm became involved in overseas work—starting with projects in India, Peru, Chile, Argentina, and Pakistan—communication capabilities became absolutely essential. Although the emphasis on communication began when the firm was small, the tremendous growth in the number of employees—from fifty-three when the home office left Bryan for Houston in 1958, to 290 in 1971, when CRS Design Associates went public, to nearly thirty-five hundred at the combined CRS Sirrine in 1983—made it increasingly critical that the firm have effective ways to orient new staff members and to keep the far-flung staff attuned to the firm's priorities.[2] Those were among the purposes served by "TIBs"—a series of personal notes that Caudill started in 1964 and continued almost to his death.

Just how prolific was CRS? Many firms produce a small brochure about their work, something glossy and short. By contrast, the 1972 CRS corporate brochure was a small paperback book, a volume consisting of three parts: the first dealing with the firm's philosophy, the second with CRS buildings, and the third with the CRS process and track record. That ample brochure included a bibliography of ninety-five articles and books about CRS architecture and processes written by thirty-five CRS staff members who, led by Caudill, took the time to be authors.

Interviews

WILLIE PEÑA

Bill Caudill, our mentor, had the idea that great architects wrote about their architecture. Frank Lloyd Wright wrote books. Le Corbusier wrote books. Walter Gropius wrote books. I don't know that Mies wrote terribly much, but at least we read articles *about* him, if nothing else. Bill believed particularly because we were modernists and our public didn't quite understand our buildings, they needed to be explained. Bill would take every opportunity he had to explain our buildings—dedication brochures, for one. In back of it all was the need to explain our approach and solution to the people. The second aspect has to do with the idea that you can publish anything if you have a good idea or [a] building that needs to be published. In other words, Bill wouldn't *think* of writing an article if he didn't have an idea behind it. Consider a magazine editor who was going to ask us for a building to publish: The only reason he would ask us was that he thought it was a good piece of architecture.

So, your first task was to do a good piece of architecture, and publication would follow: "Don't worry about publication; worry about doing a good job. Then people will ask to publish your building." That's the second aspect. I remember running into a young architect who said he couldn't get editors to publish his buildings. The truth of the matter was that he hadn't done something *good* enough to publish. Of course, I couldn't tell him that. First of all, you have to do a good piece of architecture—a significant piece or something with features in which the editor might be interested.

There was a third aspect of this publication business: "When we do something in-house, let's share it with other architects, our friends, and clients." For example, when I was a fifth-year man in college, Bill Caudill took our class to California. The architects there were very open with their material. We were students, [but] the architects would give us plans of lighting schemes, handouts, et cetera. You have to understand: this was 1948, and architects were closed mouthed about their competition. I remember once walking into a drafting room, and the manager said, "All right everybody, cover your boards because CRS is here." I thought it was a big joke, but he wasn't joking.

Bill Caudill decided to reverse that. He came from the university experience in which you published regardless of your competition. Out of that came a series of reports, and this is where research comes in. We had three research report series. One called "Rese*arch Arch*itecture" [was published] between 1950–60, so we called it the "Arch-Arch Series." There were twenty-two reports [in it]. Subsequently, we had the Research Series. These are reports we published in pamphlet form. The other was an Investigation Series [published] between 1960 and 1970.

Q: That's a lot of reports. We're looking at twenty in the Investigation Series, and twenty-two in the Arch-Arch Series.

A: And some fifteen in the Research Series.

Q: These would be a combination of promotional and informational material?

A: That's right. They were our open policy. We had a list of two hundred to three hundred architects and educators throughout the country on our mailing list. They would write and ask to get on the mailing list. Some of the reports were very basic, like "Selecting the School Site." We put [in] everything we knew about site selection—which wasn't very much, but we put it on paper.

Some were not mailed to our competition, educators, or friends because they were specifically client related. "The Laredo Schools" was number two: a report on the growth of the enrollment and population spread on the map of Laredo, how many schools they were going to need for the next ten years. Obviously, it was [for] one of our clients—a report we gave the client, but we printed enough copies to give to somebody interested enough to ask for one. [It was] not for general distribution. This was probably before the mailing list was compiled. "The Design of the Brazos County Courthouse and Jail" was another nice, thick book. "Developing a Catholic Church School Center in Corsicana"; "Programming the Liberty Schools"; "School Planning Clinic at San Angelo"—we met with all the architects in town [and] produced the clinic. Different men from CRS lectured on education, school lighting, materials—you name it. [We] spent two days lecturing to these architects and answering their questions, et cetera—a clinic on school design. So we published it.

Right after that is a report on programming the San Angelo school needs. We did a survey on their schools. In 1950, Bill Caudill wrote a little pamphlet called "Take a Good Look at Your Schools: How to Do a Long-Range Planning Study." Out of that came all these programming projects. That same pamphlet was published in *The School Executive* magazine over six consecutive months. In other words, the magazine took parts of it [and] they did the editing, and out of that pamphlet [they] made six articles. So here's a pamphlet he had done for TEES [Texas Engineering Experiment Station]. It got national distribution through *The School Executive,* which was the best magazine for educators at that time.

[In] "An Approach to an Industrial Plant Design," a microchip company, Texas Instruments, asked us to document our approach to the design of their plant as part of a competition between three or four architects. Out of these approaches, they were going to select the architect who would design the new plant. We documented it and called it an Arch-Arch report.

"An Approach to College Design"—our first college, [which] was a small one in Oklahoma. "An Architect's View of West Germany"—Bill Caudill was invited to go to West Germany and committed his views to letters every day. When he came back, he put his sketches and the letters together and published it. This was the first of a series of travel reports. He went to Russia and made a report. That one is rare now—"Memos from Russia." "Memos from Egypt" [and] "Memos from Indonesia" were all done the same way. Then we would distribute them. By the time we got to "Memos from Indonesia" it was rather more sophisticated. So these reports were a kind of potpourri.

Some of these, like "The Core: A Scheme for Facilitating Back-to-Back Classrooms," came out of our research. We needed to get a very compact scheme at Laredo. Bill arrived at a scheme that could be tested at the Texas Engineering Experiment Station for ventilation and sound transmission, and it was built. On the basis of that, he wrote this little report. True, this was the beginning.

By the time we started numbering these research reports, *American School & University Yearbook* said they would publish any report we would do. They wanted to know if we had some back issues we could give them, and we agreed. Thus "The Quadruplex," "An Approach to the Design of High Schools," [and] "The Core" were picked. Then we would do individual ones for *American School & University* that were written and designed according to a format. They could have only four pages: a front, two inside, and a back. The front page would state the problem and a quick introduction, [so] we had two pages in the middle and one on [the] back to do the whole thing—no more. The reason? Once they published them, we had access to reprints for our own mailing list. So that was our marketing, our research, and our publications. . . .

We became known as leaders in the industry. We knew what we were talking about, and we were sharing it with our friends. *Why* were we sharing it with our friends? Because 80 percent of our jobs were with associate architects since we were practicing in thirty to forty states. There were architects in these communities who would ask, "Would you like to collaborate with us on this high school? I know you are an expert. I'm local, so together we might get the job." That's the way it worked. Bill, with his open policy, attracted this kind of architect who wanted to collaborate with us. So it worked out as an indirect marketing scheme, indirect promotion. The idea of secrecy among architects was being dispelled. We were among the group who began to tear down that wall, establishing ourselves as experts at the same time.

"Domes for Schools" was an Investigation [Series report]. We had used domes for gymnasiums [and] auditoriums. Can we use them for classrooms? In it, Bill said we might. It wasn't two years later that EFL asked us to design a school for team teaching inside a dome.[3] It was built in New York. It was the first school designed for team teaching, and the dome protected the method [because] they couldn't put partitions in it if they wanted to. It was go for broke; either sink or swim. You can teach in groups—malleable groups—but you can't go back. You can't put partitions up twenty feet high. It worked and was used as a laboratory school for Queens College for teaching teachers how to teach in teams. Here was a report that preceded that commission. . . .

In the long run, I think the indirect promotion was more successful. We would go into an interview absolutely unknown, but there would [often] be an educator there who knew about us, and he would say, "Oh yes, I've seen your schools published in magazines." We thought we were unknown, but there would often be a superintendent at an interview who had other educator friends who would say, "Oh yes, I know Caudill Rowlett and Scott." That came through indirect promotion. Some of it came from clients.

One time, Bill gave a speech in San Antonio, and two weeks later a superintendent called him and said: "Bill, I want you to design a high school for me. I heard your speech in San Antonio." Bill didn't even meet him while [he was] there. That was extraordinary, but [it was] still sort of an indirect/direct kind of thing.

In 1950, I went to Laredo, my hometown, and visited the school superintendent. I said: "Mr. Nixon, I understand you have a school bond issue. I'd like our firm to be interviewed." He said: "I'm sorry, Willie—I've already selected my architect. His name is Bill Caudill. I went to a school conference in Austin, and Dr. Walter Cocking said the best architect in Texas was Bill Caudill." I said, "He's my partner!" Nixon said, "Bring him over, and we'll have him meet the president of the board." We already had the contract by the time we got to the board. It was indirect promotion. Bill had gone to a conference; Dr. Cocking was editor of *The School Executive* magazine.

TOM BULLOCK

When we were first mentioned in *Life* magazine—the old *Life*—that was really something. We were hired by *Life* to do a *Life* school—very special. It covered two to three pages in the magazine in the '50s. We built that *Life* school, too—in Bartlesville, Oklahoma, just like it was [in the magazine]. We also built modifications of it in different places. We used Oklahoma as a testing ground for buildings. Being recognized nationally and this sort of thing were very important to us at that time. Just think: a firm from Bryan, Texas, in *Life* magazine! . . .

[I'd say it was] open communication, if you want me to tell you what really made the company. We've always been very open about our business—about what we do, our so-called secrets, or our unique way of doing design.

Members of the team for the *Life* magazine project, a national publicity coup, are, *from left:* Cleon Bellomy, Bob White, Frank Lawyer, Doyle Hammond, Bob Reed, Al Martin, Charles Lawrence, Roland Chatham, and J. W. Hall. *Photo courtesy Roland Chatham.*

We would publish everything. Wallie would keep saying, "Why are we telling our competition what we do?" That's to make us better, make us stay out in front of things. We were open, maybe to a fault at times, [but it was] very important [and] kept us going.

Bill was criticized for distributing our research reports—our own self-produced research reports about what we were doing on different kinds of schools—and that criticism also came from colleagues. It's a wonder we weren't strung up on an I-beam for doing that. We only sent it out to people who requested it, so we got around this business that it was a promotional technique. I think we were as good at promotion as we ever were good at design, and we called it "development." . . .

We can talk for days on promotion that built the company. Without it, we wouldn't be sitting here. We had rules: You don't go to an educational convention without being on the program. You can take somebody in CRS with you and have them sit in the audience, but you've got to be on the program. We called it "indirect promotion." Direct promotion was going to a board meeting where a decision was to be made on the architect. Indirect was going to conventions [or] meetings, [or] writing articles. But you know, indirect promotion was . . . the most direct promotion, the best promotion. It got us a national and international reputation.

We published from the very beginning. By the time we moved to our Richmond Avenue [Houston] location in 1961, we had an R&I section: Research and Information. Willie had set that up. The guy who generated the ideas, managed it, and made sure it got out into print was Bill Caudill, backed by Peña. Bill had the relationship with the architectural publishing field—not just in architecture, [but also] the education-consulting field. Not just consulting, [but] educators and education. "How many superintendents do you know?" "How many college presidents do you know?" "When did you see 'em last?" We were on the road all the time.

However, communications at CRS meant more than simply writing books and articles and giving talks at professional meetings and conventions. CRS developed a communications style for notes and letters that became part of its corporate culture. Brevity and informality were basic to it. The pocket card (measuring 5½ by 3¼ inches) with the corporate logo on it was employed heavily for brief, personal, handwritten notes from CRS staff members to each other, to clients, to prospective clients, and to prospective associate architects.

The firm's stationery, or letterhead, was 8½ inches square—distinctive not only because the shape was different, but also because it encouraged brevity. [It was] a style honed to perfection by Bill Caudill and adapted by other partners and staff members. The word *dear* in the salutation was dropped as archaic and ineffective communication. Letters began simply with "Barbara" or "Mrs. Anderson," and ended when the message was complete. As with the omission of the traditional greeting, the complimentary closing disappeared for the same reasons. Sometimes, letters closed with "Best regards from Bill," or "Wallie," or "Tom," or "Merry Christmas." Such tritenesses as "Sincerely" or "Very truly yours" were not part of the style.

In an effort to communicate architectural, philosophical, and moral ideas to the staff, Bill Caudill wrote a series of TIBs—short for "This I Believe"—which eventually numbered approximately four thousand. These were distributed within the firm and, along with comments made in the margins by recipients who read them and passed them along to other CRSers, were a form of internal intellectual conversation.

HOW THE TIB WAS CREATED

The day after April Fool's Day in 1964, Bill Caudill started to write down some of his thoughts under the heading of "This I Believe" so that his daughter Susan and his son Bill Jr. could get the benefit of fatherly instruction. Broadcast journalist Edward R. Murrow had hosted a syndicated radio show called *This I Believe* from 1950–55, interviewing prominent figures about their personal philosophies. Caudill himself had been interviewed on television by Murrow in 1955, so the title was a natural one to borrow. The two teenagers apparently did not open the folder their father prepared. So, Caudill said, "I aimed my blurbs at partners and associates of CRS—a captive audience. One reads what the boss writes." He abbreviated "This I Believe" to "TIB," and over the next eighteen years wrote about four thousand of the messages, which were folksy, reflective, pontifical, reminiscent, and sometimes earnest. Some employees hated them. Others found them refreshing. Whatever reaction they inspired, the TIBs consistently injected a leader's personality and ideals into a large company. The following is a TIB from March 29, 1972:

A person's lack of deep intellectual capacity quite often is compensated for by his energy and enthusiasm. But it is not quite true that a person's lack of energy and enthusiasm can be compensated for by his deep intellectual capacity. If I had to rate these three characteristics, I think I would place them in this order:

1. ENTHUSIASM
2. ENERGY
3. INTELLECT

How fortunate for you, dear reader, that you have all three!

Open communication meant lots of photocopying. CRS communication meant distributing copies of letters and memos among the staff through the use of buck slips. The notes on these were again a form of conversation.

"Brown bags," another form of CRS interoffice communication, were held whenever an important voice was available in Houston. The firm would buy sandwiches and everyone would sit on the floor in the reception area during lunch hour. These informal gatherings helped to keep the staff up to date on architectural issues and ideas. In short, internal and external communications were intense and well managed.

JIM HUGHES

I think the communication thing was all related to marketing. It was one of Bill Caudill's geniuses. The guy was extraordinary. Just an aside story to show you how great this guy was and how well thought of he was: When I got involved with community colleges, the first thing I did was go to California to a meeting of the California Association of Junior Colleges with Caudill. He was to make the keynote address at this big conference. [There] must have been a thousand people there. We went a day or so early and spent one day attending some of the meetings. Bill knew a number of people there, and he introduced me to some he knew.

The afternoon of the banquet, Bill told me he was going back to his hotel room to work on his speech. It was thirty minutes, and he thought it was too long, so he wanted to cut it down. The name of the speech was "The Whale's Hipbone." The whale having a hipbone was considered a vestige of a time when the whale was an animal walking on land. Bill related this idea to the concept that community colleges were trying to identify their own image separate from secondary schools. He identified where they were at that point in time as still having a whale's hipbone. So that night, I met him in the lobby and we walked over to this big ballroom full of round tables accommodating eight people each.

Not knowing anybody, I just sat down at a table against the wall. Of course, Bill went up to the head table—a long one on the dais. They served dinner before the speeches. I was sitting with my back to the wall, which was an undulating wall made of plywood. The waiter coming behind me was carrying a tray of eight plates of roast beef and mashed potatoes to serve the table. The tray hit a projecting portion of the undulating wall and came down on my back—I was drenched! Some splattered on the lady next to me, and the guy on the other side, but they weren't damaged too much. Fortunately, we were staying in that hotel, and I just went to my room and changed. Bill didn't know anything about it—and I'll come back to that in a minute.

After the meal came the preliminaries to Bill's speech, one of which was awards to some of the community college alumni from California, one of whom was an Episcopal bishop. There were five or six others—people who were products of the community college system and had excelled in their fields. When it came time for him to give his speech, well, somehow, Bill picked up on this Episcopal bishop and would stop every now and then and throw a barb at him—you know how he could inject humor into his speeches. He had the audience rolling in the aisles. He spoke for an hour and a half and got a standing ovation, which must have lasted five minutes. They just loved him.

Next morning, we had a feedback session. The idea was to allow the participants to question Bill on some of the topics he discussed in his speech. I was concerned that he had [used] so much humor [that] the message had not gotten across. I was dead wrong; they asked very pointed questions. After the banquet, I told him what had happened to me, and he was distraught that he hadn't known about it so he could have picked up on that, too.

Bill's instigation of these wonderful small things and large things he published over the years brought the firm a lot of recognition and also stimulated the need for the building type specialists to produce publications, which all of us did, [although] not nearly to the degree Bill did. I think the publications the firm produced over the years were a big reason for our national recognition.

Q: Is this very loosely marketing or is it image building?

A: The genius behind that was Bullock, of course. He's a marketing genius. I'd almost give Tom the full credit for putting the firm on the map. He didn't do it alone, obviously, but Tom made a business of CRS when he first came aboard. I even heard stories when I was a student at A&M before I knew a soul at CRS. Occasionally, somebody from the tiny little CRS office would come and make a presentation to us. Bill spent the firm's money on design and producing beautiful books with drawings and diagrams. He published everything he did. The stories I heard at the time were that the firm's profits went to hell. But Tom came in and made a business out of it—not only by putting the firm in a business posture in terms of profit, expectations, et cetera, but also in terms of efficiency and things that eventually made the business what it was. At the same time, Tom recognized the benefits of a very broad and comprehensive business development effort within the firm. It wasn't a shotgun thing at all. Everything was purposely conceived, intended to produce some desired result. As you say, the mailing list we had was very extensive: people in all different fields representing all kinds of projects.

If you spent $10,000 on a publication, and that brings in a million dollars in fees, it pays off. I guess we were about five hundred when I managed business development. We had a division called DV [Development], and it had thirty-five people who were nonproductive people—overhead. We did nothing but promote work. They were extraordinary people, though.

When I joined the firm, the stationery was [8½ inches square]. . . . It's not used as much as it was, [though. T]hey've gone to the standard stuff.[4] It was designed that way because it was one fold over. That was only one reason. The other was that brevity was key to our correspondence. Bullock and Caudill were masters at it. They taught me so much about how to write letters that were brief, to the point, warm, friendly—never "Dear Sir;" always started "John," or whatever the first name was. Of course, if not known well, "Mr." or "Mrs." I used to get comments from clients and associates all the time about the warm, friendly letters CRS generally wrote. Again, that was stimulated by the leaders of the firm—like Bill, John, Tom, Herb, and others—it sort of permeated the organization. Little things like the pocket cards CRS invented—a wonderful device. People all over the country are using them now. The firm was loaded with [this kind of inventiveness].

STEVE PARSHALL

Traditionally, marketing was done through indirect business development—writing, publishing, speaking—and after the contacts were made, a very personal maintenance of contacts [through] letter writing. . . . Right now, in my opinion, we do not do that well in a systematic way.[5]

[The company's success] was individuals. It was Caudill writing constantly and maintenance of these national and international contacts—kind of like advertising, but in a different form. You can't advertise for one day. You have to advertise every day so when the buyer has the need for what's in your ad, they'll see it. Same thing with indirect development: You've got to be out there speaking and publishing as a continuum. Then, when the need arises, they will attach to you. If you don't communicate, you will perish. Because we have done indirect [development] well for forty or fifty years, our reputation is an asset. What I mean by reputation is that every day—I exaggerate—a request for proposal comes in. We're a big firm, and every day, something comes in the door unsolicited. The problem is what to say "no" to. I saw a phase where we were everything to everybody.

In the beginning, what attracted me to the firm was their reputation for research. I've almost forgotten that. It's one of the things that differentiated the firm. Research at CRS, as I understand it, began with Bill, and there was a kind of litany or cycle to that research process as he defined it. In some ways, there wasn't a lot of opportunity to do basic, fundamental research. There was a very specific model for research, and it had a lot to do with leveraging your resources by collaborating. The research material was focused on clients. . . .

The research reports did two things. Bill called them "calling cards"—the exchange format, you know. He paid meticulous attention to the wrapper. You notice on these reports, he put the red ribbon around it where our name would be [and put] the marketing message right on the front. . . . Of course, the point of the report was the information it contained. But the marketing—the wrapper, the package, the calling card—was the value to the company. . . .

What was published ultimately became a calling card and served direct marketing. [Bruce] Wilkinson once summarized that research and the service industry: "You can't get a patent on it very well, so to get a return, it's got to improve your marketability."

■ CHAPTER 6

MARKETING

■ TIB: 24 NOVEMBER 1965

When we get our name in the magazines or in the papers for the work we have done, an immediate reaction sets in. We are invited to make speeches. We are invited to cocktail parties. We are invited to interview for jobs. . . . This is why we should have a program of publicity which will give us a continuous flow of interesting material which has public appeal.

But to do this, we must do outstanding work. First, you have to do good work. *Then you have to let the right people know about it.*

■ For about thirty years after World War II, architects, like doctors and lawyers, remained subject to professional rules prohibiting overtly competitive behavior. Each profession behaved as a self-governing organization, enforcing its own regulations aimed at curbing the ruthless (or tasteless) marketing practices in which ordinary American businesses engaged. The architectural profession continued its attempts to avoid commercialism until the federal government's insistence on unfettered competition finally overrode decades of professional decorum and proscriptions.

Architects during those years needed to attract work, and that meant finding clients and developing proposals for them. However, until legislatures and courts embraced free-market doctrines and swept away the old professional codes in the 1970s and 1980s, marketing continued to be looked upon as the grubby side of the practice, and was limited by tight American Institute of Architecture (AIA) rules. Typical of the prevailing attitude was the following assertion made in the 1963 edition of the AIA *Architect's Handbook of Professional Practice:* "The use of paid advertising to increase demand for an architect's services violates ethical ideals."[1]

In this restrictive atmosphere, how is an aspiring firm supposed to make itself known? Caudill Rowlett Scott answered the challenge by entering its projects in architectural exhibitions and awards competitions, by submitting materials to architectural journals, and by disseminating the results of CRS research among other architects and people in fields such as primary education. Even in a constrained environment, CRS managed to assemble a carefully thought-out marketing plan, one that emphasized knowledge, quality, and a commitment to specialization. Nowhere was CRS's focus on marketing more evident than in the detailed strategy Bill Caudill laid out for the partners in May, 1954, six months after winning the commission for the Brazos County courthouse and jail:

> We have a good start in breaking into the courthouse field, but we must definitely have a plan on which a systematic operation can be conducted. Here's a plan which I would like to propose:
>
> 1. Start a file on every commissioners' court in Texas and Oklahoma.
> 2. Determine the date and the condition of the existing courthouses.
> 3. Obtain the names of the county judge and the county commissioners.
> 4. Start a public relations program that will give the Bryan courthouse the greatest publicity that is possible.
> 5. Prepare article for COUNTY PROGRESS.
> 6. Find out what the official organ is for county organization in Oklahoma.
> 7. After the survey of the existing courthouses, make a list of the counties who most likely might build within the next five years.
> 8. Start building up friendship among county judges.[2]

As CRS's marriage of expertise and marketing developed, many employees matured into specialists: Jim Hughes, Bob Reed, and Tom Hooker in community colleges, Bob Brooks in elementary and secondary schools, Phil Williams in higher education, Bert Ray in systems building, Ed Finlay in city planning, Jim Gatton in civic and performing arts centers, and Chuck Thomsen in the lucrative field of construction management. From outside the firm, CRS also imported experts, including Jonathan King in schools and industrial building systems and Jim Falick and Bob Douglass in hospitals.

A core principle of CRS marketing was that "the people who promoted knew what they were promoting."[3] Thus, much of the task of seeking commissions fell to the specialists. This set CRS apart from most of the profession, where an unspecialized salesperson—often but not always a partner in the firm—did the selling. "There were several times we tried to hire a person who only knew about promotion," Bullock says. "It didn't work."

The specialist would win the clients' confidence, understand their priorities, and avoid mistakes that a generalist might make. Nonetheless, marketing was a team activity. A principal, such as Wallie Scott or John Rowlett, was part of the team that went to the initial interview with the client, demonstrating that the project had the attention of the firm's top echelon. At some point in the interview, the principal would hand the discussion over to the specialist, who would impress the clients with his knowledge of their field and his interest in their concerns. The firm might also send a designer to accompany the principal and specialist during the client interview. The specialist would be placed in charge of the project, but would not be the chief designer.

Each building-type specialist spent about half his time leading work on projects and the other half on direct and indirect promotion. Direct promotion involved courting clients to obtain jobs. Indirect promotion included conducting research, along with writing and speaking in their area of expertise. This kept the firm abreast of innovations and trends, and planted the seeds for future commissions. The system was very productive. Some specialists pursued clients with such zeal that the firm had a hard time keeping up with all of the projects they attracted.

By emphasizing quality, the marketing program helped lay the foundation for a satisfying design practice. As Tom Bullock observed, "If you raise the expectations of quality to a level that excites the client, you're going to get his support all the way through."[4]

INTERVIEWS

TOM BULLOCK

I have to take credit for moving the families out of Bryan and Oklahoma City into Houston. We got settled in Houston about 1959–60, closed the Bryan office, and more or less called an end to the Oklahoma office. We left what projects remained with an associate, who ran his own practice in our office space. We were out of Oklahoma. Again, growth, you see. We were going to places we hadn't been before. We depleted the old cotton field; we were going to some other crop. We arrived in Houston with a backlog of work, but not too much.

The low point was—I remember this very well. I mentioned John Stambaugh, Bill Caudill's classmate. John and I were not close until I was given the job of managing partner. Then I realized I didn't know anything about managing and knew John could be a big help to me businesswise in telling me how to project fees, all that sort of thing. I made an effort to get him involved as a kind of consultant. . . . Not only did his firm, Touche Ross, take care of our tax accounting, he became a friend and counselor. . . . So he made a trip to Houston at my request.

I said to him, "John, we're out of work. We've got all these people in Houston—forty-two families—[and] we're out of work." He had heard that before: "Well, what are the prospects?" Me: "Very little."

Bill Caudill was in Corning, New York, then, working on schools that were never built because the bond issues failed. We were paid only our costs. Bill and I met in New York at the old La Guardia terminal. I was ready to return to Houston, and he was going back to Corning. We had met in New York to try to figure out what our next moves might be. Bill said, "Let me call Walter Cocking. Maybe he knows where there's a superintendent who intends to build another school."

Walter Cocking, the editor of *The School Executive* magazine, became a great kind of "father confessor" to architects who devoted most of their lives to school buildings because he had been a superintendent in San Antonio years before he became a publisher, editor, and writer. So naturally he liked the Bill Caudills, John Lyon Reids, Larry Perkinses—these people.[5] Well, Bill came out of the phone booth—it was right by the parking area—and said, "I knew there wouldn't be anything. He said he didn't know of anything but cutbacks." I also knew it was very difficult for Bill to ask anybody for a favor like this, and I'm sure he got that message over to Cocking. Cocking didn't have any idea of where building might be going on.

So I came on back to Houston and called John Stambaugh, and he flew down to Houston. In those days, we might get a call the next day from somebody in Phoenix or Reno or someplace. But we weren't getting calls and were working on what you might call "finishing up" projects. So when John came down and asked what was going on, I told him we did have a project: a cotton gin. "A friend of Jim Gatton"—Jim and I are still laughing about this—"is going to build a cotton gin in, I believe, Victoria, Texas, and he wants an architect," and I think he [Stambaugh] said, "Really?" And I said, "I know what you're thinking, John—there's never been an architect on a cotton gin. But he wants to do one. Maybe he has an esthetic curse." John asked, "What does this mean?" I told him, "It will help us for a couple of months, and we're working on it." John asked, "Is he paying his bills?" I said, "No, there's an account outstanding on that, but he's a friend of Jim's."

When I took John to the airport after that, he turned to me [and said], "I wish I could have done more." I answered, "I wish you could have, too. What do you think we can do, John?" That was the first and last time John ever said, "I don't know." We were at the end of the road at the airport, the end of any kind of business. So I said, "Well, John, we still have the cotton gin."

The next day, guess what? The cotton gin was a phantom project. The fellow didn't have any money. He was trying to build this as a speculative kind of thing. Gatton feels guilty about it to this day, but it did keep our doors open—a little hope. I called it a phantom that worked. The cotton gin was a very low point, though.

Within a month, we were able—again, through indirect promotion; meetings, conferences that had taken place over the years—to get a project in Saginaw, Michigan. Superintendent of Schools George Mills called Bill Caudill [and] we did the whole Saginaw school system. There were three local associate architects. [It was] an outstanding opportunity: probably a $10 to $15 million building project, the largest we had at that time. That low point taught us something: You've got to hold on and have that indirect promotion working for you.

JIM HUGHES

Early on in the 1960s, Tom came up with the concept of what we called building-type specialists. It sort of started, as I remember, with John Rowlett. . . . Among many wonderful traits, John had an extraordinary ability to make lasting friendships with people. He had been attending the American Association of Junior Colleges' annual conventions, held in different parts of the country, for several years. These were not big things in those early years; they may have had 250 to three hundred people attending. He had made a lot of very good friends at those conventions in what was called at that point the junior college field.

About 1962–63, the convention was held in Dallas. Tom Bullock, Wallie Scott, John, and I think Herb Paseur all went to Dallas, booked a suite, and entertained a lot of these junior college presidents. They came back all excited about the potential of this building type in terms of CRS's marketing strategy. . . . That was at the beginning of what became the community college movement in the U.S. [It was] an extraordinary thing [that] lasted probably fifteen years.

Tom called me in one morning and said, "You are now a junior college specialist." As a matter of fact, we had just gotten this University of Petroleum and Minerals project in Saudi Arabia, and I had been designated as the project manager. That designation had been made maybe three or four weeks before. After they came back from this Dallas trip, I was dropped from the UPM project and made the junior college specialist because they could see the enormity of the potential. It was a brilliant concept on their part. They needed somebody within the firm to concentrate on this building type who could walk among these educators as an architect and talk their language as well as the language of building. . . .

At that time, there was a real goal to develop a unique kind of community college. Most of the junior colleges in the country—they were trying to get away from the term "junior college"—were housed in secondary school facilities in the community. None of them had their own image. The first thing I had to do was find out what a community college was all about because I wasn't all that familiar with it. But that began a new thing in the firm: a marketing strategy on Tom's part. There were several specialists identified. I was the community college specialist. There was Phil Williams, the university planning specialist. Don Wines, one of the CRS designers who had done many, many schools, became the school specialist. You have to realize that, up to this point, I would guess 90 percent of the work the firm had done was schools. Not very many [were] university projects, either. They were mostly elementary and secondary school buildings all over the country, not big projects. Don Wines was pegged a secondary school specialist.

Along about that time, Jim Falick was brought into the firm as a hospital specialist, and he was joined by . . . Bob Douglass, both involved in medical facilities. Then we had Jim Gatton in office buildings.

We were organized in one area [of the office], and our job was to promote each of our building types through developing within ourselves a national presence. At least, this was the objective, to develop a national presence in that building type. In my case, this meant I attended all the junior college conventions. There were two held in California because California was sort of the leader of the pack in the '60s. I think they had some eighty junior colleges established when the rest of the country began to get on the bandwagon. So I got deeply involved in junior college activity all over the country. At that point in time, there were many, many opportunities for contracts to design new facilities.

Wallie Scott was a wonderful, wonderful promoter, [and] one of the best interviewers I've ever seen, probably the best in CRS. He had a way of going in to meet a college board or school board and absolutely charming them with his East Texas humor. The guy had a sweet way about him. He could both charm people and sell a specialist like myself—what I could do for them and their project—as well as sell all the other attributes of CRS, the other specialties and uniquenesses of the firm, which were many. We barnstormed all over the place. In a period of not very many years, we brought in a total of, I think, thirty-five community college projects—nine in Illinois, for example. We had them in Kansas, Florida, California, New York, Michigan, Ohio—all over the place. . . . It was a really exciting period.

The first community college we got was from John Rowlett's real good friend, Leroy Good, president of Monroe County Community College in Rochester, New York. I think, at the time, it was the largest contract the firm ever had. . . . John had met Leroy Good through his contacts at the junior college conventions [and] they had become close friends. So when Good was ready to build a new campus in Rochester, he hired CRS.

That project was the first time, I think, we had entered into a multiple association. We had three local architect firms and one local firm of mechanical engineers involved in that project. We interviewed them jointly with the client, and with the client, we selected the three firms, and they brought in the other engineering firms. This team was a unique thing that we put together. It was a $22 million project in the 1960s, a pretty good-sized job at that time. As we did on many, many projects, we would do the design and design development part of the project, [and] the local firm would do the working drawings and supervision. I spent a week a month up there for about four years on a commuting basis, coordinating the work of those other firms with our own to make sure everything was moving along as it should.

At any rate, that was a major concept of Tom's, the concept of specialization in terms of building type. We wrote publications, articles, we made speeches at the conferences, made presentations of our work. The more work we got under our belt, the more we had to show.

JIM FALICK

In 1965, I was working for a firm in New York named Westerman Ellis, which was a small firm that specialized in hospital work or health care facilities. I had been working for them less than two years after graduating from Columbia in a program that was designed for architects who wanted to specialize in health care. I had a fellowship from the AIA and the national AIA Committee on Architecture for Health to study health care at Columbia. I spent a year on a Columbia University fellowship in Europe looking at health care facilities as part of the rebuilding of postwar Europe. So I had the background in health care [and] was working in a health care firm, although with less than two years of practice. I had written an article for a magazine called *Architectural Forum* on some part of health care design.

From what was told to me later, none of the principals of CRS were interested in going back and specializing [in health facilities], so they wanted to buy somebody. They asked two people who knew me rather well—one was Ed Romieniec, who had been part of their A&M background, had worked at CRS, taught at Columbia, and was my senior year professor and friend. The second one was Charles Colbert, an architect from New Orleans who had . . . been connected with CRS in some fashion and was the dean at Columbia in my last undergraduate and graduate school years.

John Rowlett contacted me in the spring of 1965 and asked me if I would come down [to CRS's New York City office] and talk to him. I was fairly naive and didn't quite know who CRS was. I had been knowledgeable about the New York architectural scene but not outside of it, except having seen the name published. CRS was a firm "out there." There's a wonderful *New Yorker* cover by Steinberg which shows New York, the Hudson River, New Jersey, and then Japan—I mean, the rest of the world is "out there" in far smaller dimensions. From the architectural magazine's point of view, architecture had a few big firms and New York. The New York architects got a far more prominent play. But CRS did have a reputation: it was in schools, and they were published.

I went down to visit John Rowlett. There is something in my memory that says I was wearing inappropriate socks for the interview. When I realized it was an interview—when I realized, "Wait a minute; this is John Rowlett of Caudill Rowlett Scott," and I was not wearing the right business socks—I remember to this day being anxious about all this. John was a wonderful man, as warm and sweet an individual as you could find. He talked to me, told me what they were looking for and what they were interested in. I thought, "Gee, this is kind of interesting."

I had no idea of leaving New York. My ex-wife and I were both from New York. I had worked in New York. So it was only kind of interesting—but the idea was very attractive. He mentioned he was talking to other people. One of the other people he talked to was George Mann, who preceded me in the program at Columbia and had been my friend since we both started at Columbia.[6] I told George I had talked with them. When they called him, he told them that since they were talking to me, he couldn't talk to them because he was my friend, which was very nice. . . .

Within a few weeks, I got a call from John Rowlett asking if I would go to dinner with some other people. Actually, Tom Bullock was in town, and Rowlett had told him about me. He would like to meet me but was up on business, and the [only] time he had available was dinner. Well, I was very excited at that and again, not quite sure—I don't know that I was that young chronologically, but I was certainly that young as far as experience goes. When somebody is calling you up and saying, "Shall we go to dinner?" that's very heady.

CRS was in what was then the Grand Central Building, which was on Park Avenue—[at] the head of Park Avenue. I went down there in time, met Mr. Bullock and a friend of his who was also joining us for dinner, somebody he had been in the air force with in World War II. We got outside, and they stood on the sidewalk and said, "Let's not go to the Cattleman for dinner. Let's go to the Four Seasons." Well, at that point in my life I had been to the Four Seasons four times: once each season to get an ashtray, which every architectural student did. You went for a drink and stole one of the seasonal ashtrays. The thing was to have a set of ashtrays—one with each emblem for the four seasons—but I had certainly never eaten at the Four Seasons. We went there, and it was time to order dinner after chitchat. I ordered something I really love—I love duck, and I ordered duck à la orange. They all ordered steak. Why we didn't go to the Cattleman, I don't know, but we went to have steak at the Four Seasons. Let me tell you, duck à la orange is not what you want to be into—I mean, you don't order something that requires dissection for an interview.

John Rowlett said they were interested and would like me to come to Texas. So I arranged a trip and came down on a Thursday. I spent the day with CRS on Friday, stayed with family friends Friday night. Ed Romieniec came in and met with me on Saturday. I was interviewed—put through the mill. I was passed from person to person and was taken to lunch by Bill Caudill and Chuck Thomsen, among others, at what was then a private club on top of the Fannin Bank Building overlooking the medical center. Sometime later in the afternoon, Herb Paseur and Tom met with me and offered me a job. I was delighted and told them I needed to talk to my wife and family and would let them know the following week. I told CRS I would accept, but my wife was expecting, early in November. I said I would like to stay in New York and work in New York from whenever I joined them to about three months after the baby was born. I think I joined them June 1, 1965. . . .

So I went to work for John Rowlett in the New York office and had nothing to do. It was a construction administration office. My graduate thesis was on community mental health facilities, which was a new area of architectural practice, and I started meeting people. When I talked to CRS on that Friday, one of the things was a clear understanding that I would not do marketing. I had never done marketing, didn't know anything about it. My job was to lead in the specialty, to lead in the specialty of this design category, which was what I had been trained in.

I was coming to start a health division. That was the reason for my coming. The excitement was that CRS offered the chance to create something. They offered a career opportunity that nobody offered. And I've got to say, of all they told me that could happen . . . they didn't tell half of it as far as career and opportunity and the chance to be somebody in the field, to create a star of yourself. That is what they held out. Their idea then—and their idea restated—was that you find somebody who's got a desire to do something, you attach your tail to that kite, and you let it fly. They did that with me, they did that with Phil Williams, with Jim Hughes, and various other people who helped create whole areas of business.

Anyway, I was in New York with nothing to do [and] Bill Caudill suggested I write an article. He told me that to write an article, you first meet people and find out what they want you to write about. So, I went and met the editors of the health care magazines. I wrote one article, which I think was the third one I published. I remember Bill taking it and [critiquing] it. He gave me five things. I learned that you always watched his criticism very carefully because he said four positive things. [So,] you had to watch after you got to number four as to what the real point of the criticism was. There were "tremendous ideas" and "wonderful this" and "magnificent that" and "by the way, you might find it easier if you put in subheadings." To put in subheadings, I had to rewrite the whole article because it was just a mash of stuff! He had a wonderful ability to teach in a subtle way. So I wrote a couple of articles. I was in New York from June to the following [spring, and] I moved to Houston March 31, 1966. I didn't have anything else to do, so I got work.

We talk about marketing in a very different sense today. Looking back, I can package it much more easily than it actually happened. I had already published. I had one article on health care published, I had a college project published, [and] my graduate thesis at Columbia was published. It was the only time [a thesis project] was ever used on the cover of *Hospitals* magazine. So I had been published already. There are people who can write articles, and they are going to write articles; and there are people who talk about wanting to write articles, and they don't write articles. Somehow, I was going to write articles. I loved what I was doing, and I was very driven to be successful. CRS, I think, saw that and said, "The guy can market himself, which means he can market." I think they saw marketing potential—I didn't know anything about marketing.

The way I got work: I did my thesis research with a guy who went to work for the National Institute of Mental Health. We talked, and he told me about a community mental health center in Brooklyn that was in trouble. . . . They didn't know what they were doing; would I help? So I got into that. It was an association with a firm named Kahn and Jacobs on Maimonides Community Mental Health Center. Through that, I met a woman named Marge Frank, who was assistant commissioner for mental health in New York City—a very wealthy woman. Marge hired us to do work for New York City.

My thesis was a community mental health center for Columbia Presbyterian, and we got hired to do a community mental health center owned by the city—working with Columbia. So I got hired to do my thesis. Norman Hoover was the designer for it. It was a very exciting thing. The only trouble was they wanted to build it on the site of the Audubon Ballroom, which was where Malcolm X was killed. The community revolted because Columbia was across the street and lived behind its walls across that side of Broadway. Now it wanted to cross Broadway into the community and tear down a building which was a shrine in many ways to a certain group of people. So the project never got built, but [it] was very exciting to work on.

The second job we got from them was the Manhattan Community Health Center on Ward's Island; Manhattan State Hospital. I think I got those jobs, and we were working on those. This was making the people in Houston very nervous. One, they never had anybody come into the firm at the level I came in: I came in with a promise I would be an associate and was elected an associate almost immediately. So that was hard to absorb. I hadn't been trained and hadn't grown up in the CRS system. Second, they were getting all this work and didn't know *why* they were getting this work.

My next interview was in Baltimore for a community mental health and retardation center for the State of Maryland. The commissioner of mental health for the state somehow got my name and asked me to come to the interview. CRS sent Chuck [Thomsen] to help me. Chuck said, "Where are your slides?" I said, "What slides?" I didn't know anything about slides, about interviews. I didn't know anything about anything. My graduate training in part was in the Department of Community Psychiatry. This was legislation passed in '63 and was just being implemented, so I was one of the few who knew what they were talking about. You went in and talked on a basis of experience in an area where people had less experience than you did. So we got the interview. Then I got myself on a talking circuit for CRS—really for the National Institute of Mental Health. They held meetings all over the country. I think I did about one a month for eighteen months.

The first hospital [we got] rather than a mental health [facility] was a project in Chillicothe, Ohio, in 1966–67. The first project was $15 million. The second, in Louisville, Kentucky, was a $20 million project. CRS had no health care facilities built of any scale, and this was sold on my energy and the fact that this was a national firm that had delivered nationally. In Chillicothe, we were not associated; in Louisville, we were. But you know, you sold the CRS reputation and you sold this "young Turk in the field" [image]. The fees on the Louisville project were the largest fees CRS had ever gotten. They had never had a fee over a million dollars. When I joined CRS in 1965, there were 103 people, and by 1973 it was four hundred people, and 70 percent of the volume was in health care. . . .

Marketing is so much more sophisticated now. First of all, we recognize it as such. CRS recognized marketing. It was called Business Development—you were in DV, but it was nowhere as sophisticated, and the clients weren't as sophisticated. When we got Midland Memorial Hospital, I remember I flew in, met with the board, chatted a little bit, got the job, and left town. There was much less competition, much less sophistication, and very few people were specialized. The fact that you really were specialized, that you knew the language they were talking administratively, that you could talk the language the doctors spoke, you could talk about nursing patterns and organization—that was extremely impressive early on in any area. These were all people who specialized, and they respected the fact that somebody else was a specialist in their field because they all felt they had been screwed by architects. In one sense, marketing was relatively easy. It felt easy. It was work, but it was fun, a challenge.

The opportunity to travel, to learn this country, to work in so many places and work with the power structure of communities where you were somewhat of a voyeur, but you were there. You were intimately involved in what was happening in the community for a period of time. It was extremely exciting and very wonderful. The people you met, the learning about America, it was the most wonderful gift I could have had. I was given the support to write, to lecture, to speak. It was all seen as good for the company, so I was applauded for that—although the work had to be done on weekends and evenings. I worked enormously hard. . . .

I called up the AIA Committee on Architecture for Health and said, "As part of CRS, I think we ought to be represented on this committee." The committee now has 150 to 200 people—it was 12 to 13 then. Muscling your way in took a level of guts I could have in my corporate position but that I certainly would never have had personally. So I became part of a national committee then on its way to becoming very powerful. I think by the early '70s, CRS was the preeminent health care [design] firm in the country. . . .

I was in a teaching mode. There were very few people who did health care. George Mann went to Texas A&M, and we were able to get some people out of the program that Romieniec had him start there. Many of those people have been extremely successful in the field, and I feel like I had a piece of their career, which is nice and makes me very proud. . . . Even when we're competing, I feel proud of them. CRS, in essence, formed the Texas health care industry today. The leading firms in the state, except for PSP [Page Southerland Page in Austin and Houston], have people who all came out of CRS. It spawned its competition all over the country. . . .

I brought people in; I brought in a superb guy from Leo Daly named Bob Douglass, who later left CRS and founded what became one of the major hospital consulting firms in the country, Robert Douglass Associates, which has been sold and merged with Touche Ross. . . . I brought in a guy named David Scoular, who's brilliant.[7] There was a designer we taught—who was really into his capacity to conceptualize how this mini–inner city operated—named Hank Winkelman, who came here with me and later left and is now with HOK, St. Louis, and has done some very special work. [There's] Anderson DeBartolo Pan—ADP—in Tucson, all three of whom came from CRS.[8] [Jack] DeBartolo and [Solomon] Pan were part of the health care group. Brooks/Collier, Watkins Carter Hamilton—all of them were part of that original stew of people. It was a very heady environment.

BOB DOUGLASS

Well, I think I was about the twelfth person in the country to receive this joint fellowship from the AIA and the AHA [American Hospital Association]. Jim Falick, I believe, was maybe the second in this order of people who did that particular thing. I had been with the Daly Company in Omaha for about four years, resisting being specialized in health care. I was a good designer and designed lots of different kinds of buildings and enjoyed that. I was just unwilling to be specialized. Then, when I joined CRS, it was obvious from the beginning that my real purpose there was to be a hospital specialist and, even more than that, a specialist in programming and planning rather than design. So even though I resisted, it quickly became obvious that it was the smartest and best thing I could do. I realized I had a bad idea and that specialization was really good for me.

So I got in the groove. As I remember the story—the numbers may not be right—health care accounted for less than 1 percent of the firm's business when I joined them. Jim had been there for a couple of years, maybe, and had done some mental health related projects but didn't have much hospital experience. I came in with good relationships with a couple of good hospital consulting firms that, as a favor to me, provided us referrals. Jim was a good enough salesman that, even without a track record, we started getting those jobs. As you know, we got some big hits early—prestigious clients. Our process created a lot of excitement, drew a lot of attention, [and] made the consultants look great, so they continued to refer more work to us. Most of the early referrals I can recall came through Dick Johnson at A. T. Kearney [or] Jim Stefan and David Danberg, who were partners in the James A. Hamilton firm and my mentors when I was a grad student at the University of Minnesota.

Q: Both of those were hospital consulting firms?

A: They were both hospital consulting firms, and by different routes, these people had sort of adopted me at some point along the way to help me. . . .

Concerning the health facility success, there's no taking away from Jim's gift of salesmanship or his energy and tenacity. I also think we just happened to be there at the right time. The wave crested nationally, and [there was] the perceived need for hospitals and improvement in hospitals. The Carnegie Report came out about the time I joined CRS, saying we've got to have twenty-five new medical schools right now. Things like that worked just right for us.

I don't think just any firm could have done it. The fact that CRS had developed a pattern of practicing nationally, had evolved this believable way of bringing a team in, squatting, and making it happen right there was very, very important to our success in the hospital field. The fetish among health care people was experience: "If you haven't done fifty jobs just like ours, it's too big a chance to take." I had quite a bit of experience—probably stretched it to be more than it was, [but] my consultant friends were willing to reinforce that.

Jim had developed a relationship with Newell France that made it seem like CRS actually had something to do with all the new buildings over there [in the Houston Medical Center].[9] In fact, it was mostly Frank Lawyer picking the brick color on the outside of the tower, but Newell let clients believe we had done the whole darn thing when we'd take them over there for a tour. But the fact that we would take our team out to our client's place and let them see everything that was happening, I believe, had a lot to do with overcoming their sense of risk—the biggest thing hospital clients had to overcome. They were terrified of architects.

As I started to say earlier, when I started, health facilities was less than 1 percent, as I remember. When I left [in 1971], it was said to be 54 to 57 percent—can't remember precisely, but about that—within a little over a three-year span. When Jim left [in 1975], somebody told me it was about 70 percent.

I'm not quite sure why that happened, because I'm not as sensitive to other markets as I was to the health care market, but we definitely hit a wave of intense interest in building in the health care field. I also think community colleges and other work the firm had previously thrived on were on the downside of their lifecycle curves. I believe it's also true that when I joined CRS in the summer of 1968 there were something like 150 employees. When I left, I think there were about 350. So it was not just hospital work replacing other kinds—it was a net growth across the firm. I don't know really why that happened, but I believe CRS's credibility as a national firm enabled us to blossom instantly into a nationally credible force. . . .

Our biggest jobs were with the universities. They were universities that maybe CRS had done a campus plan for or some other kind of work. So our bed was sort of made for us.

Before I came to CRS, I had published one article in *Hospitals*, the AHA journal, and I had helped conduct a seminar for the Hill Family Foundation at the University of Minnesota about some work I did there. But that was the extent of my public speaking. Being a kind of shy person, I was terrified of standing in front of any group of people saying anything. I would watch Jim do his thing and feel physically uncomfortable to hear him say such dead obvious, insultingly simplistic things to these intelligent and sophisticated people. Then the second thing I observed was they loved it! They were impressed.

I learned so much from Jim. [It] sounds like I'm being insulting, but I'm not. I learned that what seems obvious usually isn't, and there's some kind of equation along the lines of what Marshall McLuhan said: "If you write a book that's more than 10 percent new information, nobody will be able to read it." So the message needs to be couched in a lot of sugarcoating, in some familiar thing. That was Jim's gift. He would say so many things to these people that seemed obvious and simplistic that he would get them comfortable, [and] then lead them across the line. Whether to get the job or a decision or win the point, he had that way of doing it. To the extent I've been effective in building my own business, I've learned most of that from Jim.

■ CHAPTER 7

GOING NATIONAL

In the early days, we made a decision, which has had a profound effect upon CRS's present-day operation. We decided that we would go anyplace to do a job if there were an opportunity to produce good architecture. So far, we have been in luck. Opportunities come with good clients, and good clients from all over the United States have come to us. We respond by going to them—in the areas of Los Angeles, Boston, Miami, Minneapolis, and points in between. There are CRS projects in a majority of the states.

Some people might think that we can't make a living at home. They are right, in a way. We can't do all the things we want to do in Houston or New York—or for that matter, in any other one place. . . .

We like to travel. And we have devised ways to be proactive successfully most anyplace. That's why any day, you may find six suitcases standing in the lobby of CRS. We may be sending to an out-of-town job our secondary school specialist, our mechanical engineer, a top-flight designer, a construction systems expert, plus the project architect and a partner.

Couldn't one man have done the job? Maybe. But at Caudill Rowlett Scott, we offer specialized services. Our approach is interdisciplinary. That's why we need a team. And that's why we travel so much. It is most difficult to solve a problem away from the problems.

—Where Do We Work?
CRS brochure no. 4000.0601, ca. 1972

■ In the 1950s, architects who wanted to practice nationally had two choices: establish branch offices or form associations with other firms capable of handling the distant projects. Caudill Rowlett Scott did both.

The firm's first branch office opened in 1952 in Oklahoma City, a metropolitan area twelve times as populous as Bryan–College Station.[1] It was a natural choice: Oklahoma had been the source of many of the firm's best early projects, including schools in Blackwell and Norman, and Caudill was a native of the state—born in Hobart, brought up in Durant and Oklahoma City, and educated at Oklahoma A&M—that helped to generate work there. But Caudill, as the firm's leader, stayed in CRS's home office in Bryan with most of the staff. His partner John Rowlett and a young associate, Tom Bullock, both Texans, were sent to establish the office in the Oklahoma capital.

A second branch office, in Big Flats, New York—just outside the small upstate city of Corning—opened in 1957, after CRS was chosen for an important planning and design project for Corning's school system. The Corning project was considered so important that Caudill himself moved there.

In most cases, a branch office was established for one of two principal reasons: to tap a new region for a variety of commissions or to be near a particular project. Few of the branches were permanent. Oklahoma City's

The CRS Office in Oklahoma City, about 1954. *Left to right:* Tom Bullock, Wes Harper, Herb Paseur, Ruth Sarkoff, John Rowlett, unidentified, Frank Davies, unidentified, and Wendell Locke.

closed in the early 1960s, and Corning's was moved to Stamford, Connecticut, in 1959, then relocated again, in 1964, to New York City. Additional offices were opened in other locations, including Chicago and Los Angeles, in the early 1970s.

Rowlett, with his friendly, nonconfrontational manner, was the person most often selected to help open new offices, whether as the partner in charge or as an adviser. "The architects in the city where you're opening an office are going to hate you because you're competing for their work," observed Willie Peña, but "they would not find fault with John. He did not offend. He was not aggressive. He was a pleasant organizer."[2] Besides having opened the short-lived Austin office in 1946, Rowlett was instrumental in opening the New York office and a Hartford, Connecticut, project office, and he assisted the employees who opened the Chicago and Los Angeles offices.

However, the most common method CRS used for national expansion was association with local architects on projects distant from CRS's home base. As early as 1949, CRS relied on Philip Wilber, head of the architecture school at Oklahoma A&M, to carry out some of the work on the schools in Blackwell. The firm also had Wilber supervise construction for a schools project in Stillwater, where Oklahoma A&M was located. For the high school in Norman, CRS teamed up with an established force in school design, Perkins and Will of Chicago, with CRS taking the lead in design, while the more experienced Perkins and Will acted as a design consultant and produced the working drawings. The right chemistry helped to make the association click. Caudill and Larry Perkins were complementary personalities: Perkins suave and cosmopolitan, Caudill humorous and down to earth, each appreciative of the other. At one point, Perkins and Will approached Caudill about buying CRS, but the firm was not interested in being acquired.

At first it was common for associated firms to receive a small portion of the work—often 25 percent—with CRS retaining the rest. In the early 1960s, the assumption was that CRS could do nearly everything, including the working drawings and even putting construction supervisors on site, but that practice hampered the firm's ability to get work, since local architects viewed CRS mainly as an adversary. Consequently, in the mid-1960s, Herb Paseur and CRS developed new arrangements that greatly expanded the local firm's role to include preparing working drawings and performing construction administration while CRS handled site selection, programming, schematic design, and design development.

Because public institutions such as schools and colleges usually try to spend their money at home, local associates were crucial to winning many of the commissions. Associating with local firms also made project management more efficient for CRS. The goal was to achieve collaboration between CRS and the local firm throughout the project. In each phase, one firm or the other would be the quarterback, but both would be apprised of progress. Typically, CRS got 35 percent of the fee, and the associated architects (sometimes more than one firm) received 65 percent. The associated architects would be named first in any local publicity announcements, and CRS would get top billing in national publicity releases. These arrangements were fair to local architects, and as soon as the CRS method became widely known, local architects began calling Houston with prospects.

INTERVIEWS

HERB PASEUR

You have to see the move to Houston as one of the most significant points in CRS's history. At that time, we went through consolidation. This organization has been like a breathing apparatus—it would expand and contract in terms of centralization and decentralization. We really centralized in Houston. [We] brought our best people from Oklahoma and New York into Houston. That was the thing to do at that time [1958].

One thing I was involved in [as] my first chore as a partner—I was the eighth and last partner—we had reached a plateau of about a million dollars in revenue in '61, and we stayed at that plateau for a year or two. I was given the responsibility to get us from plateau number one to plateau number two, which was $2 million. The plan we ultimately put into effect to do that called for closing the Oklahoma City office completely, opening an office in Chicago, and strengthening the office in New York, and we set out to do that. We did close the office in Oklahoma City. We tried to open an office in Chicago, [but] we never got it opened then, [and] by the time we went through all of this, we had gone through $2 million like that and then shot up to about $3 or $4 million in revenues. This was not because of what we planned to do, but because we realized we were losing a lot of work nationally by trying to do it all. So we developed a new concept of associating where we would do only 35 percent of the work, doing what we did best: programming, schematic design, and design development. Then the associate architect would do the rest of it. Of course, we were still involved all through the total process.

The work just poured in! Architects from all over the U.S., particularly in the community college field and hospital field, started calling us. The growth that took place was incredible as a result of not being greedy about the fee. Give it away, and it comes back to you. So we got up to $4 million real quick. I took credit for that, of course, because I was supposed to get it there. But we didn't get there the way we thought we would.

Q: You said you were given the responsibility. Who gave you the responsibility?

A: Tom, with the blessing of the other partners. Tom, of course, was the executive partner. CRS had a board that included some people who were not partners. Understand that we practiced as a partnership but operated as a corporation. Partners, at that time, were still the most important part of the decision making, but the corporation carried out the wishes of the partnership. That changed later on, and the force of the partnership began to diminish in the mid-'60s.

We were prompted more by events than by planning. I say that in a broad sense. Events seem to be more of the controlling factor in our destiny than a lot of things we wanted to do. We've had a bunch of failures. We were proselytized on systems building back in the '60s. We thought that was going to be the next real movement. . . .

We like change and new things. We weren't reticent about undertaking these things, and we could well accept failure, too—and there were certainly times when we failed. That gave everybody the motivation to try new things. When we first got into computers, which was a new thing, we spent a lot of money. Even buying a computer back then was a bunch of money: about a quarter of a million dollars for just an IBM 130. We even formed a new company called Computing Research Systems, CRS2, that was going to market our computer capabilities. We actually organized . . . to take it public [but] it never got off the ground. There wasn't a market out there. It was just too early. People would come in and take up our time, wanting us to explain what we were doing, but nobody bought anything. But that was the forerunner of CM Associates [the construction management group established by CRS Design Associates in 1971].

JIM HUGHES

CRS had a lot of uniquenesses. One of them was our ability to enter into associations with other architectural firms. For many years, at least 40 percent of our work was done in association with other firms. For many of those projects, we did only programming, design, and design development—and master planning, if that was needed. The associate firms did the working drawings and supervision. . . .

There were a lot of reasons on our part for wanting to associate with local firms, and those were primarily political. . . . Let's say John Rowlett had a wonderful relationship with Leroy Good in Rochester, New York, who's going to build a $22 million college. Politically, Leroy Good could not hire CRS from Houston, Texas, to do the whole thing, a tax-supported project. Leroy needed to spread the wealth [locally] as much as possible, and it was a large enough project that he could. So I think he determined there would be a minimum of three local architectural firms involved with us. That's sort of how that came about.

Wallie and I went to Rochester and spent a couple of days interviewing several firms. At the end of the process, we decided on the three firms with whom we eventually formed an association agreement. We had two narrative pages to the agreement and about three graph or chart pages—something CRS developed over the years. We used it [the association agreement] for years and years and years with some, but not many, modifications. It worked beautifully because the narrative spelled out the responsibilities of each firm and who had the prime responsibility with the client.

The contract was written either in our name, which we preferred, or in the name of the associate architect. In some cases, it had to be that way due to the wishes of the client or politics. Many times, local firms would choose to associate with us because it was a learning process for them. The firm had attained a national reputation at that time for doing some very unique things. These things were exciting to a lot of small architectural firms—some rural, some not so rural. These firms were most excited about an opportunity to work with a firm like CRS, to participate in the things we did that were considered unique. Also, they realized many times that they didn't have the experience necessary for the project in terms of design; for instance, never having designed a university building. But they could produce a good set of working drawings, so we made a good team.

We sought out firms [that were] only interested in association. We didn't want anybody who was a reluctant associate. That never works because when you marry a firm like that, it's not only a business venture, but they become an integral part of the team. The job they do, as well as the job we do, affects the welfare of the entire team. It's an important decision. Also, on the projects where we did design and design development, we had to do a pretty darn good set of design development drawings. They had to be very comprehensive so the local firm had a good sense of exactly what we intended in the design. Also, our designers were so thorough they not only designed the special layouts and the visual concept of the building, but they got into detail conditions—almost down to the hardware in some cases. That may be an exaggeration, but our design development drawings included a lot of detail, as well as basic layouts, elevations, and sections you normally find in a DD [design-development] package.

There were some that weren't too successful, but by and large over the years, our associations were very successful. That ability to associate and other firms' willingness to associate with us allowed us to work in many parts of the country and accounted for a great deal of the firm's growth. Again, it was the process thing. [It was] almost totally unique to CRS at that point.

JIM GATTON

Q: How did CRS evolve from a local to a national practice?

A: Well, through reputation, through the reputation that Caudill had . . . developed in education, through publications, through awards on projects. The CRS renown for education projects became widely known among the architects and among the educators. So we were sought out by both potential architect associates or clients who wanted a CRS school. Wallie Scott and John Rowlett, sometimes Peña, and sometimes Caudill, spent an awful lot of time in Atlantic City meeting with educators every year.[3] Why they always picked the winter to go Atlantic City, I'll never know. Maybe it made for warm meetings once you got out of the cold and off the boardwalk!

Q: Atlantic City?

A: Yeah, that's where [the meetings] were always held. All the superintendents and a lot of the school board people would trek to Atlantic City for what was new in education. [It was] a chance to get out on the town. John Rowlett developed a long list of friends out of these sessions—along with Herb Paseur, Tom Bullock, Charles Lawrence, Frank Lawyer, and everybody else who went up there. I never did get to take one of the Atlantic City trips. . . .

The national practice, I started to say, evolved from the reputation that we had earned in schools and schoolhouse design. And we started getting calls from all over the place—all the forty-eight states—and I guess we started doing schools even in Mexico and other foreign countries.

Q: Oh, so schools went international?

A: Now that you say that, I'm trying to think of other examples beyond Mexico. I know that when we did the American school in Monterey, it physically was in Mexico, but it was still for Americans and American expatriates. I'm not sure how many public schools we did. Eventually, we did a lot of universities in international situations—Saudi Arabia, in particular. I guess Mexico was our first international experience, unless you count Laredo as being an international experience. We did a lot of schools in Laredo, and we had the same associate all the way through on every school we ever did down there. Pancho Leyendecker was our associate from start to finish. . . .

Q: How important are ethics in practice to you? What does that mean to you, first of all?

A: Well, it's the application of the Golden Rule, number one—realizing you are going to be treated the way you treat other people. Ethics in practice, to me, is one of equity . . . but if you try to get all the chips on your side of the table, it's never going to work, and you're going to resent the other guy's doing the same thing. The chips have got to be equally distributed, whether it's between you and the owner, or you and an associate. It's an attitude of fairness and equity. . . .

Q: Do you remember any jobs that were ethically difficult to work on? That turned out to be sticky situations?

A: Sure, a lot of them, [especially] where the client was trying to cut corners in everything he did, including us and the fee payment or slow payment or nonpayment. We've had clients I considered to be very unethical.

We had one client who believed in getting to everything and everyone, and the architect was just one of the people. Unfortunately, he [the client] was the head of a university, [yet] he believed in getting to the students and to the faculty. For instance, he made everybody who came on faculty an overnight Ph.D. and gave them a raise—and a country club membership that they could pay for with the raise that he had just given them! He built a dormitory for the students without doors. But he also owned a hardware store where students could go down and buy their own doors. And they were in unpainted rooms, but he also sold paint! So we've worked with some unethical clients along the way, too.

Q: How do you recommend dealing with those people?

A: Walk away, as quick as you can!

Q: But how do you deal with them if you don't discover this fact until the job is halfway through?

A: Walk away as soon as you can.

PHIL WILLIAMS

Starting in the Oklahoma City office was a really pleasant experience. John Rowlett was running the office. John was a real gentleman and a kind of quiet coach. The office was about twenty people, a great size. We were dedicated to our work, and John was dedicated to us, and it was a really pleasant experience, a good way to break in. . . . And it was deliberate, part of what you mentioned earlier. It gave people a chance to get responsibility that they couldn't get in a larger group.

TOM HOOKER

In July of 1966, I believe, I was invited to New York City by John Rowlett and Jack Smith. So I went up there, met with them, went out, and met with a client on Long Island for a school project there in Roslyn. I was transferred to the New York office in July, 1966, to wear three hats. It was kind of interesting because, while I had been involved with squatters for programming and master planning as well as design, I had never actively participated as a programmer or project manager. At the time, Willie Peña was in charge of programming, and Jim Gatton was in charge of project management. They had each developed huge three-ring binder manuals on how to program facilities and how to be a project manager.

As I walked down the hall—this was when CRS was in the Dow Center [in Houston]—by Jim Gatton's office, he said, "Hey, Tom, aren't you going to New York City?" I said, "Yes." Jim said, "I've got something for you," and he stuck a big project manager manual under my right arm. As I proceeded toward the door to catch the airport cab to go to New York, Willie stepped out of his office. Willie could never remember my name. He just said, "Oh, buddy-bub, are you headed to New York?" I said, "Yes, sir." He said, "Wait a minute—I've got something for you," and he stuck a programming "how-to" manual under my left arm. That's the way I went to New York.

I was prepared for everything and, in fact, I had a wonderful time there. They allowed me to be the project manager and programmer and even designer up there on several projects.

When I met with Herb [in 1970], he invited me to go to California with Truitt Garrison and Paul Kennon to establish the West Coast office to be located in Los Angeles. I, of course, thought that was a wonderful opportunity—never dreaming I would be going out there to do marketing by myself, thinking that John Rowlett, who seemed to me to be the spearhead in opening new offices, would go out there for some period of time to help establish the market plan and approach and give me some guidance on how to be a marketing person. When I saw John and mentioned how excited I was to be able to work with him again, I was surprised [when] he looked at me quizzically and asked, "What are you talking about?" I said, "Aren't you going to Los Angeles with us?" He replied, "No, you're on your own." I was startled by that, quite honestly, and had a lot of trepidation, if not absolute fear, of not being successful in the marketing they asked me to do.

In any case, I joined Truitt Garrison out there on February 1, 1971, and helped put the rest of the light bulbs in the fixtures. We opened our office and started interviewing people to join the firm. We were quite fortunate in successfully landing the San Jose County Administration Building almost before we opened the doors. So we literally opened the doors with a major project to help us get started. I was happy to be part of that interview team, but like everything else at CRS, no one person was responsible for getting that project or winning the award. A team went out and interviewed for the project. Wallie Scott led the interview, starting it off and introducing everyone. He did it as only Wallie could in his charming way that really won the clients' confidence. The interesting thing about it was that, while we had good design and good capabilities, we were not that well versed in county administration buildings. I believe the thing that sold that project was the programming process.

Q: A couple of people who worked in CRS branch offices have commented that it was an unusually wide-open opportunity to be there on your own, away from the "heavies" in the firm. You worked in two branch offices. Did you find that to be true?

A: Yes, it was. In my opinion, that was probably the thing that made that office so successful. Herb Paseur put three people out there who had never really worked together. How he found the right combination, I'll never know, but the chemistry among Truitt Garrison, Paul Kennon, and me was—I can't explain it. We were totally supportive of each other. With one exception, we never stepped on each other's toes. We always worked as a total team, and I think that's what made the office successful. . . .

It was so easy to go out and sell a client with confidence that we could do their project when we had in the office the best project manager I had ever worked with in Truitt and certainly one of the finest designers. I can't say Paul Kennon was the finest, for there were so many outstanding designers at CRS, but certainly he was at the top of the list. Paul was so strong in all phases of architecture, not just design. At that time, we would do design through design development and hand it off to Houston. Paul insisted on reading the specs, every word, to make sure that what he intended to be in that design was there and [that] it was going to serve the client. Paul was not just a designer; he was an architect, an excellent architect.

Paul Kennon, *left*, speaking with *Megatrends* author and CRS director John Naisbitt.

We had a wonderful experience out there in L.A. At that time, Mike Trower was general manager of CRS, and after we had been in L.A. for about a year, he called and said he was coming out. We kind of looked at each other and said, "Why is Mike coming out here?" I finally called Mike. I had known him when I was in New York and he was in Connecticut running the Hartford office. I had worked with him on one of his projects as project manager, on loan from the New York office. So I finally called him and asked why he was coming out. He said, "Well, I've never been there." We asked, "What do we need to prepare for?" He said, "Nothing. I just want to find out why you guys are so successful." I don't know what he learned from that trip, but we had some anxious moments wondering why he was coming. While he was there, we enjoyed having him and then went on about our business. I don't think he ever returned, so I guess he was happy with the way things were running.

CHUCK THOMSEN

When I was at MIT, I wrote Bill Caudill and told him I would like to teach at Rice and work for his firm—simultaneously [Caudill was director of the Rice University School of Architecture during the 1960s]. I decided while I was at MIT I wanted to return to the Southwest [to] teach and practice both. I thought it would be stimulating, keep life going.

Bill wrote back, arranged to meet me, and I went to meet him. I sent him my brochure. I'll always remember—Bill said, "I showed your brochure to Frank Lawyer. He said it was the best brochure he's ever seen." [It was] one of those nice things somebody says that you never forget. Frank is a lovely person whom I always liked after that. That's how it was that Bill said, "Look, you can have a job either place, but not both. I'll hire you at Rice to be on the faculty, or I'll hire you at CRS, but we don't want employees of CRS working at Rice."

Q: Why did he say that?

A: I think it was probably the deal he struck with Tom: "OK, Bill, if you want to go out and do this, but we're not going to let everybody else do it." And I think, by the way, that's a very good deal. CRS had a national practice, and we all had to travel a lot. If you had a teaching schedule, there would be a real conflict with serving clients, going on squatters, running off for meetings with joint venture parties, clients, et cetera. I think it's a good policy. I later came to believe it was a good policy. Anyway, I thought it would probably be a lot easier to teach at Rice and then go to CRS rather than do it the other way around.

I taught design at Rice and history. He [Caudill] made Clovis Heimsath and me share the history course. I knew nothing about architectural history, [but I] had more fun teaching that course than anything I've ever taught. I'd stay a chapter ahead of the students. I think that's what probably made me a good salesman: I really learned to wing it. I taught at Rice for three years [and] worked for CRS during the summers—did some part-time research. [I] did a really important study for the Ben Franklin building back in '63, '64; the first application of computer technology to determine the optimum size of an office building for downtown. I think Tom was impressed that I was innovative. I kind of worked with Tom that summer. After three years, I got pretty bored with what was going on at Rice and thought I wanted to do something else. Bill Cannady and I had a little practice going on the side, so I decided I'd either spend all my time on that or go to CRS, and wound up joining CRS.

My first two years there, probably, I would have been fired from any other firm. I think Tom, Bill, Wallie, [and] Herb all from time to time sort of protected me from getting thrown out. I'm sure I was abrasive, [a] smart-ass, arrogant beyond my capabilities.

Most organizations have some brilliant people at the top and then they have a middle management whose role in life is to put in place the direction and vision of the leadership. Typically, those are people who are less inspired and less inspiring. I had no truck with those people and offended every one of them. I'm sure I caused a lot of frustration for Bill and Tom, who evidently saw something I could contribute to the company and wanted to hang onto me. So I guess they figured out the best thing to do was to send me to New York to run that office where I wouldn't be causing so much grief.

Meanwhile, my first job had been to look at computer applications, which is very characteristic. I think that was Tom's idea. He thought computer technology was something that was going to grow, and if it was going to grow in the world, then CRS ought to figure out what it meant to the practice of architecture. We were one of the first two or three firms to explore the territory.

I think that's the first important point I'd like to make about the success of the company. Some people had a gut feeling about something that might be important. They didn't know. They didn't understand it or how it might be important, but they thought, "If this is happening in the world today, we better look into it and know something about it." Over the years, we looked into lots of things like that. Many of them led nowhere, but the fact of the matter is, CRS was always up front in the world of computer technology, and it began then [in the late 1960s]. . . .

Tom came in the office one day and said, "I like what you've done, you need to be a project manager." So I was a project manager on a community college. Then he came in one day and said, "How would you like to go to New York and run the New York office?" I heard from three different sources—Tom, Herb, and Bill—that when either Herb or Tom suggested it, Bill said, "That's the best awful idea I ever heard," expressing the notion that this young guy who had caused a certain amount of friction—I had only been with the company a couple of years—and had not had a lot of solid experience in the actual design and production of architectural projects should go head the major branch office. That's the kind of high-risk planning those guys did. And I can tell you, they failed in a lot of them, but the winners more than paid for the failures. . . .

Bill, of course, in the early years when I first got there, was very much the engine to drive the company. Bill tended to surround himself with excellent people who specialized in some area, but he would pull the strings. At the time I joined the company that had already begun to wane a little because Bill was spending a lot of his time at Rice. Because he did that, somebody had to take responsibility for the company, and Tom Bullock really emerged as the new leader. Herb, being Tom's close friend—they had worked together in the Oklahoma branch office—they were very synergistic personalities. Herb [was] very stable, cool, deep keel. Tom [was] mercurial, innovative, inspirational. Tom had highs and lows; Herb was pretty steady. Herb was one of the best two or three managers I've known in my career in the business. He was a better manager than anybody else in CRS—ever. He was never in competition with his people. If you look back over the years at CRS, you wonder: What did that guy do? He came in late, left early, never missed a weekend, [and] got out of going on squatters fairly early in his career. He didn't invent the technology of programming, [he was] never a great designer, but he had this infallible judgment, [he] would quietly listen to people and decide who should be supported and who should not.

You'd get together with Tom, and by the end of an hour dealing with the problem you'd be wound up so damn tight and so full of enthusiasm for solving the problem. He had this kind of gut sense of what might be important, [he was] an avid consumer of current events. A lot of what he did was wrong. He was the Babe Ruth of the company: he had more strikeouts but [also] more home runs.

I share a characteristic with Tom that is good or bad, depending on who you have around you. Tom could be impetuous. He sometimes did things on impulse that weren't carefully thought through. On the other hand, that kind of visceral management is something you could never teach anybody—produce by analysis or strategic planning. It was a gut kind of thing, and the gut was right a lot.

New York really did work very, very well. I learned how satisfying it is to move away from all these people you respect and admire—who are close by and can be asked for advice regularly—and discover that "I know the subtleties of this situation better than anyone else and am probably the best one to make this decision." I made some mistakes, but we were growing, making money. That's a hell of a thing to happen!

I remember very clearly when it occurred to me. It must have occurred to others in the company because when I was president/CEO of the holding company, we used to have an executive management meeting, and we would have the president and executive vice president or chairman of each of the subsidiary companies come in and have lunch on Mondays to talk about the issues in the company. Maybe it would be twice a month. One day, I looked around the company and realized everybody except one of those had run a branch office.

Let's see if I can remember who they were. Joe Scarano and Frank Whitcomb were running the CM Group then; Paul Kennon was running CRS; Leonard Leal and somebody else were running the Engineering Group; Tom and Herb, who were part of that thing . . . [because] they grew up in the early days by running the Oklahoma office, you see. Maybe those guys wouldn't have turned out the way they did if they had been right there working for John Rowlett, Bill, and Wallie day in and day out. By the time I joined the company, Tom and Herb were having a bigger effect on its direction than John and Wallie.

We started using branch offices after we started CM [the construction management subsidiary of CRS Design Associates] to grow leadership. The attitude we developed was: You can't grow leadership under leadership, you've got to get people away so they have to do it on their own and gain self-confidence.

DAVID SCOULAR

I guess I should preface my remarks by saying I joined CRS in the early '70s and was there a relatively brief time. But I think my beginning there is, in part, telling about the nature of the firm. So I think how I joined CRS is, in part, interesting.

I was working for a firm in New York City. Having gone to Columbia and taken a special degree program in health facilities design, I was working for a health facility architectural firm and was being recruited by another firm. I gave my résumé to a headhunter in that process. She, without my concurrence, sent my résumé to CRS, who were looking for someone, and I wound up getting this phone call from a Jim Falick. I was invited to be interviewed by Jim at the CRS New York office, which I went to at the end of a long day. I remember it was in the old Grand Central building looking up Park Avenue. They had a rather contemporary conference room in this old building with a window view up Park Avenue, so it was a nice setting. . . .

We had a good interview and felt some mutual interest. Later that week, I joined Jim Falick at a squatters session at a hospital they were working on in Connecticut. . . . I was intrigued to see the amount of commotion and activity going on in this hospital setting. Though I didn't really get the dynamics of a squatters session, I was impressed by [the fact] that this many people from Texas would be camped out in Connecticut working on a project.

As a result of those interview sessions, I was invited to Houston and flew down late at night. I was met by a car at the airport and taken to the then Houston Oaks in the Galleria and put into a large room with oversized furniture. I thought to myself that this was, perhaps, some of Texas. I woke early [the] next morning [and] opened the window, expecting to see Manhattan, but instead, [I saw] a prairie full of trees—which is now a prairie full of buildings! I was puzzled by where I was. I guess Falick met me for breakfast, and I went over to the old CRS building—then the new CRS building—and proceeded through a day of interviews. I was quite intrigued with the people I met.

Q: Who did you meet in the office?

A: Well, I spent time with Jim Falick, Terry Tengler, Tom Bullock, and Wallie Scott. I guess I had lunch with some combination of Bullock, Scott, Falick—

and [Jonathan] King joined us, too. . . . I ended that day in a conference room with Wallie Scott, who was the quintessential lap dog in terms of charming me into what a great future CRS had and I could have with CRS and what a great opportunity was on the horizon for hospital design.

I think Wallie was the guy who really talked me into a serious interest in CRS. I thought he was one of the most wonderful paternal characters I had ever met. Tom Bullock, at the time, I thought was one of the stranger characters I had ever met, but I came to have a lot of affection for both. I didn't sense at the time that Tom Bullock was really the primary force of the firm.

I must say, I think the strength of CRS—still the strength of CRS—is that I was totally absorbed from the day I hit the door. Actually, before I hit the door—I was working for CRS a little ahead of time. The way CRS practiced architecture was very much to my liking in that it was a fast pace [and involved] a lot of promotionalism in the practice, something I have some skills in. Hence, I had a natural place in the firm. There was just so much opportunity turning up in the country at this time [that] I suddenly went from a rather ordinary architectural practice in New York City to a national practice of architecture—living on airplanes. I think I was readily working seven days a week and probably twelve hours a day just because there was so much to do and so much freedom to do it in that firm. There was not the usual layering of partners and egos to fight your way through or contend with. I think that was the strength of CRS. . . .

Q: CRS certainly provided freedom to fail and freedom to succeed for the people who were there when you were there.

A: I think in retrospect, what was great about the firm was also its weakness in that they never really built a foundation of practice that, say, SOM did—where there was a resource of standard detail, standard building technology answers. Every project at CRS seemed to start like we had never done one before. There was always this original exploration, original effort on all fronts—which I thought was certainly exciting for clients and a design team, but [also] a lot of building technology that should have been in a can and available to projects so they didn't need to be reinvented every time. Competent air-conditioning or electrical systems are things that don't need to be recreated for each project. Similarly, I think there is a lot of competent architectural detailing that can be much more standardized and documented in a firm than was the case at CRS.

TOM BULLOCK

I'd like to specialize this by listing the people outside of CRS who, in my mind, made a difference. I'll start off with five. One would be Walter McQuade, the author who wrote "The Little Red Schoolhouse Goes Modern" for *Collier's* magazine in 1950. That made a difference. The next would be Walter D. Cocking, the educator/publisher who gave Bill Caudill an expanded experience in what was going on then in schools and what the future would be like by meeting with other architects and educators.

The third—not necessarily in any kind of order—would be a competitor, Larry Perkins of Perkins and Will. He gave us an opportunity to associate on a project that received an AIA Honor Award and received national recognition: Norman High School. Larry took a personal interest in Bill Caudill and CRS.

The fourth would be John T. Jones Jr., a Houston businessman and one-time publisher and chairman of the *Houston Chronicle,* who took a chance on CRS about 1962, selecting CRS to do Jones Hall for the Performing Arts, named for his uncle, Jesse Jones. I mention this one because that was our first big diversity in projects. We were known as school architects per se and this brought local and national recognition; also was an AIA Honor Award winner.

The fifth one is Dr. Harold B. Gores, educator and head of Educational Facilities Laboratories, funded and sponsored by the Ford Foundation. He was a very creative person and took an interest in architects who were willing to specialize and work hard on research for the school building business. Harold also expanded the mind of CRS.

Many of these [people] had relationships with Bill Caudill, but some had relationships with other partners. I'll stop and say [that] when I tried to think of names beyond these, I couldn't think of any big hitters who made the difference. Guess it's because these were the early years that made us what we are [and] led to national recognition, diversity, relationships with the outside world because we were a very small group here in Bryan–College Station during much of the time. [These people] gave us an opportunity to open ourselves to the world. Harold Gores did because of the Ford Foundation consulting work we did in South America and India. John Jones opened us up to Houston and another building type.

■ CHAPTER 8

GOING GLOBAL

■ TIB: 5 OCTOBER 1974

Ron Factor brings us an interesting experience from overseas. He says, "The CRS Word is now truly international.

"The other day as I was browsing through a bookstore in the Bab Idriss area of Beirut, I was surprised to find several copies of Architecture by Team. With much joy I asked the shop owner of the book's market success in Beirut; he said that this was his second order! This is truly remarkable when one considers that the selling price is 95 Lebanese Pounds or approximately $45.

"I was thrilled to see that the philosophy that I have learned to believe in was being introduced and accepted (evidently) by local professionals."

■ Caudill Rowlett Scott's reputation for creative architecture, especially schools, appealed to clients in other countries just as it did to homegrown clients. Within a few years of its founding, CRS started working in Mexico and nations farther from the United States. By the 1960s, international assignments became frequent, especially projects in countries less economically and technically advanced than the United States and Europe. The firm's squatters and programming techniques worked as well in Latin America and the eastern hemisphere as they did in Texas and Oklahoma.

One particular project, however, catapulted CRS into a global operation. That undertaking, in Dhahran, Saudi Arabia, was the College of Petroleum and Minerals, later renamed the University of Petroleum and Minerals, and still later King Fahd University of Petroleum and Minerals (UPM). From its modest beginning in 1964 as a site-selection study, the Saudi endeavor expanded and expanded, giving CRS a foothold from which the firm would grow immensely once the great Saudi building boom of the 1970s got under way.

The company was not alone in finding a bright future overseas. The Middle East construction boom, propelled by escalating oil prices, provided massive projects for many large American architecture and engineering firms, and enabled some of them to survive rather than close their doors during the severe 1973–75 recession. Even by the standards of the times, CRS

The huge University of Petroleum and Minerals project in Dhahran, Saudi Arabia, began in 1964. The campus featured Islamic architectural motifs.

benefited to an exceptional extent. Thanks mainly to work in the Middle East, by 1975 the firm had greater earnings than Skidmore, Owings, and Merrill, long the nation's architectural giant.[1] Within fifteen years of the Dhahran site study, more than 70 percent of CRS's fee volume came from Middle Eastern projects. To produce the staggering volume of international work, the firm closed its offices in both Los Angeles and New York and consolidated its staff in Houston. "It took everything we had to do the projects in Saudi Arabia and elsewhere," Tom Bullock recalled.[2]

The firm went overseas not because of a grand strategy, but because an invitation arrived out of the blue. Moreover, despite the challenges of language, customs, and geography, CRS delivered high-quality programming and design to foreign clients. In almost every foreign locale where CRS earned a commission, the challenges were bigger and more complicated than at home. The firm, which in the United States was accustomed to doing mainly the front end of projects—programming, schematic design, and design development—had to take on broader responsibilities overseas. It was already accustomed to forming associations with other firms, but now the associates were firms from other countries, some of which were just as new to the terrain as CRS was.

THE SAND THAT WOULD NOT HOLD

The Saudis agreed with CRS's idea of building UPM in Dhahran with poured-in-place concrete, but when the first construction work began, the Americans were surprised to discover that in Saudi Arabia even the sand does not behave the same as sand elsewhere. Crews started pouring concrete and found that it slumped instead of setting in a rigid shape. The reason was that wind-blown desert sand loses its sharp, irregular edges and consequently does not bond well. The firm learned to get sand from the seashore instead. When crushed limestone and Saudi cement were mixed with sand from the coastline, the concrete attained sufficient firmness. Charles Lawrence, who led the design efforts on Saudi projects, professed himself pleased with the result: "a Saudi product, sand blasted to expose aggregate and matrix, color compatible with the *jebel* site."

The UPM campus in Dhahran was one of CRS's greatest overseas achievements. "This brilliantly sited campus stands on a limestone outcropping silhouetted against the blazing sky like an Arab Pantheon," declared architectural writer Walter McQuade.[3] The firm proposed building the school in that difficult but esthetically superb location, on an exposed limestone plateau known as a *jebel.* To generate an appropriate architectural character for the campus, Charles Lawrence and the CRS design team recommended using the forms and textures of old buildings in Saudi Arabia's Eastern Province as the starting point. The Saudis said no, they did not want anything too strongly associated with the past, yet by the time the project was under way, the Saudis had modified their stance, and CRS produced a campus that was, in Lawrence's estimation, "a clear expression of modern construction and technology, but reflecting the architecture from the peak of Arab culture."[4] It was a place of courtyards and covered walkways offering relief from the blazing sun, a place where manmade geometry was juxtaposed against nature. Large, rough rock outcroppings played off against the smoothness of poured concrete. Water was laced through a network of pools, fountains, and watercourses. A soaring water tower with a gracefully flared top acted as a landmark, visible from miles away. The design team borrowed from historical Arab architecture but abstracted it and then built it in materials that fit the desert. Inspired by the Arab architectural legacy, Lawrence devised tall concrete columns with pointed arches, turning them perpendicular to the usual organization of a colonnade, thereby giving the shaded walkways a rhythmic sequence related to the human stride. Ultimately, the campus impressed Saudis and outsiders as an outstanding wedding of buildings and site. The assignment in Dhahran went on for a quarter-century.

Caudill Rowlett Scott was followed into the Middle East by many other firms. There was a vast amount of work to be done—housing, offices, roads, hospitals, schools, whole cities—where only a few years before there had been nothing but sand.

INTERVIEWS

TOM BULLOCK

[It was] international business, [but] we didn't call it that at the time. We called it a job in Mexico, an elementary school which started about 1952 in Monterey, Mexico. Willie Peña being from Laredo, I think, must have had something to do with it. He certainly had a lot to do with its design, planning, and colors of the building. It was a good building, but we didn't leverage it. But in the early years, that was it. That would be 1952.

I believe it was closer to the '60s that we had some consulting work for the Ford Foundation: the American School in New Delhi. . . . Bill made the first trip. [It] had to be the year John Kennedy was elected [1960] because I remember we talked about his election. Bill flew over and consulted on that, and Willie followed up a year or two later. . . . I don't remember any other projects outside the States during that period.

[We did] consulting internationally, yes, but consulting at home, no. We had a policy against becoming consultants in the States for a very simple reason: If you are a consultant, you don't need a team—and we pushed team everywhere. . . . We felt it wouldn't build the team to have individuals doing their own thing. So we just did not play the consultant game, and certainly we had the opportunity to do that. Bill did many times, but it was always team first.

In the middle '60s—Bill was at Rice University at the time as director of the School of Architecture—the Ford Foundation asked Rice, Harvard, and CRS to be a partnership in designing community centers in Santiago, Chile. It was their way of putting some monies to work helping the neighborhoods, which were in desperate need of schools, community, and commercial buildings. . . . So we did that, and along the way we did work again with Ford Foundation support on the American School in Lima, Peru. We did campus planning for the Catholic University of Lima. I was able to devote some time to those two projects. Bill also provided consultant services to the University of Bariloche, Argentina. That was about it. We liked that. It exploded our minds and provided excitement we wouldn't have had if we had stayed at home.

About 1966, on the way to Peru, I stopped off in Jamaica. A Jamaican architect had called us to say there were going to be a number of middle schools built throughout the country, financed by the World Bank. So I visited with the Ministry of Education, with the architect, and we did the job. That job lasted three or four years. . . . It would not win an AIA Honor Award for design, but it would win a good, solid planning award and certainly was a step ahead of what they had. We built good buildings—straightforward, conservative design—and the important thing [was that] they got built faster than they would have any other way. They were scattered all over the island. That was the biggest job we had at the time. Don't know the size exactly, but it was considered to be important in terms of revenue, size, and what it might do for the educational system in Jamaica. . . .

Because of the national reputation of CRS in schools, we had a number of visitors in the '50s, going back to Walter McQuade, the writer from *Collier's* who did the article on the "Little Red Schoolhouse." He had heard the firm was doing different kinds of buildings. We had visitors from England in the '50s. They had gone through World War II and had to rebuild a lot of schools and do it fast, in such a way that standards could be developed. These standards would become systems for buildings.

The British couldn't afford the luxury of redesigning a door jamb, for instance, every time they did a building, or having numerous sized windows. They had to standardize sizes and shapes. We were intrigued by that. Here we are in the U.S. where we could make everything different from day one, and fairly economically. They couldn't do that. We saw this as something we might have to do someday—this was in the '50s. David Medd, architect with the Ministry of Education in England, made a visit here, and I think to this campus [Texas A&M]. No doubt, he spoke at the College of Architecture. He became a friend of the firm. We followed what he did, and he followed what we did. Anthony Part was another British architect who became well known. Again, they were trying to rebuild the buildings devastated by the war. So we all gained by this. It might be of interest that we did not do a job in England as a result, but it was a kind of spin-off research activity for us. It was in the late '60s before we returned to what we called the beginning of building systems in this country in schools. . . .

It was about 1964 that our Mideast activity began. It began with a visit from a building committee member [Dr. Robert King Hall] from the College of Petroleum and Minerals, now called the King Fahd University of Petroleum and Minerals, Dhahran, Saudi Arabia. He called on us, having visited with the Architects Collaborative and probably Perkins and Will—maybe several others. He called us out of the blue from the Shamrock Hilton Hotel in Houston—or maybe from New York—and we set up a meeting in the Shamrock. I believe Willie and I went. Dr. Hall asked all about our experience and if we had any experience in the Mideast. Of course, we had not. [We] hardly knew where Saudi Arabia was, much less worked there.

He went back. We heard in several weeks that we had been selected to do the site-selection study, which meant a team of CRS architects and engineers would go to the kingdom to select the site. Again, when you talked to Charles Lawrence; Ed Finlay, a planner; Don Wines, designer; and Bill Caudill, who [all] had made the trip, they would tell you it was barren territory at the time. A study was made, a report submitted, and a site selected.

[It] turned out to be the site they wanted anyway. They [just] wanted somebody *else* to tell them it was suitable. It was right next to Aramco headquarters and the U.S.-type Aramco compound. It was a slow beginning. They really didn't have much money then. It started with a $25,000 fee.

The first-phase buildings were completed, I guess, about 1970–71. The college grew tremendously during the oil boom in the '70s, and we closed our office there only last year—1990—so you're talking about twenty-six years with some of the same team members on the project. There were a lot of additions. I'm guessing, but [I] don't think I'm too far off, [that] it ended up being over a $2 billion construction project. It had to have everything—water system, power, roads, everything—so it stretched us considerably; gave us a lot of good experience. Fact is, the chairman of the Building Committee was Sheik Ahmed Zaki Yamani, who became petroleum minister and more or less the guy who controlled OPEC [the Organization of Petroleum Exporting Countries] during the tough days.

DON WINES

Another of my CRS experiences was also pretty much happenstance. That was the Saudi work. I happened to be in the office when Dr. Hall, the American adviser to the College [of Petroleum and Minerals] at that time, dropped in the office and wanted to talk with one of the principals. Willie was the one available, and he called me in. We sat and talked with Dr. Hall, who was on a mission to come to this country and secure the services of an architectural firm to design a new college in Saudi Arabia. Willie was astounded. Talk about work coming in over the transom, this was the ultimate! It was such an incredible prospect. [It] seems to me it was in June, [and] he [Hall] was after a proposal for the work. I don't believe I was involved in the proposal, and I'm not sure who got involved with that. I'm sure Tom was, and Tiny Lawrence was set up to be the principal designer.

An unusual aspect of the contract I remember to this day was that because of cost differential, the work was to be done [in Saudi Arabia]. Since we did work on a percentage of construction cost, and that was very difficult to ascertain in Saudi Arabia, and materials cost so much more there; their approach was: "It's the same amount of work you are doing in Houston; same amount of professional thought, etcetera, goes into it." Basically, the contract was established as: We would be paid per Houston cost for work done in Saudi Arabia. All of our expenses—other than what was done in Houston, Texas—would be absorbed as a reimbursable expense by the client. That meant all travel, living expenses, etcetera, was taken care of by the client. We would perform the work just like we were working in Houston.

The ultimate kicker to all this was that it was to be based on the Dodge Reports and the relation of Houston to the national cost index. As it turned out, if you looked at the Dodge Reports at that time—we looked through books and books and books of those things—they would show examples of projects that cost *x* number of dollars in New York and *x* number of dollars in Houston. Well, the project examples didn't resemble anything near what we were going to design in Saudi Arabia.

It was a fascinating project for me as a young designer. What ultimately transpired is that in November we didn't know whether we had the contract or not—or [we] knew we had the contract, but didn't know when it would be initiated. My family had gone home to Oklahoma for Thanksgiving, and I had to pick up a rendering for something in the Dallas office of a firm that did architectural renderings. We had all taken the obligatory shots with the idea that we had to perform the site-selection service before the end of the year. So Tiny, myself, and Ed Finlay had all taken the battery of shots in the event that we should be given the go-ahead. While I was in Dallas to see the rendering, I got a call from Tiny saying, "It's go." So it was back to Houston, and we left December 1.

We flew around the country for two weeks. Bill Caudill had developed a process, the "bull's-eye graph," which we used to define a way to get input from various people. As I looked at it, it was an objective process for recording subjective thoughts. Individuals would rate a project in, say, eight or nine categories from zero to ten as their personal feeling about that aspect of the project—in this case, the site. Then you would put them all together, and through averaging, you could get a kind of graphic consensus on strengths, weaknesses, etcetera. We had nine sites identified as potential sites. We used this process, [and] narrowed it down while we were still there to the three top sites we all agreed on. Then we dug into it further to develop a better sense of what we thought was right, and ultimately settled on the *jebel* there at Dhahran.

Q: It's a pretty nice site.

A: A beautiful site, and it was Dr. Hall's preference. I think we all knew it was his preference, but he played it straight. What he wanted desperately was an outside professional—he was a domineering personality—to come in and provide professional judgment.

There was another site that was absolutely magnificent emotionally. It was called Jebel Shamali, a magnificent piece of rock outcropping. A mountain, circular in form, rose up to a flat, and then from that rose up again to the top. It could have developed a brilliant first piece of architecture but wouldn't have had the ability to grow like the campus ultimately grew. Another downside was that it was three miles from the nearest road—no utilities, no nothing. The Dhahran site, of course, was three hundred yards from the road and adjacent to Aramco, which had its own set of problems. It was a fascinating project. . . .

It was a wonderful experience. Great bunch of people over there, fascinating characters, history, everything. I was thinking the other day of that project and this happenstance thing. It was my understanding [that] when Dr. Hall visited us in Houston, the reason he was there was because of one man: a fellow named Harry Snyder. Snyder had told him he had to see Bill Caudill. We found out how this happened.

Harry Snyder was a fascinating personality employed by Aramco as an educational expert. Part of their agreement in getting the oil concessions [from the kingdom] was to give something to the Saudis in turn. In the case of the college, they had to provide a junior college, as I remember. They had an ongoing agreement to provide schools for the Saudis. Snyder had some credentials, and I'm not sure where his school credentials came from, [but] his job was as an educational expert.

Between the World Wars—in the days of Lawrence of Arabia [and] the English plots—the sheik that Lawrence dealt with had been imprisoned by the British on the island of Cypress, a British protectorate. Snyder was working for McGraw-Hill books at the time, and he got to meet this sheik—played in the movie by Alec Guinness. Snyder visited the sheik, held incommunicado by the British, to get his side of the story. Must have been in the early '30s. Harry couldn't take any books or writing material, but he did talk with him about whether there was an agreement to form an Arab state or not. As Harry told us, the visits and interview took place over a period of a week or so, which he would record on paper after each. This way, they would get the sheik's story out to the public. I'm not sure of the end of the story because there was some discrepancy about whether he had permission to publish it. To my knowledge, he never did.

Snyder was a geologist by education and an ordained minister—Methodist or Presbyterian. He'd been all over the world working for McGraw-Hill. [He] was in Saudi Arabia during the war—involved with the air force or something to do with building air bases in case Rommel took over Egypt.

In his job with Aramco, Harry was sent to this country—Aramco always sent their people to the U.S.—as the source. If it was modern math, then they had someone at the first seminars to learn it and bring it back. [Aramco was] first in everything. . . .

Harry attended conferences, and there was one in Cambridge at which Bill Caudill spoke. Harry met Bill after the meeting—shook his hand, and Bill called him "Harry," and he called him "Bill." It was that kind of chemistry. Back in Saudi Arabia, Harry and Dr. Hall were confidants, and Harry told Dr. Hall, "You have to put Bill Caudill on your list."

When we told Bill about this later, he couldn't remember who Harry Snyder was, of course. But when you or anybody met Bill Caudill, he was "Bill." The interesting thing to me is how Caudill's charisma was felt by everybody.

Q: Also, it was a good example of what they used to refer to as indirect development: You go to meetings, you meet people, and you talk. Maybe something comes of it, and maybe it doesn't. A lot of jobs were developed that way.

A: Yeah, but Bill's personality transcended that. It goes back to stuttering and the fact that he was able to overcome it. People always remembered him. Every man could relate to him. That was amazing to me, the way the Saudi project came about.

TOM BULLOCK

From '64 to about '69, we were working on and off on that project. About '69, we were able to get some work for Tapline. That was the oil pipeline Aramco ran—you see it on today's war maps—from Beirut to Dhahran. [I] believe it crosses Kuwait, maybe Iraq. We did some housing work and opened a Beirut office to do the drawings because there were no facilities for any kind of drafting or that kind of thing in Saudi Arabia. Beirut, being the great city it was, had all the services we needed. That office did odds and ends, and we didn't predict a great boom in the Mideast.

I'll tell you right now, half of success is being in the right place at the right time. In 1973, I went to the Mideast with Joe Thomas, the original engineer on the UPM project, to visit the Beirut office. [I went there] with the intent of closing it and also pulling out of Saudi Arabia. Well, I changed my mind. [I] came back saying, "No, we won't close Beirut." That was '73. Their civil war didn't start until '74, '75. "We won't pull out of Dhahran." It was almost obvious at that time there was going to be a great boom as a result of that war. So we just stayed there. Out of that came most of our business in the '70s. . . .

You can see how vulnerable we were to the bust that followed—the construction bust in the early '80s in Saudi Arabia. We did other work which helped, [like] one of the largest cities ever designed: Ruwais, Abu Dhabi. They tell me it became a great city—never there before we arrived, a city of over thirty thousand built from scratch on the coast of the Persian Gulf. We did work for Gulf Air that operated out of Bahrain and several banks there. We did a little work in Qatar, mostly construction management. We did housing work in Egypt for the State Department, [and] construction management for a French hotel on the Nile. I can hardly recount how much work we did in Saudi Arabia.

JIM GATTON

I worked in Saudi Arabia, but I never did work on the University of Petroleum and Minerals. But I did work on the Aramco project right next door, on the "other side of the fence." We did a ten-story building and some of the master planning for an expansion of five communities—drilling site communities, little villages for expatriates. I did work for Aramco—roughly '72 to '76. . . .

The College of Petroleum and Minerals was an astounding job because it was being designed in Houston for a client in Saudi Arabia who had not been out of the desert but two or three years himself and really didn't know what to ask for [in the first place]! It was put out for international bidders and was successfully bid by a Japanese contractor. We think he was probably subsidized by the Japanese government in order to be the successful low bidder, so they bought their way into the Middle East by building our project in the sand in Saudi Arabia.

So, if there was a potential for problems, it was there in spades with the mixture of cultures. And yet, the job went very well. I think our phase one of UPM was probably as successful as anything we've ever done over there—with the care that was given to it in design and detailing; the handholding and the management that was given to it. If there were failures, I think they were due to a lack of understanding of the hardships to be endured in that climate. Filters would stop up with sand. Water pipes could not stand up to the corrosion of those kinds of physical elements. We had yet to learn all of our lessons that were subsequently corrected.

I think that our first work over there was probably our best. It's funny, [but] often times our first work is our best. I don't know if we try harder or we go out of our way to learn more or if the third or fourth time around, we think we know it all. I don't know why it is [that] our first jobs—like Jones Hall or Albert Thomas [Convention Center] or UPM—are often our best. Certainly, the Bryan courthouse is a case in point. It was the very first courthouse we'd ever done, and it was probably the best that had ever been done at the time.

RALPH CARROLL

The next challenge that opened up was a place called Yanbu, Saudi Arabia. That was a small job; a city that Frank [Lawyer] had designed housing, schools, and apartments for. So I went to Yanbu as the on-site project manager. It was to have been for a year, and I stayed there three years. It was enjoyable. I met a lot of nice people—good working relations, good contractor. That was when, for the first time, I really got involved in the construction end.

Yanbu borders the Red Sea—right across from Africa on the west coast. That's when I got my first real taste of contracting and construction management. A project manager starts with a project from the beginning, works on the contract, works with the client, programming. When it gets into construction, he goes out to the job site periodically, but we have our own field representative. Yanbu was the first time I was in the field working with the contractors on a daily basis. I fell in love with it! Maybe it was because it was something new. We won't tell anybody around here, but it was a chance for this old fellow to be a little bit of a designer. Not everything gets designed on paper at the home office, and when you are that far away, you can't send anything back. This was long before the day of faxes—all we had was telex. So I'd just sit down, work it out with the contractor, and solve the design problem right then and there—and thoroughly enjoyed it! When Frank would visit, I'd show him what I did. Fortunately, he always liked it.

I came back from Yanbu and found myself in a group called CRSS Constructors—a new firm. When I left Houston, it was CRSS Construction Management, or CRSS/CM. After three years' absence, the name had changed, but like anything at CRSS, things are going to change in six months anyway. That's always been the case.

JOHN FOCKE

The international side of CRS for me was a long string of about three years of writing proposals for projects and making bad trips to the Middle East negotiating with people who didn't understand the profit incentive. CRS always seemed to be practicing in a war zone somewhere—or close to it—and always petrodollars. The difficult aspect of international practice is that all of us in the firm who had been so close to clients in the U.S. found much more structured relationships in international practice. There were still great things that happened. I think the University of Petroleum and Minerals is one of them. They happened over time with people from CRS applying the techniques they learned, but the relationship with the client—the ability to reach down into the client's organization—was seldom there.

Frankly, I was never enamored with international practice. The big projects, big dollars were always important to the company. They spent a lot of money in marketing, proposals, trips, negotiations, but it was never the area I wanted to spend the rest of my career in. So I left it alone when I had the chance. My last trip was to Baghdad with Herb Paseur—three bad weeks in Baghdad. . . .

I was sort of amused. The project we were going after was a technical university in Baghdad, and the people we negotiated with went to Princeton! But their stay in the U.S. didn't teach them very much about what motivates American business.

In my career, I've always thought that great architecture comes from great clients, and I think that's true. But some of our work in the Middle East is the result of some really great people on a team that took the initiative in spite of the client. In the highest professional tradition, they did what was right. There were a lot of projects there not done that way, but they didn't have a lot of input from the client's organization, the user—he wasn't in the country yet.

JOE THOMAS

I got heavily involved in the management of projects through the international jobs I worked on. It was a complete change in how we did business: currencies, contracts, reimbursable expenses, etcetera. I remember [that] when we first started doing international projects we hired a lot of outside consultants to tell us how they thought we should do business internationally. None of their advice was worth a damn.

Bad advice from so-called international experts rather than good advice led us down some paths we should not have followed. One of the things we always insisted on was that we be paid in American dollars. This was stupid in a way because most of the currencies we dealt with were as stable as the dollar. The Saudi *riyal,* Kuwaiti *dinar,* and other Middle East currencies became more and more stable throughout our involvement in international projects. But that was one of the recommendations we got from the international experts.

Another was [that] we didn't know anything about estimating the cost of international projects. We were extremely concerned about how to estimate the cost of a project in Saudi Arabia when all our experience had been in Texas and the U.S. We could factor from Texas to New York and from Texas to Washington, Idaho, Oklahoma—you name it. But we didn't know how to take that overseas. So we spent a lot of money learning how to do that.

Having worked in the U.S. all our lives, I thought the way to do business internationally was the same as we had been doing in the U.S. It was a shock to find I was wrong. There are a bunch of different schemes from different countries on how to do business. In other words, the difference between the way American architects, engineers, and contractors work in the U.S. versus how they work in England is as different as day and night. The role of the architect/engineer in England is entirely different from his role in the U.S.

When I started going overseas, I kept hearing about these different proposals on how we should design and construct our project. Most of them centered around doing it the British way. The British were doing business internationally, I guess, a hundred years before we were. With the British interests throughout the world, it was just natural that in Saudi Arabia, Kuwait, and other places where British influence was high, they were tuned to the British way of doing things.

Basically, it came down to this: CRS would design a school, prepare a set of plans and specs, then go out and prequalify several contractors to bid on the project and, if at all possible, take the low bid and proceed to build the project with the contractor supervising his construction. The British way was that the architect designed it, and then they had what they called a quantity surveyor who prepared a "bill of quantities" for the project. When he prepared that, he also prepared the specifications. Then the contractor took that bill of quantities for the entire project and bid unit prices on each of those bills of quantities times the quantity number of that particular item. They went through the list, and at the bottom, there was an approximate cost of the project.

But the cost was not guaranteed. We have the cost guaranteed by the contractor: "I will build this project for a million dollars." The British method says: "I think, according to this bill of quantities, I can build this project for a million dollars. But it may be more or less, depending on how many quantities."

For example, concrete. In the U.S. method, we didn't give a damn how many cubic yards of concrete we had in the project. We told the contractor, "Here are all the places we want concrete. Now then, you put that concrete in there, and we will pay you the lump sum you guaranteed for the project." In the British method, they would say, "We have one thousand yards of concrete in this project." They went out and actually measured the quantities of concrete that went into the project. If the totals were plus or minus the bill of quantities, then the contractor was paid so much for his unit price for every yard of concrete he put into the project.

You can see there were a zillion people out on the project measuring quantities, multiplying them by the unit price. Until the project ended, the poor owner had only a foggy idea of what it was going to cost him, depending on the accuracy of the bill of quantities.

When we started doing business overseas, I wanted to go the American way. I didn't know all the ins and outs of the bill of quantities system, so I told my clients we were going to do their project exactly like we do it in the U.S. More and more of the international clients we had were tuned to the American way for the simple reason [that] they had a bottom-line price. Unless there was something wrong with the plans or changes and extras—we always allowed about 5 percent for that anyway—the client knew pretty well what the project would cost. In the other method, you waited 'til it was over to find out what it would cost.

Q: No one was liable then?

A: That's right. The final price depends on the actual quantities measured, and that depends on how good the quantity surveyor is.

There were really two systems in use. We didn't have quantity surveyors, and if we were to need them, we would have to go out to England and retain them. So I said, "To hell with that, we're going to do it our way." When we first started doing projects overseas, I didn't know there was another system in operation. The client would come back to ask where the quantity surveyor was, and I had to ask what that was. After graduating from Texas A&M and doing business for ten to fifteen years, I had no idea there was another system. . . . In Britain, the quantity surveyor took off those quantities and furnished them to the contractor. So all the contractor had to do was put his unit price on each, and there it was.

It was a little different in Saudi Arabia because Aramco had been there for years before we got there. They did a lot on the quantity survey method and a few the American way. So our way was known in the international market, but not as well as the British. . . .

There was a management problem in the beginning of the UPM project in Saudi Arabia. The first thing we did for the university was to design twenty-six units of faculty housing. We went over there with the idea that we would be paid for twenty-six designs, [but] the university decided there was basically only one design that we repeated. At that point, we were ready to pack our gear and go home, which would have been the end of our international business. I was not involved with the management team. Tiny Lawrence was the designer, and the manager of the project was Don Wines. We were sitting in the dean's office, [Dean Ambeh,] who was ready to fire us. Tiny was ready to leave, and I said, "Wait a minute. Everybody in this thing is going to lose, and it's going to be a mess. Why don't we go back to the hotel and think this over for a while. Dean, why don't you think about it for a while and see if there isn't some common ground where we can meet. Let's cool off for a while."

So we did, and they did. Dr. Hall helped us a lot with the dean, and we talked among ourselves about what we could do. When we returned and met with the dean, we told him what we thought we could do, and he thought he could buy that. We went on to design and begin to build the University of Petroleum and Minerals. The next day, though, we were in a meeting with the dean and he said, "I want that man—pointing at me—to run this project." That's how I got involved with the management of international projects and got out of the mechanical engineering business of CRS. It all happened because I suggested we cool off, then come back and see if we can work out a compromise. . . .

We were over there with schematic design on twenty-six units of faculty housing. Basically, what we had done was take three different designs, put them into groups, and produce twenty-six units. We wanted to be paid for schematic design of those twenty-six units, and the dean only wanted to pay for one. We compromised by agreeing to payment for schematic design of twenty-six units, but design development and construction documents would be paid on the basis of three units.

Q: That was a lot of savings for them. It would have been better if you could have turned that around.

A: The fact is that without it [the compromise], we wouldn't have had anything. If we had gone home, that would have been the end of it. We would not even have been paid for schematic design.

TINY LAWRENCE

Aramco, as I gather from listening to some of the old Aramcoites talk when we first started going there, was genuinely altruistic when they went into the kingdom and were seriously concerned for helping the Saudis develop and understand and find better ways to do things. And part of that program was helping them develop educational systems—schools and teachers for their kids—and Dr. Hall was brought over to help run that aspect of what they were doing.

I can give you a fascinating story about this man [Hall]. Dr. Hall was with Aramco and had some political problem within the organization—which I'm not going to go into 'cause I don't really understand it accurately. He was either asked to resign or resigned. About that time, Zaki Yamani, who was the minister of petroleum and minerals there, wanted to start a new college that was sort of related to the petroleum industry. While he [Hall] was with Aramco, he had written a proposal to the king offering for Aramco to build a college for training Saudis—somewhere in the middle management level between technical school and a college education. This would sort of fill that middle management level with Saudi nationals who had a sense of the technology of the industry and a layer of management skills. They [Aramco] offered to build the college—to staff it with faculty, and to carry that faculty for several years and train Saudi nationals to come—and they never got a reply. I think it lay on the king's desk for five years—four or five years never hearing anything.

When Dr. Hall left [Aramco] and Yamani brought him in to start up a new college, he of course remembered that because he wrote the proposal in the first place [while with Aramco]. And remembering that he had written that proposal to the king and that he had never got a response, he just opened the door again.

Q: What was Hall's background?

A: He's an educator. He had a chair—probably in education, I'm not sure—at Columbia University. And he was one of the most comprehensive men I've ever met because he read incessantly and had what I thought was a rather bright legal mind. All of these things helped his position because he had to do everything. But he wrote back to the kingdom and said, "Since we haven't heard from you, we're starting this college." He told Zaki Yamani that this offer had been made and never been taken, but now, since they never said "yes" or "no," we can now say "yes" and go back to Aramco for funding our college. So he wrote back to Aramco, responding to his own proposal. He had written and built this table of how all these costs were escalating, and Aramco responded positively—negotiated a little bit, and they got money.

So Dr. Hall wrote the proposal and accepted the proposal with escalation, and that's where the early funding came from. This was in '62, probably. By 1963, he had been launched into a search for a firm to master plan and design their college. Internationally, he looked at firms in Europe and touched base with Educational Facilities Labs in New York. EFL told him about CRS, Bill's activities, and things the firm had done that got their attention. So Dr. Hall called CRS one day and said that he would like to come and talk to us, which he did. . . .

He liked what he saw. He went back to the kingdom and wrote within a month, saying he would like to hire CRS for the master planning phase—and more to come if we're happy. . . . "Can you have a team here by the first of December?" [he asked.] I think it was already the first of November. So we scrambled to put the team together. It was a tight scramble. Willie went over a week before we did and did some programming, and then we went over and did the master plan and set a design direction for the project. And they loved everything.

Q: Did you continue to do many projects in the Middle East, or did you branch out all over in the international market?

A: No, my work centered on UPM and another very large job in the Middle East, which was the King Abdul Aziz Military Academy. That occupied me almost fulltime from, I'd say, the early '70s 'til I retired [in 1981]. It was like building a town from scratch, which is virtually what happened with all of these Saudi projects because there was no infrastructure there. You would build everything from the sewage system to the road network and transportation. . . .

Bill Caudill served on a panel of the U.S. State Department's Foreign Building Office, a critique panel of name architects selecting the architect to do the next work and then reviewing what the architect would present for approval. Bill had been involved with that panel for a couple of terms. When Bill's time was running out, the man who ran the panel—I can't remember his name—told Bill that he would recommend CRS for the U.S. Embassy in Saudi Arabia because we had done the work there, but only if Bill agreed to lead the design crew.

Bill had pulled completely out of design. It may have been when he went to Rice or while he was at Rice, but there was a period when Bill just backed away and said he was not taking the leadership of any more design projects: "I'll stir things up and kind of throw things in and look to the future and all that, but I'm not going to be directly involved in design." My opinion is that he, as he did along the way, backed away to give more broad-range responsibility to other design leaders.

From time to time, different ones of us would try to cajole Bill into taking leadership on a project: "Bill, why don't you take this one?" "No, I'm not doing that." Well, when this U.S. Embassy [job] came up, it was either "Bill, you take that leadership, or you don't get the project." So he talked to the partnership and asked our opinion on it. I think every one of us must have encouraged him. He asked me about it: I said, "Bill, if you want to do this—" He said, "If I do it, I may want to use you and your design group to give it to because I don't have a design group [of my own] to work with." I said, "That would be wonderful!"

This really was delightful because I had not worked with Bill for decades! . . . When I had worked with him last, it was as a young designer, and I was sort of a thorn in his side. Here, I was going to place my team at his disposal. We really had a good time. We really related beautifully.

Bill and I enjoyed each other and enjoyed working together. I told him I firmly believe that when more than one designer or more than one heavy design firm is involved, you enjoy working on a project. To keep integrity in the design and keep peace in relationships, you have to determine in the beginning that one person makes the decisions. Then we all get together and explore things. Then you say, "What are we going to do?" And that comes back to one person.

I told Bill that if we did this, that's the way I saw it working—that we will work together and kick things around, but when it comes to decisions, you make the decisions. That suited him fine. We just had a ball. Flying back from an early programming session on this embassy [project], I told Bill that it just seemed like a good opportunity to work together, and he needed to know down the line that I was going to be pulling out [retiring] in plenty of time to get everything in order. He just seemed to be the natural one to talk to [about my decision to retire].

■ CHAPTER 9

GOING PUBLIC

■ TIB: 21 MARCH 1972

John Rowlett and I learned a lesson on response many years ago when the firm was called Caudill and Rowlett. It was this—REGARDLESS OF WHAT YOU DO, THERE IS ALWAYS SOMETHING GAINED AND SOMETHING LOST.

■ Until the 1960s, professional service firms such as architects and engineers stood somewhat apart from the business world. Professional service firms were not publicly traded; they were owned by their founders or by fellow professionals who had been offered a stake in the ownership after the firm was already operating.

However, the situation changed dramatically in the 1960s. Stock markets generated riches at a feverish clip, and professionals started wondering whether their own firms should be organized more like conventional businesses. A small New York engineering and surveying concern, Lockwood, Kessler, and Bartlett (later known as Viatech), became the first professional service firm to go public, registering in the 1960s to sell shares on the New York Stock Exchange. The proscription against public ownership was breached. Service firms in architecture, stock brokerage, and public relations—and eventually accounting and management consulting—began seizing the opportunity to sell shares to the public.[1] By 1978, thirty-three of the three hundred largest building design and construction firms had issued stock that could be bought and sold freely in the equity markets.[2]

In 1970, CRS, still privately owned, ranked as the twenty-first-largest U.S. firm engaged mainly in architecture. Its officers had been approached a number of times by companies that wanted to buy the firm, but CRS's principal owners—the first eight partners—remained reluctant to give up control and rejected the offers. From those discussions, however, came the alternative idea—a better idea, the partners concluded—of converting CRS into a publicly traded enterprise. Rather than cede control to some other company, CRS would organize its own public offering of shares. Consequently, in 1971 CRS became the first large architectural firm to sell shares to anyone interested in buying them. Tom Bullock recalled years later: "Herb Paseur and I wore out two major law firms in making it happen."[3]

There were several advantages to going public. First, the founders—Bill Caudill, John Rowlett, Wallie Scott, Willie Peña, Bullock, Ed Nye, Charles Lawrence, and Paseur—could continue to run the firm rather than hand control over to an acquisition group. Second, they would all acquire substantial personal wealth. Third, as they got closer to retirement age, they could sell their shares on the market and use the money for their own purposes. Fourth, the firm would gain enough liquid capital to go shopping for other firms in the design and construction industry. Fifth, there would be sufficient money to finance the development of new groups in the industry. The most notable of these was CRS/CM, the firm's construction management affiliate.

Professional firms often have had trouble lasting more than a generation because the younger people in a company lack the necessary funds and there is usually no one else interested in buying out the founders. Going public overcame that obstacle and enabled CRS to make the eventual transition to a new generation of leadership. Stock in CRS Design Associates, the holding company, was sold over the counter on NASDAQ with Underwood Neuhaus serving as underwriters. Later, the stock was traded on the American Stock Exchange, and finally on the New York Stock Exchange. Despite their new liquid wealth, the founders did not rush for the exit, as sometimes happens after a public offering. They stayed and helped the company prosper. Revenues in 1977 climbed to nearly five times what they had been in 1970.[4]

Doubts eventually emerged about whether going public was the right course—for CRS or any other architectural firm. Michael Baker III, a management consultant whose family had founded the Michael Baker Corporation, a Pennsylvania engineering concern that went public, asserted in an analysis in the early 1980s that there are "no compelling reasons for

Tom Bullock, ***center,*** **and Herb Paseur,** ***right,*** **in 1974, when CRS became the first architectural firm listed on the American Stock Exchange. The man at left with the ticker tape is unidentified.** *Photo courtesy Marty Cobin.*

design companies to be publicly owned." Public ownership, many analysts argued, distracts a firm from what matters most in the field of architecture and for the clients: projects. The bottom line of a professional "is not the same as the businessman's bottom line," management consultant Weld Coxe maintains. "The businessman is trained to measure success of management in chiefly quantitative terms, usually units of money, or output, or the like. In contrast the bottom line of the creative professional is most often qualitative, measured in terms of the professional's ultimate judgment about whether the output of the organization is as good as it can be."[5]

On the whole, the market's verdict on public ownership of professional firms turned out to be negative. In some professional firms, stock lost much of its value after an initial run-up. In the mid-1970s and afterward, a sizable proportion of publicly owned professional service firms bought their stock back, becoming privately owned and operated again. By the end of the century, few architectural firms, and none of the biggest names, were publicly owned.[6] Ambitious architects often want to be owners, so publicly owned architecture firms "have trouble attracting and keeping the best people," according to Coxe. Public ownership is more common in engineering, a field in which the businesses are much bigger. Yet, even there the dominant tradition remains private ownership. Engineering firms that are publicly traded "underperform the private sector," says William Fanning, research director for the *Professional Services Management Journal*.[7]

With so many pitfalls to public ownership, CRS's success as a publicly traded company stands out all the more. Here was a firm that did not reverse course, but instead remained publicly traded for more than twenty years, carrying out enormous and widely respected undertakings during that time. Whereas many of the architectural firms that went public lacked a strategy for making effective use of their new resources, CRS was keenly conscious of how it could use its expanded capital: to open new offices, to purchase architecture- and engineering-related enterprises, and to embark on entirely new pursuits. The new form of ownership vaulted CRS into areas of the economy that a pure architecture or architecture/engineering or architecture/engineering/planning firm would never have been able to enter.

Bullock expressed pride in how flexible CRS was, both before and after going public. The publicly owned corporation brought unusual individuals such as futurist John Naisbitt onto its board of directors. "We did everything we could to learn what was happening in the real world," Bullock said. "You can't learn that from a drafting board."[8]

Whether going public was a good decision continues to be debated. As the following interviews show, the postmortem is far from unanimous.

INTERVIEWS

HERB PASEUR

Back in the late '60s, there was an architect named Charles Luckman who graduated during the depression. He went to work for Lever Brothers Company and became president and CEO of that corporation. Then, in the '50s, he left that position and became an architect again in California and had a very successful practice—it was Luckman and Pereira—and then they split. In about '68, Luckman had this substantial firm of one hundred to two hundred people with good projects. He did a lot of planning. There was a big public company [the Odgen Corporation] that acquired his firm on a stock-for-stock basis. This was the first example of anyone being able to realize the value of an architectural firm in excess of its book value. It caught the attention of a lot of people, not only in architecture but engineering and other fields.

One of the first firms to start amalgamating, or bringing in companies, was Planning Research Corporation [PRC], which started as a computer company but branched off into engineering and started acquiring engineering firms. Basically, they were a public company, and they were doing it with paper—stock-for-stock transactions.

Another public corporation that started about the same time was URS, which had a big engineering background. So there were four public companies that began to acquire other firms to build their organizations. As a prominent firm, we were targets for these people, and we talked seriously with PRC [and] URS. We liked the idea that being part of a larger organization could probably bring us opportunities more quickly than we would have gotten them otherwise. But we didn't feel comfortable with giving up our independence.

At the same time, some very large corporations like Westinghouse were starting a whole division on leisure learning. We were romanced by Westinghouse to join their leisure learning group. At that time, Westinghouse had about $3 billion in revenues, and we were probably at $5 to $6 million a year—infinitesimal. But we were real impressed. . . . They flew in on one of their corporate jets, toured through the office, and all that kind of stuff.

On the professional side, no architect or engineer had ever gone public from scratch, and we started investigating the possibility of doing that. The first lawyers told us, "You can't practice architecture as a corporation." We finally had to go all the way to Boston to get an opinion from the firm of Hill and Barlow. At that time, they represented the National Council of Architectural Registration Boards, which was just being formed, and they were getting legal help on what they were doing. So we got an opinion from Hill and Barlow that in every state except New York, we could probably practice in the way we had done. The partnership would contract for the project—and that satisfied all the registration laws—then subcontract the work out to the corporation.

In New York, there were some old corporate charters that allowed you to practice in New York as a corporation. So, we had to dredge up one of these old charters and buy it. It hadn't been used in years and years. Anyway, we got a New York charter so we could practice there. We had an opinion from the attorney that we could practice as described in our prospectus.

Then we got with Underwood Neuhaus. At that time, I think our revenues must have been up to about $12 million, and we went public at twelve times earnings. Earnings were one dollar a share at that particular time. The book value of the company, which is what we all bought our stock at, traded internally, was probably about $2 a share. So we had been able to leverage the value of the company by about six times by going public. That also gave us the funds to expand. So then we started the decentralization thing again. As we described it, we were going to use the funds to open offices in Los Angeles, Chicago, New York, and to make acquisitions.

Well, we opened all those offices. We opened one in L.A., and [Paul] Kennon was the principal in charge. Chuck Thomsen was in New York, and we hired a guy [Richard Geyser] to run the Chicago office. We had a new concept of the way we were going to practice. We were going to do all of the engineering and construction documents in Houston. These offices would do promotion, design, and construction administration. That worked okay for a while. . . . Then all the offices wanted to start doing everything. They didn't want to give part of the work to Houston. They developed that "push-pull" with Houston, which in some cases is very good and in others can be very bad.

Then we started making acquisitions. We had a stock that was liquid, traded on the NASDAQ, and we made some lousy acquisitions in the beginning. The first was a firm called Interlock, a computer company. . . . We were finally going to get us a viable computer company. [But] it wasn't viable. It lasted about three years, and we gave it back to them.

Our first major acquisition was an engineering firm in California which specialized in underground work, A. A. Mathews. At that time, people were talking subways all over the world—Taiwan, Europe, U.S.—and Al Mathews was very busy as a consultant. We were going to try to leverage his consultant capacity into a real design capacity. We were never able to do it. When we acquired the company, there were about eight to ten shareholders; it was stock-for-stock. Al Mathews owned most of that company, and he ended up a bigger shareholder in CRS Design Associates than Bill Caudill. So we created some funny situations. Al left in about a year, and we bought his stock back at a very low price.

Q: As you think back about the partners, who were the key ones making some of these decisions in terms of going public, the acquisitions, etcetera? Was there a small core team?

A: That was me and Tom, primarily, and Wallie secondarily—the three of us.

Q: So Caudill wasn't involved in these kinds of decisions—not centrally?

A: No, he wasn't going out and talking to firms or meeting with analysts or things like that.

JOHN FOCKE

CRS was not only pushing and expanding in the practice of architecture, pioneering in some areas of practice; they were also exploring new business forms to bring additional resources into our profession, to expand the scope of our interest. Through my involvement with Tom Bullock and Herb Paseur, after CRS went public, they set up the parent company organization [CRS Design Associates] and invited me to join the parent company and to help—the parent company had very limited staff—to organize our international marketing and later to develop a system for corporate planning that was applicable to a professional organization, which are very difficult organizations to plan for and manage. We spent years developing those systems with the leadership of the corporation.

CRS had the resources, through the public offering, to begin to think about expanding through acquisitions. This was fairly new for a professional firm to expand in that way, certainly through a public stock offering. For several years, I worked with Tom and Herb in the acquisition program. During the time I worked with them, we went through seven acquisitions. My job was to work with these acquired companies to understand their business [and] develop their planning capability so they could input their planning into the corporate planning. At one time, I was asked to be the acting CEO for what was becoming a collection of engineering operations. During that time, we consolidated that into a single engineering entity within the firm. That had me on airplanes every week.

We had offices all over the country. It was unusual to have an architect trying to manage engineering operations. It was not an easy undertaking, but I think we were very successful in some areas in making these companies successful. Over the long run, as I look back over the acquisition program and what CRS gained out of that program—I think there were eleven, twelve companies acquired and assimilated—[what I see] was that CRS was expanding its presence on a national basis. Although some of the offices eventually phased out their original names, CRS gained a presence in these new markets. Ultimately, it was through that mechanism that the CRS/Sirrine organization . . . was put together.

Q: Do you think anything was lost in the course of that acquisitions program?

A: Well, yeah. I've discussed that with a number of people, both with the firms that were acquired and some of the CRSers I worked with. And, yeah, there were losses. I think the phenomenon I witnessed over and over was a small partnership being acquired by a big corporation and the inability of either party to come to terms. Invariably, the original partners would become disenchanted with the organization, which they had either not fully understood, or in some cases they realized they were not team players and didn't want to do that. There were some good people who would have made big contributions had they stayed with the firm, but for reasons of their own just felt they couldn't do that. There was a human cost also, a lot of people [were] uprooted in the assimilation process.

There were also gains that made the concept worth pursuing. As I look back, there were four or five acquisitions that probably should never have been done. They just never had a chance to work, but at the time, we couldn't see it. I think another aspect of it was that some of the goals a small firm will have—in terms of their expansion, how they did their accounting, how they compensated their leadership—just don't fit a corporate structure. There were some people who got rich in these acquisitions and did not stay with the firm, and I've not felt good about that. The people who sold their companies to CRS were handsomely rewarded and in the end had no loyalty to their original firm or to CRS. In hindsight, that is probably unfortunate. . . .

There's a fundamental transition in a firm that goes public, particularly a professional service firm. In the original and traditional architectural practice, the client is the focus of all activity. Obviously, the principals are interested in their income and being successful on projects, but the client is the focal point. Once the firm goes public, the shareholder becomes the focal point, and the client often is in a secondary role. In the early days of CRS, with the presence in the firm—the Peñas, Paseurs—they were able to transcend this commitment to the shareholders and hold our clients out in front of us always. As the company has matured, grown in size, and the leadership has shifted to attorneys and financial people, the focus on client is difficult to maintain at times, particularly over long periods of time. I think the people involved in projects who meet the client have a better chance of keeping that focus than those who don't.

In some cases, I can look back and see [that] while the client[s] may have been served well, they didn't feel they were the focus of the company. That's a battle that a corporation the size of CRSS has to fight every day. They fight it with the people involved in the projects. If the leadership of the company loses the confidence of those people, it has lost its connection with the client. One of my concerns in the latter days I was with CRSS—I was there twenty-two years—was that the turnover of key people in the firm was so rapid, we never felt the loyalties to clients that we had in the early days. Just to give an example: In the '60s, when CRS did its first big international project in Saudi Arabia, Tiny Lawrence was involved in design. Jim Gatton was involved. Joe Thomas, one of our leading engineers, was involved. Twenty-two years later, they were still serving that client. That was a commitment they had—a career commitment on their part. That's rare.

PHIL WILLIAMS

Q: Did CRS change appreciably in the period immediately after it went public?

A: Yes. Yes, it did. I think it was a combination of things. The main thing was that CRS's management, typical among many firms, became oriented to its responsibility to the shareholders quarter to quarter to produce good quarterly reports. So there was a short-term emphasis rather than a long-term one, and sacrifices were made in that way. There may have been an underlying assumption that the firm had sufficient momentum from its past and its people to maintain the long-term movement, and, management could concentrate on the short-term—quarter to quarter.

Part of it, quite frankly, was that Tom himself was quite giddy with this experience. He would tend to burst into a roomful of hardworking people with a corporate announcement of some kind that, after repetition, gave everyone the impression that that was what was important. At the time, a professional corporation was a fairly new thing, so there was a perception among a lot of us that you made a choice between a professional organization and a business organization. And CRS was clearly making the choice to be a business organization, and that wasn't as wholesome, so to speak. That's how I remember it a long time later and with a poor memory.

NORMAN HOOVER

Q: You were there before the firm went public and after that period. How did you feel about that turn in the history of the firm?

A: It didn't affect my perspective and the things I was interested in doing. Obviously, I knew it happened, no doubt about that. But I don't think it affected me very much in the sense of work and the organization. It seemed like a good idea.

Q: Do you think it affected your attitude toward the work?

A: Not at all that I can recall. I assumed greater minds than mine had decided it was a good thing, and that was okay with me. We were getting lots of good projects to work on, getting paid, and growing. I saw no great advantage or disadvantage in terms of the work I was involved in.

ROBERT BROOKS

Q: What do you think going public did to CRS? Did it change the culture?

A: I wasn't there the first year because of the Baltimore assignment. All of us were offered stock under various arrangements. I think I was an associate at the time, and there was a formula that told each associate how many shares of stock they could buy. I was offered more than I ultimately bought.

I think the exposure mandated when you are publicly traded, I guess mandated by the SEC, created a change in the culture. The quarterly reports became a new taskmaster in themselves. [They] made people watch the numbers more carefully than ever before, I think.

I don't know if it was a function of going public or not, but at the same time, CRS went into what I would call a decentralized management structure where different segments of the firm became profit centers, and the managers of each had a lot of authority to hire, fire, and shape the way they did things. There were a number of architects who became managers of significant numbers of people sort of overnight in that decentralization. Sometimes that worked, and sometimes it didn't. Sometimes good architects don't make good managers, and other times they do.

One of the surprising things for me in walking around as an associate of a publicly traded company was that some of the associate architects we worked with around the country in previous years thought we were the fifteen-hundred-pound gorilla. They would come up to you at conventions in Atlantic City and other places and out of the blue start seriously inquiring whether CRS might want to buy their firm. I wasn't in a role to be a real spokesman for that kind of issue.

FRANK LAWYER

How can I say this? It seemed that after the firm went public—and I can't knock it because I'm sure it was valuable to the firm to be a public organization—the whole vocabulary of our meetings was a new kind of jargon. Instead of talking about buildings and architecture, the meetings got involved with the "bottom line," "our product"—all the jargon of stock markets, profits and losses, etcetera. Probably rightfully so, but I never enjoyed our meetings when they got so involved in that kind of discussion instead of "how good are our buildings?" It seemed after we became CRSS [that] something happened, and I'm not sure what because I retired in '83, soon after. More emphasis was put on things other than people, team. I don't know. I felt something was happening, that maybe we lost something there that made the architectural arm of the firm start to die out. I don't know where the turning point was; whether it was when we went public. I hate to place blame on anybody, so I'm not sure.

JAMES THOMAS

I was made an officer [of CRS] the day the first man landed on the moon. So, every time that is celebrated, I have a nostalgic moment [for] when I got my long-awaited telegram. Right after I was made an officer, I had the opportunity to buy stock at CRS. I bought, I think, twenty [shares]. I was given the opportunity to buy twenty-two shares. Since I actually had no money other than month to month, there were simply no savings. I felt I had to buy—it was not required but certainly expected of me. So, CRS arranged a bank loan, and it was some $3,000. I think I was making about $12,000 at the time, and it seemed like an immense amount of money. CRS arranged it at Texas Commerce, and they took it out of our salary, and all was well.

When the stock went public, it was offered at twelve [dollars a share]. The split was seventy-five to one. I was just ecstatic because that was all the money in the world to me. I remember going over to the underwriter, which was Underwood Neuhaus, and [I] was asked to be interviewed by this broker as to what we should do and not do. So I explained my situation, what I had: one old car, a very small house, three children, and no savings in the bank. He advised me very candidly to not buy any CRS stock. With my holdings, I had sufficient [collateral only] for that. . . . Any other investments, he would be happy to help me with, but I should diversify. Well, I didn't diversify—I couldn't afford anything else—but within three days, the market had jacked the stock from 12 to 18! Then for many, many, many months, it stayed at two. I was grateful to that broker, and to this day, I don't know his name. Later, I sold my stock after a bunch of splits for I think $58,000, which put my children through college. It was just about the best investment I've ever made, even though if I hadn't been expected to, I would not have done it. Going public was a very exciting period at CRS. Nobody really knew exactly what was going to happen, but we all felt it was going to be positive. I think I left there probably two years later.

RICHARD ANDERSON

I remember one day getting a dictum from Mike Trower [then general manager of CRS] saying that for [us to reach] the goal to build the bottom line for going public, we needed to try and hit a 70 percent profit on the Buckley and Weaver high schools.[9] Back in those days, those were $25 million schools, and we had a 6 percent fee. That's $50 million of work at 6 percent, and not a bad fee. Of course, I was young and dumb at that time, and being dictated to concerning a profit—I never imagined anybody could make that kind of profit, and we didn't. Considering how it was delivered and by whom delivered, it probably didn't get my utmost support anyway. I couldn't understand why anyone would want to go public and why the focus on the bottom line had to be as strong as it was.

Now of course, having run my own business [Anderson DeBartolo Pan] for twenty years and into a transition strategy for the last ten years, it's crystal clear to me why. I understand it very well now and applaud it.

Q: But you still couldn't come up with 70 percent profit.

A: I think there are a lot of projects where 20 to 25 percent profits can be expected. Occasionally, we'll hit 30 percent, but the truth is, our firm [ADP] has not been as profitable as it needed to be because we've been slow to make the transition from practicing architecture to running a business. That slowness has run vertically through the firm. Where we've had as many as thirteen to fourteen partners, we're down to eight or nine now—and mostly because we couldn't convince guys they needed to do what needs to be done in order to run a successful design practice. We've also had a difficult time in that regard making the transition into computerization. I'm told we have one of the largest CAD operations in the country here, but a lot of our people still haven't figured out how to understand what's in that box and figure a way to test it frequently enough to get a good indication of what percent complete they are on a project.

I was talking earlier about our transition plan [at ADP]. We made a decision to make the transition internal. In order to do that, we've got to be able to pay the new owners enough money to buy the stock. In order to do that, we've got to generate enough profit to cause that to happen. If we set aside 5 percent of our profit for transition, and 5 percent for growth, and 5 percent to allow the proper compensation to take place—the kind of money everybody wants to make—we're talking about a bottom line of 15 percent that this firm has to make year in and year out. I can tell you we're not doing that. We'll have years when we make 12–15 percent, and then years when it will be 5–8 percent. That puts a real kink in the transition strategy. So we're wrestling right now with market segments, new business ventures—the kinds of strategies that will help us be more profitable. Before we brought engineering in-house, we consistently would run between 15 percent and 20 percent profit. Since we brought engineering in, we probably average 8–10 percent.

With intent to be a truly big A, big E firm for the sake of integrating architecture and engineering, we've had a "love me, love my dog" mentality. We are only architects for the work we engineer, and we engineer only the work on which we do the architecture. The reality of that is we continue to establish our growth goals to increase our revenue, but we can't grow the company fast enough to do what the company needs to do. We are finally realizing that. So one of the changes we'll be making . . . is to think more in terms of affiliations, associations, and consultancies in order to grow revenue [and] offload the staffing up and risk involved in growth onto a broader base of colleagues and people who can help us get the work done.

Q: That worked very well for CRS. The association agreements managed to increase our national presence and at the same time got more people promoting for us, and the projects tended to be quite profitable; in fact, more profitable than when we did the working drawings ourselves.

A: Absolutely. You've got somebody else taking the risk and somebody else doing the ramping up in order to produce the back end of it. That kind of flies in the face of the trend today, when clients are more and more wanting to buy single-source responsibility . . . to be responsible for 100 percent of the task.

Q: Is this sort of the "virtual corporation" notion in which you put together a complete team?

A: Right. We will continue to want to be prime and take the responsibility for 100 percent of the project but defer from doing it all ourselves. We will be finding firms to help us do it. It will allow us to cover more territory, sell more work, earn more revenue, and hopefully increase our profit line. Sounds a lot like what Tom Bullock might have thought about a long time ago.

Q: I think it probably is. I've always thought one of the problems with doing all the work in the home office was that the people who did construction documents and that kind of thing never saw the buildings they worked on.

A: We have that same problem. Fifty percent of our business is on the West Coast, [and] 25 percent is on the East Coast. I don't think we have more than one active project in Tucson [where ADP's home office is located] today, and typically, probably less than 5 percent of our revenue has been earned in Tucson. Two hundred of the three hundred people we have work in Tucson. Most of the guys never see the buildings they're drawing.

Q: So if they've got a really poor detail, they keep right on using it project after project. Local architects don't have that problem because everybody goes out to see the job.

A: That's true.

Q: When you developed your succession plan or transition as you called it, what other options did you consider?
A: We never looked at going public. If the truth were known, I think that's the major thing that caused Jack [DeBartolo] to leave CRS. . . . I know Jack and I decided we would just as soon not go public and try to do it in-house.

So we really only looked at an interior transition plan. We've had firms approach us who were interested in acquisition, but [we] never had a reciprocal interest.

ED NYE

Going public was good for the firm. We discussed it for years before going public.[10] Some of the guys said, "We want to keep control of our partnership and don't want a bunch of stockholders making us go through this and that and getting involved." But I think it was a smart move.

Q: What do you think it did to the office as a place to do architecture and engineering? Good things? Bad things?

A: I don't believe it was detrimental. It might have caused some to think the bottom line ought to be improved. It's possible it had a subconscious effect on design. But I think overall, it was beneficial for the firm. It gave us more financial room, more financial benefits.

Q: How do you feel about the whole collection of mergers and acquisitions that took place largely as a result of going public?

A: Very good. I really do. I think Sirrine was one of the smartest things we did. I haven't been that close to it, maybe, but I'm sure without Sirrine, we'd be worse off now than with them. General construction has been kind of slow.

It's fairly obvious, I think, [that] if we can get a wider scope of operations—a different type of building besides just schools—I would certainly be in favor of it. I wasn't too conscious of the need to get more and more people just for the sake of being big. If we do a job well, get big because people know about it and want us, then [fine]. But the first thing is a job done well. The fact that we got bigger would give us the benefit of bringing good people in.

BRUCE WILKINSON

I would be remiss in my duty not to give you a little bit of philosophy about public company versus private company because others in the organization have an opinion on the issue.[11] The question is raised often. I would say we are a little bit of [an] anomaly in that, and I've sort of come full circle in my philosophy. I've never worked for a private company, so my entire business and professional experience has been in public companies. One would think that would be my natural bias.

In the *Engineering News Record's* "500 Largest Design Firms," the fiscal reality is that 95 percent of them are private. It is not a world that is generally traded publicly. When you look at the rest of the world and try to draw analogies: What is the nature of things worldwide, not just in this region? In Japan, most larger design firms are small parts of bigger conglomerates. They are the 2 percent of Mitsubishi or Mitsui, a firm buried down in there that—compared to the manufacturing, engineering, construction, banking, [and] other things they [big conglomerates] do—is relatively small. But again, it's privately held, or at least part of something bigger, so you never quite see it by itself.

When you go to Europe, you see concentric circles. There are some general patterns that say the design group tends to be more within a construction company or part of construction. In most of the big construction companies, certainly in England and France, there is an affiliate operation in real estate development, homebuilding. Or some own big aggregates of construction materials. Our partner, the John Mowlem Company, happens to be the largest owner and renter of scaffolding equipment to other contractors throughout Europe. Again, looking for where in the world there are large, publicly traded design and construction companies that do nothing else, there aren't many of them. In this country, certainly the largest one most people think of would be Bechtel, which is privately held, and Fluor would be the largest publicly traded. I think the issue is not necessarily public or private, but well managed or poorly managed.

There are lots of privately held firms in which families or one man owns everything, and that allows him to do what he wants in this lifetime and with the ownership upon his death. I think one of the disadvantages of being public is that everybody reads your mail, and you don't read theirs. We produce annual reports, dissect our revenues every way imaginable, produce a document that says what the five highest-paid people make and how they make it, what the rules are on how they get it.

There's part of me that's kind of evolved over the years that believes privately held is more in the natural order of things for a design/construction services company because, in general, it doesn't need lots of excess capital. One of the arguments for being public is access to the public marketplace so you can raise capital. But if you don't need it, then why are you public? The other issue is liquidity for the shareholders or owners: "What will I do when I get old and want to cash out?" That can be resolved another way.

I think there's a pretty good argument that says a design firm might be at its best as a privately held venture. I raise it because we are public—have always been public [and] kind of run ourselves that way. Certainly the electric power cogeneration business, CRSS Capital Independent Power, is probably one about which you could say the opposite. You could say right now there are only two types of utilities: investor owned and publicly owned, but no private or family owned. The reason is that a few hundred million here and there all add up, and there is a need for public access to finance. I make the great argument that we may have a situation where the baby that's been created—CRSS Capital—I believe has the potential of growing to a size and scale beyond the parent which created it, and it needs to be public, probably forever.

DAVE THORMAN

Q: Were you around when CRS went public?

A: Certainly was.

Q: Do you think it changed the firm a great deal?

A: I think it did. I think it had a very strong impact in probably two ways. One, it made us accountable on a short-term basis rather than long term. We had to watch the bottom line on a monthly or quarterly basis. Our focus became that instead of long term in terms of where we should go and how we should get there. Second, it diverted a lot of energy and balance into accounting and other activities that had to be done because we were a public company.

It would be interesting to talk to a financial person—go back and look at history and see where we'd be today if we hadn't done that. We certainly had a very solid foundation before we went public, [but] going public enabled us to spend a lot of money buying other firms, all of which fizzled out for one reason or another.

That's one thing I think is interesting in our history: Of all the companies we bought over the years, the only one that is still a viable culture is Sirrine. The rest have been absorbed into what is now CRSS. Of all the good things each of those companies brought, only fragments still exist.

■ CHAPTER 10

FAST TRACK, BUILDING SYSTEMS, AND CONSTRUCTION MANAGEMENT

■ TIB: 21 MAY 1971

"Fast Track" is a common word, not only in CRS, but in the profession. How did it get started? As Tom Bullock, who was in at the beginning, said, "It's hard to trace. Chuck Thomsen's memo to Jack Smith dated 30 March 71 is close if not accurate."

So let's read Chuck's memo:

"Jack I'm not absolutely sure how the 'fast track' term got started. The only role I had in the initiation of the phrase was in the report to the construction firm.

"My understanding of it all; however, goes like this. Tom was using the term around the firm to emphasize driving some projects through in a nontraditional way. He talked about the way projects get 'sidetracked.' And at one point a number of years ago, I heard him say that we had to develop a 'fast-track' to get some kinds of stuff through the firm. John Focke used the term in an in-house report.

"Simultaneously, Matzke was talking about planning projects by plotting all the possible ways to get them done from the start. When he said those words he would draw a typical decision tree starting at the present and branching out in many directions showing the alternate ways of getting the job done. Frank would say, 'What you really need to do is find the FASTEST path through that sequence of decisions.' As I understand it, Frank and Tom got together and somehow sidetrack and fast path got together and we started talking about fast-track construction.

"Fast track was a marvelous image. It connoted the inside track—one that doesn't make every local stop along the route. That's the big idea, isn't it? We don't ever stop the project for approval, various or comprehensive evaluation. Everything moves all the time. It is all overlapped.

"At any rate, somewhere in the synergy between Matzke and Bullock, fast track became more of a specific term describing accelerated project delivery processes. During this process, of course, we started the study of accelerated project delivery processes for the New York Construction Fund. Somewhere along the course of the study, we decided to put the fast track name on it—and I think we alternately credited Tom and Frank for the title. Frankly, I think Tom was the one that invented the expression. But it was Frank's supporting the study that probably institutionalized it. I only evangelized.

"Let's say it like this: Tom was the prophet; Frank was the Pope; and I was the faith healer."

—CHUCK "BILLY GRAHAM" THOMSEN

I felt that in the interest of history, this classic memo should be tibbed. So be it.

■ In the late 1960s and the 1970s, CRS developed new specialties aimed at improving the processes of architecture and construction. This was less the result of a strategic pla0n than of CRS's penchant for identifying talented individuals and providing them with plenty of resources, along with ample praise and criticism.

When Chuck Thomsen joined CRS full-time in 1965, Tom Bullock asked him to investigate whether there would be uses for a computer in an architectural firm. Thomsen visited the firms of DMJM and Ellerbe Becket, which already had computers, and went to an IBM school. Soon a strategy was developed to buy a computer and design a Management Information System (MIS). The computer, an eight-kilobyte IBM 1130, cost $60,000 and had about as much memory capacity as a $10 calculator today.[1]

The management system that came out of this was one of the first in the industry. Soon afterward, to avoid the drudgery of estimating construction costs that Herb Paseur had assigned him, Thomsen teamed up with Byron Stennis, CRS's great estimator, and in 1965 wrote what is thought to be the first computer-based construction-cost estimating system. After that came programs for specification retrieval, elevator design, and parametric estimating (a form of estimating that establishes achievable budgets early in a project, before designing has been completed). Jonathan King, executive vice president of Educational Facilities Laboratories, provided a grant to develop software that would help in the development of master plans for college and university campuses.

In the late 1960s, CRS established a computer affiliate known as CRS2, with Bob Mattox as its president and Frank Whitcomb as vice president. The objective was to provide computer services to CRS and, more importantly, to sell computer services to design firms that had not been as quick as CRS to embrace the latest technology. Herb Paseur, CRS's president, had institutionalized computer-aided cost-estimating capabilities so that CRS could produce reliable estimates at an early stage in a project's development. By 1970, the firm was outstanding at estimating. With its three-person estimating group under Stennis, CRS was one of the few companies that could really do parametric estimating early in design.

Yet CRS2 never sold a dime of anything. Perhaps the business world was not ready for the idea. Certainly architectural firms did not feel comfortable revealing all their financial data to a company owned by a competitor, nor did they want their clients to think they needed CRS to do estimating, economic analysis, campus planning—or anything else.

Another process-related specialty pioneered by CRS was fast-track design and construction. This idea yielded better rewards. In the late 1960s and the 1970s, when inflation plagued the construction industry, the need to accelerate building and lessen the impact of rising prices was acute. Fast track's virtue was that ground could be broken, foundations started, and structure ordered *before* the last design and purchasing decisions had been made. The process was phased, with some phases overlapping, speeding the building project enormously.[2]

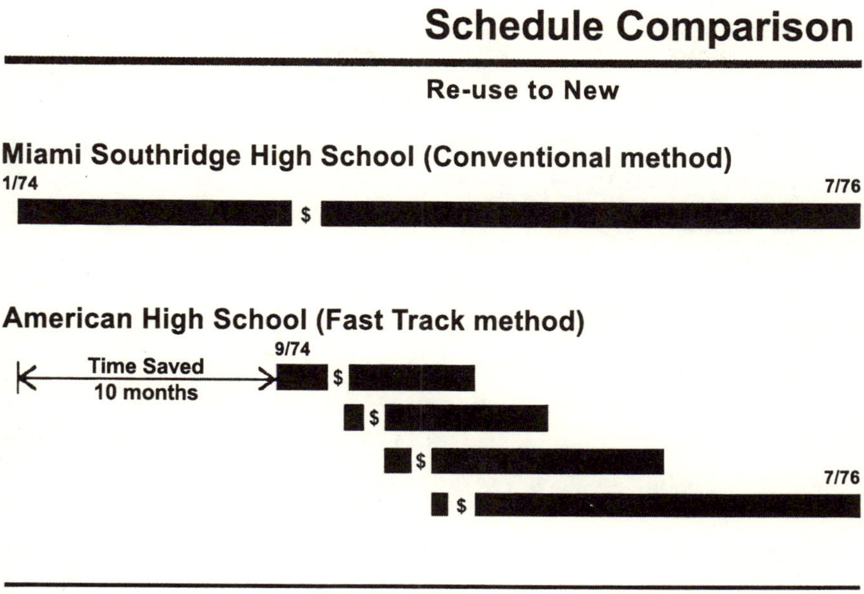

Fast-track schedule for American High School in Dade County, Florida, showing time saved by this method of design and construction.

Preliminary attempts at fast tracking were made for schools in Florida and on Long Island. The first true fast-track project was a school in Phoenix for Bell and Howell Schools (a chain of electronics-engineering and accounting schools run by Bell and Howell), designed by Norman Hoover, overseen by the New York office in 1970–71, and built by Kitchell Construction. The entire design and construction schedule was eight months, and the results were so good they won a design award from the Arizona AIA.

The firm introduced industrialized building systems into schools and housing and, to a limited extent, hospitals. These systems, which had first taken hold in post–World War II Europe in an attempt to bring the benefits of mass production to the building industry, at their optimum reduced project costs, lessened the need for on-site labor, and improved promptness and quality. Caudill Rowlett Scott went so far as to propose an industrialized building system in a competition for Johns Manville's corporate headquarters in Colorado. Although CRS did not win the competition, it did establish an important goal: that of bringing high design quality to a systems building process which, on the whole, lacked design distinction. Norman Hoover was later made a fellow in the AIA for his accomplishments in that area.

A third process-related specialty—one that paid off spectacularly in growth and in profitability during the 1970s—was the CRS affiliate for construction management. The construction management group, initially known as CRS/CM and quickly renamed CM Associates (mainly to keep "CRS" off competitors' job signs), was established with some of the capital that had been generated by going public. It turned out, however, that only about $18,000 was needed, because CM was making money within just four months.

The new firm's first significant construction management project was a $3.5 million high school in Opelika, Alabama, designed by CRS. The entire design and construction process took eleven and one-half months, shaving a year off conventional construction time.[3] Thomsen had strongly argued for establishing CM, and he was placed in charge of it when it was created in early 1971. By the fall of 1975, CM had 125 employees and had supervised construction projects totaling about $1.8 million.[4] By 1980, the company was managing $12 billion in projects worldwide. Although CM Associates worked on a number of CRS jobs, it was proud that it did not need the parent firm in order to flourish. Most of CM's projects came from other clients. In Thomsen's view, the architectural section of CRS had reached maturity by the 1970s and was having trouble with growth, profit, and a leadership transition, whereas CM, its dynamic progeny, "was very much the inheritor and carrier of CRS's culture and commitment to professional innovation."[5] It had the long coattails of the company's reputation and none of the burdens of age.

Construction management began in complicated private-sector projects like refineries and manufacturing plants. The first major government project to use CM's services was New York's World Trade Center, which in the late 1960s obtained that capability from Tishman Construction, a subsidiary of a large New York developer. Size was the determining factor in that project. The two towers, containing nearly 8 million square feet of office space, were simply too big to be bid in one contract, and few organizations had the financial strength to bond the job. By contrast, most public institutions that chose construction management did so because, with construction costs rising about 18 percent a year in 1969–70, they wanted a process that would reduce inflation's impact.

Construction management of some sort became common for schools. The firm's representatives would give a school board convincing proof that they could deliver a school in a year. If two years could be saved, that meant over 20 percent savings—or 20 percent more school. And good cost control in what had been a poorly managed process saved another 10 to 15 percent.

Hospital operators, who were already an important market for CRS's architecture, also liked the construction management idea, since those buildings were complicated—filled with special functions, complex equipment, and unusual building systems—and usually had a board of directors that lacked hands-on experience with building programs. Construction management of some sort also became common for universities, prisons, and certain building projects of large corporations.

After success in the domestic arena, the demand for projects of immense size began to rise overseas. The modernization of countries around the world generated a tremendous market for management expertise, so CM and other U.S. construction management firms revised their operations to suit conditions in countries where the design and building industries were much different. The ultimate size of the projects was mind-boggling. A telex that CM sent to its project manager on the University of Riyadh read: "BID DOCUMENTS ACADEMIC AREA ARRIVE ON SAUDIA FLT #60. MEET PLANE WITH FORKLIFT THEY ARE SHIPPED ON 9 PALLETS."

Big things were afoot, and CRS, with its strong CM affiliate, had become master of the megaproject.

PUTTING SCHOOLS ON THE FAST TRACK

For the American High School in Dade County, Florida, the local school board wanted to test innovative processes, so it offered to run a race between a traditional method and the construction management idea. School officials had a design for a prototype. They proposed that CM build one school, and they would bid the same design to a general contractor; then they would compare results. Thomsen told the client he wanted to do more than that: Both firms would start simultaneously, but CM and CRS would totally redesign the school—and still beat the cost and schedule of the other school. They succeeded, saving about 11 percent ($1.1 million on a $10 million project) and beat the other project by a year. The project also won a Florida AIA honor award for design.

Thirteen months were required for design and construction of a one-hundred-thousand-square-foot Bell and Howell School in Chicago that used construction management and fast-track scheduling. Placed on the corner of a wooded seventeen-acre site on the outskirts of the city, the school was built with closed walls clad in weathering steel on the street sides and with mirror glass on the other walls, looking out toward stands of trees and landscaping. A structural skeleton of bar joists and eight-inch tube columns extended beyond the ends of the building, in anticipation of further growth and to expose the industrial components. The school was designed so that 50 percent of the cost—the structure, ceiling-lighting "sandwich," heating and air-conditioning, and metal movable wall partitions—could be bid nationally. The project was a huge success: economical in initial and lifecycle costs, and at the same time esthetically pleasing.[6]

Interviews

CHUCK THOMSEN

The New York office [led by Thomsen in the late 1960s and early 1970s] worked very well. After we came off the high of selling the Manhattan Community College project, I began to realize it was going to take a year to get the contract negotiated through the city bureaucracy. We would spend a year on the master plan, another year to negotiate the design contract, probably two years to go through the design work, then we would bid it; and they were looking at close to a ten-year construction program to complete it. I thought, "I'm thirty-five, and I'll be fifty when this is done. I can do another project, then retire." Two jobs—is that what I wanted for my career? I called Jonathan King. . . .

I asked Jonathan if he would put together a program for me to study systems construction. He had been behind that SCSD [School Construction Systems Development] Program [to develop a building system for schools in California]. He put together a little agenda. Of course, CRS was never one to restrict the expense if somebody wanted to do something with big implications. Well, I got on a goddamn airplane, flew all over the U.S. and Canada, and talked to all the people doing this. Meanwhile, Jonathan persuaded my friend Frank Matzke of the New York State University Construction Fund to do a study of how they could accelerate control of design and construction of projects for the State University Construction Fund. John Focke was doing a little research on how to accelerate projects [and] project delivery, and he started using a funny little term: *fast track*. I thought that was a neat term, so we put it on the cover of that report, and the rest is history.

The press of the time, [including] Foxhall's book on construction management, gave us the credit for inventing the term. I always thought we ought to take that credit—everybody else does.[7] That was an important report, and I thought we ought to start doing that [fast-track construction]. I remember flying into Houston on a Friday, talking to Herb [Paseur] in his car back from the airport and talking about the opportunity to do a couple of rinky-dink schools out in Long Island with fast-track scheduling, industrialized building systems, and construction management. Herb's comment was, "Someday, we've got to quit talking about it and really do it. Go ahead." So we did. Then we got a bunch of schools in Florida, some schools from Bell and Howell Schools [previously and subsequently the DeVry Institute of Technology], and suddenly we had about five schools doing systems and fast track.

We were trying to get all five schools designed and constructed within a year. I had the idea that what we really needed was to quit screwing around with these projects—spending three, four, five, fifteen years. You know, get some feedback on your ideas. Who's interested in something they did fifteen years ago? What architect cares about a design he concluded two, three years ago? So, I went to Tom and Herb and asked if I could start a special group at CRS that would concentrate on fast track, construction management, and systems schools. I had in mind a group that would include architectural designers, construction managers, and construction technologists who would understand the technology. Our objective would be to develop the procedures to deliver a building in less than a year—big buildings. They said, "No, you can't do that. Things are going real well in New York. You need to stay in New York."

God love him, Phil Meathe [then chairman of Smith Hinchman and Grylls, a major architectural firm in Detroit] called one day and asked if I would like to be considered for the presidency of Smith Hinchman and Grylls. I promptly called Tom and told him. I didn't feel I ought to answer Phil surreptitiously. In a few days, Tom and Herb said, "Let's talk about this new business idea you've got." I think they realized I was pretty impatient with what was going on and was just as troublesome as I had been in the beginning years.

Tom and Herb did not want to pull any of the designers in. I think they saw properly and clearly that if they pulled a design team into this company oriented to systems construction, there would be a lot of talk between it and the existing CRS. Of course, I didn't know whether I was talking about a corporation or division of CRS or what. They said, "Looks to us like managing

The DeVry Institute of Technology in Chicago, built in 1971, was one of several Bell and Howell Schools that used fast-track scheduling and systems building to produce award-winning architecture in record time within an impossibly low budget.

the process is what's new and special here, so why don't you do that?" So, CM was started just as the company went public. Of course, they liked the idea of a multicorporate structure, so making it a corporation was a good idea at that time. I think it was essential that we did that. CRS's growth forced us out of the White House [CRS headquarters in Houston] into the Transco Tower. So, we created a whole new culture and a whole new business idea.

The company grew from Frank Whitcomb, Byron Stennis, and Robert Finley, and me. Seven years later, we were at three hundred people—something like that. Just made a ton of money; a very, very prosperous company—extraordinarily innovative. CRS has been an innovative company, and CM took that and rarefied the environment, and that resulted in an explosive growth market. We all thought it was because we were smart and worked hard!

The '80s humbled us all. Our philosophy was, "Nobody knows how to do this business, so there's no sense in hiring experienced old guys. Let's hire well-educated, very bright, highly vigorous young people." Consequently, we made a lot of mistakes. Jack Eimer, when he was officer in charge at the University of Riyadh, which was a $6 billion project—the biggest construction management contract in the whole world, ever—was twenty-eight years old. Fortunately, we did hire some few older, more sagacious people. I've also got to say that the young people in the company really did make a lot of mistakes. Yet we really, as much as anybody in the '70s, defined what construction management was.

We had a strategy that saved our neck. Whenever we went somewhere to do a construction management job, we would joint venture with a local general contractor, and we would pick the bluest chip, finest firm in town and get the job. We were the charisma—the sizzle on the steak—and they were the people who knew how to do it. So, these fine blue-chip general contractors kept these young, cocky whippersnappers out of trouble, and yet they provided the innovation and energy. Jack Eimer, the guy who managed the University of Riyadh, we sent to Denver to run a project when he was twenty-four. Within six months, he had eight projects in his office—all in joint venture with Petry. Max Morton took Jack under his wing, kept him from making mistakes, and we later started calling Max "the professor." Max treated Jack like a son, and, of course, Jack worked his heart out—sixty hours a week—and Max provided the judgment. That was the kind of formula we applied. Our company grew and grew and grew. We had offices all over the U.S., and offices all over the world: Mexico, Saudi Arabia, Hong

Kong, London, Cairo, Puerto Rico. [I] can't recall them all. The company was really a roaring success.

We also developed the best internal management system. I give a lot of that credit to Frank Whitcomb, general manager of the company the entire time I was there. Frank could remember on Wednesday what we decided we were going to do on Monday. I used to tease him, "Damn it, Frank, if a client comes in with a $50 million job that's not on your schedule, you won't even see him!" Frank would say, "Chuck, every time you have a new whim, you run off with a new program." He accused me once of having a "whim of iron."

There was a lot of confidence and friendship between the leaders of the company, so we all kind of kept each other out of trouble. We created most of the management systems and internal controls that were later adopted by the other companies. The marketing and financial reporting documents that became standard were invented at CM. I give Frank a lot of that credit. The company never would have grown as a division of the Caudill Rowlett Scott architectural firm. I would have gone to work every morning wanting to succeed on Bill's value scale, and our success had nothing to do with Bill's value scale.

I don't think it had to do with an ethical conflict; I think it had to do with aspirations to be a designer that Bill had. He was very interested in architectural design, in architectural programming, the esthetics of the building. And CM's reason for being was to control costs and schedules and deliver a predictable result to a client.

Q: How big was CM? You said three hundred people.

A: It got to be about three hundred.

Q: And how big was the old design group?

A: It may have been four hundred; it may have gotten down to two hundred–plus. To add insult to injury, on the operational side, CM was making a lot more money than CRS. CM was growing, and CRS was shrinking. I was being my insufferable, cocky self—giving Tom and Herb enormous grief by not being sensitive to some of the traditional founders and senior managers in CRS, who probably deserved a little more respect for what they accomplished. Probably the success of CM produced by all those "smart-asses" over there rankled them a little, but once more, it's to CRS's credit that they were able to tolerate CM and keep individual frustrations and irritations from destroying a very good thing. . . . A lot of growth, profit, and innovation in the construction industry was going on over there.

The basic centroid of attitude from Wallie and Bill and the older founders was never anti-CM. These were irritations, not fundamental attitudes. They were irritations I think we would have all done a lot better without. If we had been more statesmanlike at CM, we could have avoided those, and everything would have been smoother. I think Bill probably felt about CM like you might feel about a misbehaving adolescent child who was nevertheless bright and you saw had a lot of potential. Irritations were not fundamentally distancing.

I think CRS tolerated the difference in the corporate culture at CM because we were growing and making so much money, and I had such a good working relationship with Tom and Herb. It really was good. Those guys would lineback for me. [They] did [the] downfield blocking. Whenever I'd stumble, they'd do damage control, give me advice and counsel on what we ought to do. I clearly remember four or five strategic events over the almost decade of CM where a few one-liners from Tom and Herb made all the difference in the world in our company. In the early days, there were about thirty of us, I guess. We had been in business two or three years—didn't know what we were doing trying to invent a new profession. Everybody was doing a project for the first time in his life. People hadn't done construction management jobs before. We were doing systems, fast track with a bunch of guys we had hired who had never done it before. Neither had we.

Frank Whitcomb looked at me one day and said, "Do you realize we are all doing jobs all over the country—big important jobs—and none of us has ever done one before?" Every one of our clients was mad at us. I went down to have lunch with Herb at the Coronado Club, and I told him we just weren't doing our job right. He said, "Chuck, you're going to have to figure out somebody who stays home and minds the store and manages the company." He knew I was marketing oriented. I liked cooking up new ideas, new ways of doing things, [and] was not patient with the everyday challenge of making sure the company's resources were properly deployed to the priorities of the demands. I went back that afternoon, sat down with Frank, and asked if he would quit marketing and managing projects and instead manage the company. He said sure, he'd do that. Frank turned into a really good manager. Frank kept me out of a lot of trouble over the years. I'll always remember Toni King [Mrs. Jonathan King] wrote a poem for my fortieth birthday party, and two of the lines were: "If Chuck can't make it, Frank will fake it."

There will never be another company quite like CM. The unique structure of events, the entrepreneurial ferment that existed at CRS, the basic notion you should develop new ideas and take them to the marketplace, the expectation that you commit yourself to eighty-hour weeks [and] do the best job you can, the belief in young people. . . . All those things were part of the CRS heritage that CM picked up. But then we picked that up in an explosive marketplace, which began with the growth of construction management, systems, and fast track in the U.S. and then was fueled—put into turbo—by the Mideast/Saudi Arabia [projects]. Then you populate that with people less than thirty years old, primarily. They were all making more money than they ever thought they would earn in their lifetime, let alone before thirty.

NORMAN HOOVER

Those [fast-track projects] worked fine. One of the reasons, I think, was there was a very clear idea of what the goals were and what systems were to be used. The important thing was the schedules were so incredibly tight that nobody had the chance to rethink any of the decisions. The good ones and bad ones all got built. By and large, they were very good, very well-designed schools, if I do say so myself. They won a lot of awards, and I guess people are still using the buildings. I know I'm getting old when I drive by the place where the Bell and Howell School was in Phoenix, and it's been torn down. It was torn down three or four years ago for some higher and better use of the site. There's an uglier and higher building in its place.

I think what made those projects work well is that we had a client who really wanted high design quality. George Dougherty [then president of Bell and Howell Schools] challenged us to create award-winning architecture on an impossible schedule and an impossibly low budget. As long as people don't get in your way, you can do that.

JONATHAN KING

When we at EFL started the SCSD Program to develop school building systems for California and, by extension, the United States, we got Tiny Lawrence to serve on the SCSD advisory committee. I had wanted to get Bill . . . but he had other fish to fry and thought Tiny ought to be involved. I think Tiny may have been at least as useful on the committee as Bill because we had huge problems of how you manage to mass-produce the components for buildings while maintaining design freedom for the architects. This sounds like a contradiction in terms, but it's not entirely a contradiction. . . .

Architects don't usually design all the pieces from which they make buildings . . . and this was an effort to . . . restrict that menu even further in order to develop a kit of parts that would be, on the one hand, more technically efficient for building schools and would develop schools that were more suitable for contemporary learning situations, and at the same time, schools that were architecturally of high quality. That project, which Tiny was involved in for three or four years—and I was involved in forever—was a fairly intense effort to do something that never quite worked: to develop a generic way of dealing with a generic problem. You know, architects were fond of taking Sweet's Catalogue and inventing an architectural vocabulary every time they did a building.

Q: What was your role in CRS? I know you had been with EFL.

A: I came to CRS in the summer of 1970. . . . I had been talking with their [CRS's] New York office, particularly with Chuck Thomsen and Norman Hoover, who was the New York designer at that time. I had been involved, as I mentioned earlier, in the development of building systems—with SCSD and building systems for Toronto public schools, Montreal public schools. We were beginning to work on one for college housing, and I was frustrated by the fact that most of the building systems projects seemed to be third rate. Some were second rate, and a few were first rate. [It] seemed to me the system was better than the buildings; that nobody was taking this technology and doing anything with it that made any sense.

I thought if we could get together, put a team together and a process that utilized building systems already in existence for design and construction and did it well, we could make a contribution. It was pretty apparent that the construction industry was one of the things that militated against this. You specified a product you wanted, and you had an "or equal" clause on it, so you weren't sure what the hell you were going to get. The closer the components got interlocked with each other, the worse off you were in terms of the ability of the contractor to play games with the pieces. In any event, in terms of design, construction, and promotion, we thought if we could put together a team that took industrialized systems on the market and went after school districts and other clients, we would be doing something new, exciting—good architecture—and it would make us all rich and famous.

So, we worked on this idea and tried to persuade Tom that it would be a good idea for CRS to set up a subgroup to do it. I didn't much care about the business end of things—whether it was a separate corporation or division didn't make any difference to me. Chuck Thomsen . . . is a very impatient person. He had been in their New York office for a while, had been very successful, and was ready to do something else. Chuck and I were very good friends. Norman thought it was a way to get him out in the limelight. CRS was pretty interested in this. Then suddenly, Tom turned around and said, "Hell, building systems is the way it's going to go. If it makes sense for this group of weird people to set up and do this, it's got to make sense for the whole firm. And if it's got to make sense for the whole firm, you've got to come to Houston and do it here." So, that's how it happened: I came to Houston [and] Chuck stayed in New York.

It was very hard for somebody to come in who was not educated as an architect and persuade large numbers of this firm's staff that they should do things this new way. So, I came in as a partner and director of systems building and was charged with doing this. We did a bunch of systems projects—some of them really pretty good projects. We made, I think, a timid effort to get into systems buildings for hospitals, a tougher design problem than schools because hospitals are sort of four or five buildings types all mashed together in one ugly mass. But it was always the problem of whether you can find some allies and make it happen. The only way you could make it happen is to sell it to the client. If the client said, "I want a systems building," then you could settle down with a designer and say, "He said he wanted a systems building, get going." That's what I was doing. I think we did some pretty good stuff. I never worked on a project that came out as well as I hoped, but some were at least close. I felt some conflict with Caudill at that time because he was enthusiastic about anything you wanted to do as long as it didn't mess up the architecture, but he wasn't quite sure that all this systems stuff coming into his group wasn't going to mess things up.

Q: What did he feel would be lost? Some of the creativity?

A: The primacy of the designer. With the likes of me saying, "No, you've got to use this stuff on the ceiling and this stuff on the partitions, and this is going to be the structure." Then you've hemmed him in, as indeed you have.

Q: Bullock was a good designer and critic, but he said "design isn't everything." He didn't view the primacy in quite the same way.

A: No. Caudill by that time, as I say, was moving more and more into design as he got older. So there was a difference in attitude there—fairly distinct. Bill wasn't around for some of that period, for he was over at Rice. Then he came back, and after a while, he got interested in doing a system. We played around. . . . I had gotten Bill in with the Herman Miller people, and he was made a director of the corporation. We talked for a while about doing a package with Herman Miller for small office buildings. If you needed a fifty-thousand-square-foot office building, Herman Miller would make the partitions and furnishings, known as office landscape, and we'd provide a shell, ceiling lighting system—that was before task lighting—and the whole thing would be made up of known components. Thus, we'd have a known module, known components, and known prices and could put the whole thing together in twenty minutes. [It] could be quite elegant.

Then we also spent a couple of weekends on a *charette* doing design for a system for small schools. That was the kind of problem we ran into—nobody could sell small schools anymore. Management militated against it. Wallie Scott wasn't going to get off his duff to go out and sell a million-dollar schoolhouse.

Todd Lee, of the New York office, and I sold one up in Massachusetts. [We] came back to the office, and everybody said, "We can't do that! We can't afford to send four programmers to Plympton, Massachusetts, for a week." I told them we'd program it ourselves and charge it to promotion.

We actually made some money on this project, which was done out of New York, and it was quite a nice building. It was very difficult. You really had to shake the administrative structure of the firm to deal with anything that small. If you really got good at this and began to bag lots of million-dollar schools, it just wouldn't have worked. Some of the programming people had difficulty shifting to modules. If it was forty-three square feet per student, when they added that all up and we were working on a five-foot module, those forty-threes weren't going to add up to anything that was divisible by twenty-five square feet. The programming people were so well developed in their habits that the notion of their shifting to multiples of five feet or twenty-five square feet was hard for them: "That isn't the way we do it at CRS."

Just like when we got into fast-track construction. The worst problems we had were with the guys who deal with billings. They had been brought up on other arrangements: you do that much and you bill that much. How do you bill some of design development before you finish schematic design? And how do you bill construction documents before you finish other aspects of design? It shook them up because that's not the way they had always done it.

JANE STANSFELD

I certainly worked on quite a few fast-track jobs. . . . We were doing a different [bid] package every week. I found that challenging, too. In fact, I used to tease Paul [Kennon] because I had a wall set up in the studio, and if we had the window wall going out in a week's time or whatever, I would stick all the appropriate details on the wall with little arrows pointing down: "These are the details going out with the bid next week, and if you trip over them on your way through the office and don't approve them, they're gone." Pretty soon, he figured out that on my wall I had all the latest details he had to look at before they went out. It worked extraordinarily well, and I thought fast track worked to our advantage because it forced us to focus on solving this problem, solving that problem, solving another problem. Sometimes at CRS, we tended to keep on designing, designing, designing until the last minute. So, fast track worked well to production's advantage.

■ CHAPTER 11

GROWTH

CRS is committed to growth. To keep the people we want to keep and to do the things we want to do, we simply have to grow. It has been a natural thing for us. When we felt that an engineer was important to team operation, we brought in an engineer. When we thought we needed a planner to help us with outside spaces (as in the case of the high school in San Angelo, Texas), we added a planner to our team. We acquired interior designers and graphics designers as we needed them. It was not a deliberate plan on our part to get big—at least not in the beginning. We grew because we had to. It is another story today. We are growing because we want to. We believe in the expanded team. . . .

I suppose from the beginning, without realizing it, CRS was committed to growth. Deep down, we are expansionists.

—*William W. Caudill,* Architecture by Team, *11–12*

■ Caudill Rowlett Scott went public partly to expand its role in the design and construction industry. It did this in two ways: first, by acquiring companies in segments of the design and construction industry in which CRS did not already operate, and second, by starting companies from scratch when that seemed a more intelligent way to penetrate new markets.

The company did phenomenally well with some of the new activities it started, especially its construction management subsidiary, CM Associates. By contrast, few of the acquisitions panned out. A fundamental problem with acquisitions—which remains to this day—is that in buying a firm whose success depends on brainpower, there is no way to guarantee that the crucial leaders will remain on board and continue putting their heart and soul into the operation.

In the early and middle 1970s, the stock market was enamored with purchases of professional service firms because they generated enormous profits when measured against the amount of capital they employed. But the buyouts turned out to be a Wall Street fad, which collapsed within five years because, says management consultant Weld Coxe, "the asset that was sold was people. The people have feet, and they walk."[1] Bright, energetic leaders in quest of bigger rewards could move to another firm or start a new one.

Caudill Rowlett Scott was at its best when it seized opportunities by developing its own staff (or hiring new specialists) and entering promising fields, as it did in schools and hospitals. When CRS bought outside firms, as it did after receiving the infusion of money generated by going public, the results were rarely good in the long run. The most successful foray into acquisitions and mergers was the combination with the J. E. Sirrine Company of South Carolina. From an economic standpoint, that transaction—some called it a merger, others an acquisition—had benefits: It created a company with big domestic capabilities, especially in Sirrine's specialty, engineering. The decline of the market for big projects in the Middle East in the late 1970s and early 1980s made a stateside investment of this kind attractive. Caudill Rowlett Scott had let its leadership in hospitals languish while pursuing the huge overseas projects, and by the early 1980s it seemed dauntingly difficult to rebuild its domestic operations. Chuck Thomsen, in a March, 1982, memo about CRS's profitability, wrote: "During the last 35 years, CRS has consistently outgrown its interest and its ability to profit in one increasingly larger market after another. Bill [Caudill] is right, we are a big-job junkie and it's getting harder to support our habit. We may . . . finally have outgrown most everything and have little available at the size we can do profitably."[2]

The general rule today is that outright acquisitions of professional service firms should be avoided. Many firms have found that if they need the strength of another firm, whether for economies of scale or to become multidisciplinary or for other reasons, they should merge with the desired firm rather than purchase it. There seem to be more incentives for the middle managers to stay after a merger and help the combined firm prosper.

Caudill Rowlett Scott changed because of going public. It became increasingly finance-driven as it joined with Sirrine and continued diversifying into other fields. The original emphasis on professional innovation in architecture, design, and construction fell into relative neglect.

INTERVIEWS

MIKE MYERS

I got acquainted with Caudill Rowlett Scott, CRS, back in 1967. At the time, I was administrative assistant to [Texas] Gov. John Connally, and Governor Connally had committed himself, the governor's office, and the state to a project called HemisFair. He wanted to build a project to be called the Institute of Texan Cultures to really tell the story of our heritage in Texas, of all the cultures that make up our state. The building was to be funded by the state [and] built at the HemisFair in San Antonio. The governor set up a structure through which to select the number one architecture firm in the state to do that wonderful project.

My first meeting with CRS was with John Connally in about '63 or '65 or '66 in their Houston office. They ended up getting the job. [They] designed the Institute, and I had some brief contacts, although they were pretty limited, with the two or three partners who were involved with that project. Governor Connally would, from time to time, meet with them to see what they were doing, for he got personally involved. When he got involved with something like this, he was really involved instead of just hitting the high spots. I was traveling with him at that time wherever he went, so I was exposed to some of the questions and comments from the people actually working on the design of the Institute of Texan Cultures.

So, that was my first experience. Then, some six or seven years later, I was on the board of a company called Sam P. Wallace in Dallas and was invited on a couple of trips by Ghaith Pharaon, who was a stockholder in CRS, and Sam P. Wallace. I spent some time with the Paseurs and the Bullocks and got to know them on these trips. I had met Tom in the earlier days.

I resigned from the Wallace board, and Tom invited me to come on the CRS board about 1980, I believe. I joined the board at the time when Bruce [Wilkinson] had been CFO [Chief Financial Officer] for a couple of years. It was a pretty dramatic time. CRS was winding down its Saudi involvement to a great degree. They'd had all those very lucrative jobs that paid those big margins: a lot of government work in this country [and] in Saudi. All of a sudden, it went from being a very profitable company to . . . losing money. . . .

It became apparent to Tom and Herb that architecture was going to be a really tough business. Here we were, the largest architecture firm in the country, stock traded over the counter; and the future didn't look good to Tom, Herb, or to Bruce either. Someone . . . recommended to the board that they hire Arthur D. Little Company and Stanford Research Institute [SRI] separately. The fee, if my memory serves me . . . was $100,000 each to tell the board what we could do with CRS. They [the board members] were farsighted enough to know they couldn't keep doing what they were doing. They were one of the top professional firms in America but couldn't keep doing things that were not working. Hiring those two highly qualified firms to do the study was a very dramatic turning point for CRS.

They each wrote independent reports. All the board members read them, and I remember—being in the real estate development business—I was particularly struck at how true and farsighted [those reports were]. In terms of office buildings, for instance, we are [now] seeing a glut all over the country, which they predicted. . . . All the things we see today, they predicted. The future for architects didn't look good.

They were even more specific and said that about the only office buildings built in America in the coming ten to fifteen years would be suburban office buildings in corridor areas all around the country like North Dallas, West Houston, [and] Orange County, California. They said that, and yet insurance companies were lending huge amounts of money on downtown office complexes—maybe they should have read these reports. That was just one part of the reports; they went on to say that the business of architecture was declining, and you had to diversify. So, we wanted to know not that it was a declining business, but what we could diversify in, and what made sense. That's how we got into the engineering business. It was obvious it [engineering] had a future. We went on to acquire Sirrine a very, very outstanding move. . . .

[Tom and Herb] had worked on Sirrine prior to my coming on the board. In fact, they ended up firing the president [of CRS] over the situation just prior to my joining the board. . . . So they had already made a run at Sirrine, but it didn't work at the time.[3] So the Sirrine acquisition was really in the works before the Arthur D. Little and SRI reports were written. But the reports went on to say we needed to get into such things as cogeneration [the simultaneous generation of electrical energy and heat, and the use of both]. They listed a number of different things that made sense for us to get into that had a great future, [and] they were right about the cogeneration business. . . .

We were in the design business and were looking for things that were not totally unrelated, something that made sense. As time went on, with

Sirrine in [on] designing some of these big plants, we had some liability anyway, so it made sense since we were already in the design business, were a public company, had cash. We were in a situation where no other firm in the country, except for Bechtel or some of the huge conglomerates, [could compare]. . . . For our size, we were in a position where we could leverage that up, if you will. . . .

I remember reading a book called *Future Shock* by Toffler about eighteen years ago.[4] People thought his was such a cold concept . . . the rate of change, how fast the world is changing. Ten or fifteen years is not that long, even at age forty-five, and when you realize how much the world has changed [and] how great the rate of change has been, it's absolutely mind-boggling. . . .

The whole point is that here is a professional firm that's having to make big changes. Although you think the best architects in the country shouldn't have to change, they will just be out of business if they don't. I think the greatest thing Tom Bullock and the CRSS people have done is to be flexible enough to make changes. I've been on some other boards and in the banking business, as well as other businesses. Sometimes we haven't done it [changed] as quickly as possible, and sometimes we made mistakes, but I think Tom's leadership and willingness to explore new ideas and make change—so typically, when people get older, they have a tendency to [say], "Well, we did it this way successfully before; why change?" I find myself thinking that way. It's a basic instinct. CRSS has been willing—Tom, Herb, Bruce—to change. . . .

The NaTec thing turned out to be a mistake. The construction thing was a mistake. That's one I had a feeling about. Getting into insurance was a mistake, in my opinion, and [I] thought so at the time, [too].[5] The point is, even though they were mistakes, they [the founders] were not afraid of change. Had they not changed and not made so many mistakes . . . [then] the party's over [anyway]. . . .

[CRSS had] an open board, and they let people speak their piece. In the corporate world, it has become pretty obvious there are many people—and I'm pretty cynical about it—who are hired as board members to do what management wants them to do for $25,000 a year. Sometimes they sell the stockholders down the drain because they are serving management. I don't think that's ever been the case here. . . .

Bruce and Tom let there be open discussion and disagreement on things like compensation, for instance, which is a pretty touchy subject. When you start talking about disagreeing with the chairman or the president over what his compensation is going to be—we've had those kind of discussions, and

I think they have been wholesome, constructive. And I applaud management's part in being mature enough, I call it, and honest enough to say, "I don't have all the answers." Tom, particularly, is constantly probing and asking questions. I think Bruce has a brilliant and gymnastic mind. I've known two, three, four people in my life with what I call a gymnastic mind. They have ideas and are reaching and grabbing all the time. Bruce has that kind of mind, and I think Tom has been the sounding board through the years. He hired Bruce and then chose him to take on this job. They [made] a good combination. There's no question that nothing would have happened if they had remained just an architectural firm.

Q: How about the acquisition of Sirrine? Were you there during that time?

A: You bet. They [Sirrine] would say it was a merger, but it was really an acquisition. That was an older company, a lot older than this one. It started in [1902] as J. E. Sirrine—a [firm with a] lot of engineers with a long history, a couple generations, in some cases. The transition was not painless. It was difficult changing from a philosophy, I would say.

Bill Carpenter [CEO of Sirrine at the time] stayed on the board. . . . He made a real contribution in nominating a wonderful man, Wilson Wearn from Greenville, who was board chairman of MultiMedia Corporation and a distinguished businessman in America. The two of them—Wilson, particularly, in terms of leadership ability—had a soft way of alleviating the inevitable conflict of the transition.

I give a lot of the credit to Wilson and everybody involved for at least hearing their side of it. We made some mistakes and lost some people we probably shouldn't have lost. Right after we made the acquisition, business got bad—it's a cyclical business—and we had to lay a lot of people off. [It was] a real emotional, gut-wrenching experience for Bruce and everybody involved. When you have people who have worked someplace for twenty-five, thirty years, and you have to ask them to take early retirement, that's always emotional. Then to be asked to retire by someone from Houston rather than Greenville makes it tougher. . . .

We added Wilson, and Bill Carpenter stayed on the board for a number of years. He stepped down just recently. We sold him one of our companies. I don't know of many corporate mergers or acquisitions where in six or seven years there's anybody left from the acquired company. . . .

In my twelve years [at CRS], I think the Sirrine acquisition was the most significant highlight. In the long term, I think the cogeneration business will end up as the biggest single right decision. Again, during my twelve years, getting into the construction business was a bad decision. The NaTec business will turn out to be a bad decision for different reasons. It was a question of timing rather than a question of concept. . . . Our timing and spending all that money . . . to get into business and then not to have anybody to sell to was a huge problem. Everything, particularly in business, is timing. The concept was sound, but [the] timing was off.

BRUCE WILKINSON

I joined the firm in November of '78, but I'd say for a year, year and a half, two years maybe previous to that, I had known Bob Bridwell [then serving as CFO of CRS].[6] From time to time, free of charge, when he'd come ask about international things, I'd sit and consult with him. And through him, I met Herb Paseur briefly, and I think I met Tom Bullock. So, Bob resigned—must have been in the summer of 1978—and gave my name as somebody he thought would be a reasonable replacement for him in his role. That's how I was introduced to them. So, I went to work originally for Herb Paseur, who was then president [and] CEO. I was chief financial officer from date of hire—I believe late November, '78, to March of '82, when I became president and CEO.

Thinking back on it, I remember two events that had just taken place: Ghaith Pharaon, a Saudi investor, had bought about what was then nearly 20 percent of the company stock from the founders. They had 40 percent ownership, and he bought about half, or 20 percent. That was in, I believe, about July or August, 1978. The other thing that had just occurred: They [CRS] had acquired the engineering firm of Clark Dietz and Associates of Urbana, Illinois—I guess in about August of '78.

Q: Up in Urbana?

A: Yeah. Urbana, Illinois. At that time, Clark Dietz had revenues of about $18–20 million in fees. CRS before that acquisition probably had about $30 million, so it was a benchmark. The whole company probably had about $50 million in revenues then.

That had already been done before I joined them. Candidly, what I remember is that I made one trip to Urbana, Illinois, before that calendar year was over—may have been in December of '78. I had this sinking feeling [of], "Oh, shit, this is not a pretty picture," because it was my opinion then that there was a massive amount of things not done with due diligence. For instance, it was an old firm. [It] had lots of people who had lots of retirement benefits, and the actuarial cost of that I don't think had been considered in the acquisition price. It was in a facility that had a lot of leases with principals in the firm, so there were sort of complex interests. . . . It was my opinion from the first trip that this was an old, stodgy place in downstate Illinois with yesterday's technology, and somebody paid a lot of money for them, and it may not be a pretty picture.

Q: Did they have a lot of clients?

A: It was based on an environmental firm that had water, wastewater treatment markets, and, to a lesser extent, their so-called marketing future was railroad business. They did a lot of engineering for railroads.

Q: What kind of impact did Pharaon's stock purchase have?

A: The aura around it at the time was one of excitement because of the Mideast being a great market already and, theoretically, a bigger potential market. I believe there was a lot of excitement about what this might mean.

Q: Did it pan out that way?

A: No. In fact, I know that by October [or] November of '78, my recollection is—and this is on a price before various splits we've had since, so it's not a current price, but a "then" price—he had bought at about $20 a share, I believe, and within 120 days of when he bought at that price, the stock was down to like $13, $14 and was falling even lower. So, on the short-term basis, the excitement went away pretty quickly—at least in the stock market.

That was kind of the benchmark of the lay of the land when I joined the company. My recollection is that the first year or so after that was still the very best of the Mideast era when we were doing a lot of work in Saudi. Major projects [were] coming in. The King Abdul Aziz Military Academy was already well under way then.

It was a huge facility: academic environment, military housing, officer housing, academic housing. It had the famous—what we called the "rim row" up above this one oasis sort of north and west of Riyadh. It's where the old King Abdul Aziz was from, kind of his home. It was a spectacular site. Beautiful city. So, it's their West Point. In '78 [or] '79, the Internal Security

Forces project was coming in—the beginnings of what became the University of Riyadh, which we now call King Saud University—with the HOK + 4 Consortium. I would say the period from about '75 through '81 was the "golden era" of the Saudi experience. Even though we did work before and after that, it was sort of the epicenter of a good environment.

Q: How did the embargo affect business?

A: As a company, we benefited dramatically from it. . . . The more money that went into the Saudis' pockets, the more that came back to us—probably with greater benefit than for other companies. To some extent, both of the big knee jerks—[the] oil price run-up and OPEC running the show—probably benefited Texas and the oil industry generally, but certainly in our case, it was a net benefit.

Q: It peaked '75 to . . . ?

A: I would say through '81. To give you an example [of] when I became extremely concerned—I came there [to CRS] in '78. Our fiscal '79 was a really good year. Our fiscal '80 was still good, but beginning to wane. I was the one who took away the separate treasury functions of all the subsidiaries and created the first centralized treasury function and kept it. In the old days, CM operations, all the civil engineering operations—the old A. A. Mathews, Stevens Thompson & Runyan, Clark Dietz, and Caudill Rowlett Scott, CRS—all had their own business development group, board of directors, chief financial officers, and treasury functions. So I felt a lot of that had to go, but I was the new boy on the block and couldn't attack the central fortress, so I practiced attacking the flanks where I felt I could have some impact. One of the first was the treasury function, and so, as a result of just centralizing treasury and having an automated receivables collection system, it simply accelerated the speed at which we collected receivables and automatically fed it into the treasury function. We were starting to earn significant interest income.

We were cash rich. . . . We had front-end loaded them [those projects], so we had the cash, and labor was going down. The point is, by our fiscal 1980, my recollection is that . . . probably 30–40 percent of the consolidated earnings of the whole company became interest income. By 1981, it was even worse, because by then we sort of had the tail end of runaway inflation at the end of the Jimmy Carter inflation era where you had [a] 20 percent prime [interest rate]. All of a sudden, we had this anomaly: The big projects in Saudi were all over, we were collecting cash more efficiently than ever before because we had created this "real business world" treasury function, [and] we were throwing it against the highest paying Eurodollar market in history. So, it looked really good, but I kept telling Herb Paseur and the others in the company of my concern that, "As good as this looks, you can't live on it forever. It's not our future." I used the example of eight hundred to one thousand employees downsized to two hundred. Then we could really make some money, but we'll be in danger, it won't be a design firm. That was the "golden era," and I got in on the last two and a half years of it.

Q: When did the consolidation actually take place?

A: It has ebbed and flowed. I would say we began to consolidate a few other functions. But as a practical matter, the corporate headquarters in those days was downtown in the 1100 Milam Building, the CM group was in the Transco Tower, [and] CRS was on the West Loop.

Q: So you were physically separated?

A: Yes, we were physically separated as well. I would say the first time we began to integrate a number of the traditional corporate and management functions was when we physically moved everybody to the West Loop. I believe that was [in] late 1983.

At the time, we felt there was enormous efficiency just on a cost of space basis achieved, which was compounded by the fact that it was the year we acquired J. E. Sirrine. They also had a Houston operation, which at the time was way down from its high point. It once had as many as 400–500 people in Houston; I think at that time, they had maybe 100–120. They were way out in West Chase, [and] we were in corporate headquarters downtown. We were all over the city and had no visible signage on any building—no name recognition, plus enormous travel time just to be able to talk to one another.

Q: When you started, what types of projects—aside from those in Saudi Arabia—were going on, and what markets were you in?

A: The civil engineering group was really in kind of the worst of all worlds. They had two environmentally oriented, water-resource type firms in the old Stevens Thompson and Runyan in Portland and Dietz in Urbana—both of which had some regional offices, both doing water and wastewater treatment, primarily municipal and state-oriented work. No single project was huge or terribly noteworthy from an engineering breakthrough or notoriety standpoint. I'd say some years they made money, [but] it was never much money [and only] some years. . . .

They also had a firm whose specialty was underground tunneling type work, A. A. Mathews. It was in Rockville, Maryland, and a little place called Arcadia, California. I had never met Al Mathews, [but] he was infamous in that they acquired his company for stock, and in one day he became the largest single shareholder in CRS. This goes all the way back to '71 or '72. Although he was on the board, he was by reputation a very difficult guy to deal with. That firm, more than anything else, I think, reflected his personality. When he left the company, a lot of what the firm was left with him, at least spiritually. So, that part of the company [civil engineering] really didn't have any great, noteworthy projects going on.

The CM operation was doing very well, just hitting its stride because construction management was then a relatively new alternative to the general contracting mode of building. It was a period of ever-increasing inflation, runaway inflation. One of the selling tools of construction management, of course, is to begin the construction process much earlier in the design phase. . . . Its appeal in a period of rapidly increasing inflation was very high. The CM group was doing very well then, not only in the Mideast, but with some of the big projects that followed on our design assignments through our office in Miami. They had an office at the time in Denver, so they were doing a number of projects coast to coast at the time, primarily in educational markets and, to a lesser extent, health care. That group was growing. In fact, of all the domestic or U.S.-based activities, the CM group in that period was by far the largest moneymaker.

At the time, CRS—the old Caudill Rowlett Scott—from my recollection, was making all or about 85 to 90 percent of its revenues internationally. I do remember that by 1982, one of the anomalies was [that] . . . I was finally asked to be on the board of Caudill Rowlett Scott, the architecture operation—one year after I had been a board member of the parent company! That shows how self-contained they were. They had their own board with Bill Caudill. . . . It was a self-contained world, and they did their own thing.

I remember at one board meeting being shocked by the reality . . . that the mighty Caudill Rowlett Scott had only about $7 million in domestic revenues at the time. I pointed it out at the end of that meeting, and it kind of offended everybody. In a six-hour meeting, they had allocated about forty minutes of it to Truitt [Garrison] and the people doing the international work, although 120 percent of the bottom line was coming from that. I can tell you by that point, at least in the domestic markets, Caudill Rowlett Scott had sort of shrunk to be just a small domestic activity compared to the big international work. The big joke was that everybody in Houston said we were the firm, that group of guys out on the Loop that only knew how to get to Intercontinental Airport and knew nothing about what was going on locally. The reality was probably close to that. . . .

I remember the Internal Security Forces project—ISF we called it—in Saudi, which would be like our National Guard, as one that sort of drifted around before I was with the company. [A Telex arrived about 1978:] It wasn't a request for the whole world to propose on something, it was almost like: "Fill in the blanks because we want you to do this." It was one of those huge design fees that came in, and it was almost like: "Can you get started tomorrow?" We had to figure out how on earth we were going to produce and staff it. I remember its being extremely profitable, and yet it also was one of those projects on which, I think, the biggest concern at the time was—with all the new people being brought in off the street—whether we could turn out the quality that would be required. We had several like that come in. The Ministry of Interior's—MOI—project was a similar one with multiple sites, multiple facilities. There were very few firms anywhere in the world with that building type experience and the project delivery system to do that many buildings simultaneously. I remember that as being pretty damn spectacular.

If the truth were known, from all of these huge projects we did in Saudi, we got very little spin-off in other markets. Maybe one or more helped us get the big Ruwais project in Abu Dhabi, where we did a massive housing project for ADNOC [Abu Dhabi National Oil Company]. But it would be hard for me to say I can remember a specific instance where major American corporations or public institutions in the U.S. hired us to do things in the U.S. because they perceived the experience we gained in the Mideast was applicable. It's almost like there was a megaproject world, and there was the rest of the world.

It's almost like the Mideast was a mixed blessing because for CRS at the time, we became known as the firm that did all the work in the Mideast and really didn't do anything else. So that's why I say by 1982, my recollection is that domestic revenues had dwindled to a very small scale. The other thing I can tell you for sure is that by far our most successful experience abroad was in Saudi—second most successful was in Abu Dhabi—and everything else was downhill. Bahrain was a disaster, Egypt was a disaster, and I think it's because all of those [CRS] people went where the biggest projects were, and the biggest projects were in Saudi. That worked against us because it was common knowledge that, "Yeah, they're great guys, real smart, but all the good talent is over in Saudi. [They're] too busy for my little project." That was our reputation. . . . It was not only reputation, it may have been a deserved reputation.

Q: Could you have done anything differently?

A: Probably not, if you look at it in the relative pecking order of who really mattered. The organization was run by the residual of the eight founders who were still actively involved. It was Caudill Rowlett Scott and, to a lesser extent, the construction management team, including Chuck Thomsen. And by then we had been a public company since 1971. The profit motive is always admirable whether you are a public or private company, but you went just where the action was.

The collective energies of the top management of the companies were driven toward the Mideast market—particularly the Saudi market—for a long time. I remember lots of philosophical discussions and sat in many meetings where we talked about diversifying our markets. We talked about balance, domestic versus foreign—all those things. But in the greater scheme of things, if an RFP [Request for Proposal] comes in over the transom, and it's bigger than any fifty projects you can sell in Texas or New York, what would you do? You'd do the same thing probably. So, I don't find fault with anybody for chasing that market. I think we could have done differently and probably should have been more dedicated to reinvesting some of what was being made in other markets.

Beginning certainly in late '79 and by '80, '81, it was my belief—I told you of that phenomenon where we were starting to make more money on interest income than from our real business. I was actually uptight about it twenty-four hours a day. I was jumping up and down at Herb Paseur, and, after he retired, I reported to Chuck Thomsen that if we didn't get back into the domestic market, didn't diversify, my greatest fear was that the market would just simply go away. I guess in '82, when the bottom fell out of the oil market and the bust hit, it was like that market did go away in one day. So my time, beginning '81 through '83, became almost totally consumed with acquisitions. . . .

Basically, we set out on this acquisition trail on the theory that time was too short to sell our way back into the local market. We had to buy our way back into it.

Q: Mergers and acquisitions. What kind of things happened? How did they evolve, and what acquisitions and mergers took place?

A: Well, the acquisitions were what I call "the good, the bad, and the ugly." Some were probably two of the three above. The acquisitions include Preston Geren's firm, Geren Associates; EPR, which was probably the fourth largest interior design firm in the country at the time, headquartered in San Francisco; Western Empire Constructors, a general contractor in Denver; and, finally, the J. E. Sirrine Company in Greenville.

The Geren firm was acquired mainly through the personal relationships of Tom Bullock. That was done while I was chief financial officer, reporting to Chuck Thomsen [then president and CEO]. . . . There's no question that the relationship was Tom and Preston. It was Tom's belief, consistent with what I was saying, that we needed to be more back in the domestic market, and here was a fine Texas firm that was Preston's father's firm before. It was in north Texas, did work down on the UT and A&M campuses [and] all over Texas—except in the Houston area. . . . I guess the strategy was [that] we acquired a very strong regional architectural firm. But they weren't experts in anything. They were experts in their backyard, their geography.

Geren did institutional design on college campuses. He [also] designed some churches [and] office buildings. I think he was designer on the renovation of the Ridglea Country Club in Fort Worth. He was the Fort Worth associated architect on the DFW [Dallas–Fort Worth] Airport. It was a firm centered around him and one or two of his closest colleagues, a sort of classic regional architectural practice.

Chuck Thomsen was president of CRS at the time, and my recollection is that Chuck met Preston certainly after the deal was done in spirit, and maybe after it was actually signed. I think he visited Fort Worth one time. My point in all this is that he really was not involved. It was not his idea, and he basically never showed up on the screen. Even though he was my boss, in fact, all the analytical work—all activity that took place in making that acquisition happen—was me doing it for Tom Bullock, who had recently come back into the firm active after having been in a two- or three-year retirement period. He [Bullock] was chairman of the board but not president [and]

CEO, and I didn't report to Tom. In fact, the guy I reported to really had no involvement whatsoever in the acquisition and had hardly even met Geren.

The acquisition that followed quickly on the heels of that was EPR, located in San Francisco, with an office in Washington and one in L.A. After we acquired them, we jointly opened one in New York. They were a premier interior architecture firm with a specialty as that.

I don't think there was anything erroneous in the strategy of acquiring Geren as a strong toehold in a major growth state like Texas. Likewise, in the case of EPR, it was a recognition that the world is not all new buildings, that what went on inside of existing buildings could be an integral part of the future world, that our interiors practice had always been a poor boy second to architecture, that while we did some interior architecture projects, it was never the flagship, it was always the rudder behind the ship. EPR was a premier firm in that market, so we acquired EPR.

I'm talking about what went wrong with both of those because there are some common themes. . . . In the case of the Geren firm, we finally sent a guy named Chuck Nixon up there to sort of be second in command to Preston, to be his heir apparent. But we could not make the transition from a firm totally dominated by one man and his father before him.

The structure of both these acquisitions was such that key numbers of the principals got stock in CRS. They had various incentive compensation programs designed to prevent them from walking out the door the day the deal was done. [It was] a sort of "golden handcuffs" deal. I was intimately involved in the financial structure in both of those . . . cases from day one. We did everything possible to invite as many people as possible to stay in the deal, keep working hard, and be part of what went forward.

But in both, it was a classic case of almost cultural genocide that took place. The acquisition team, if you will, was a pure corporate team: me, a guy named Steve Gilliland, the board, [and] our general counsel, Richard Daerr, who had recently been hired. It was a very few of us who made the acquisition happen, but we weren't the ones that were going to run it after the fact. In both instances, it was turned over to Caudill Rowlett Scott, and the cultural genocide that took place was almost shocking.

In the case of Geren, I think we still had the mentality of the megaproject CRS, which in the greater scheme of things didn't give a shit about churches, country clubs, and small office buildings up in north Texas. . . . Then, to top it off, we had a very strong personality in Preston Geren as he went through his three- to four-year phase down. . . . Because it was a one-man band, we bought a massive insurance policy on him that scaled down by a million dollars a year over a five-year period. [We did this] to address the issue for our shareholders that if he died eighteen months after we acquired the firm, and the firm disappeared and our shareholders looked over our shoulders and said, "What in hell were you thinking about?" we would have cashed a huge chip and answered that question. As you know, he's alive and well today. He lived through it, and we killed the firm, in my opinion. . . .

It's sort of like once a deal is done and you hand it over to Paul Kennon, then [to] Ray Martin and the others running the firm, and say "This is now yours," [it] just didn't change the fact that they didn't give a shit. I don't mean that in a cynical way, I just mean that their collective mind-set and that of all the others around them was somewhere else.

The case of EPR was slightly different in that there we had a very, very strong culture that was more than one individual. It was not only Darryl Roberson, [but] Chuck Bowman, Dave Morning, and four or five others. That group—unlike Preston Geren, who was a one-man band reaching retirement age—was a premier firm headed by a guy who was probably in his early forties, and all his colleagues [were] key movers and shakers who were between twenty-eight and forty-five, in their prime. That became such an ego battle between EPR's culture and the culture of what was then CRS—and more specifically, a personal battle between Darryl Roberson and Paul Kennon. Almost everything degenerated into who was going to survive the battle. It got so bad. . . . that . . . after we acquired the J. E. Sirrine Company, [when] we were trying to figure out what would be the new logo, . . . [and] who would get to design that—whether it was Kennon and the architects, or EPR—got to be such a bloody goddamn political battle that Tom Bullock and I ended up going to outside consultants.

The net end of that deal was that it was a total clash of cultures, sort of the megaproject institutional architect culture on one side and the miniproject—five thousand square feet was a big deal project—high-end design interior architect, [or] "boutique" practice, on the other side. It was cats and dogs. In the end, I was [the] CEO and attempting to referee this thing.

I'll never forget one day, I called Darryl Roberson and asked him to come to the Houston office. I told him that I hated this, but it was going to be a divorce, that somebody had to go, and if I had my choice, both he and Kennon would go because I couldn't stand either of them by that time. It had gotten so brutal. But . . . Paul had been there much longer. He had the traditions of the firm, and if somebody had to go, it was going to be Darryl. That was it. I told them I'm presiding over a really sad chapter, but it has to end, and it has to end with the newest kid on the block leaving.

The other acquisition of that time was Western Empire Constructors. That was an idea that had been kicked around and almost done while Chuck Thomsen was still president. It was something he felt strongly he wanted to do.

They were a general contractor in Denver with operations around Colorado, New Mexico, Wyoming. They had an industrial division that did civil works projects, primarily bridge structures and wastewater treatment projects. But by far, most of it was buildings. They had an excellent track record. Again, that was one where, going in, the structure of the acquisition was such that we put no more money out in cash than they had in their treasury when we acquired them. The rest was all in stock. We put four or five of the key people into incentive programs. We thought it was structured pretty well.

Looking at that one with twenty-twenty hindsight, I would say we probably underestimated again the cultural gap between somebody in the construction management end of things and a bid general contractor. A bid general contractor, which Western Empire was, viewed our construction management group as a bunch of "kissie" architects who really didn't know anything about building anything—just pretended to be in the construction business. Our Construction Management group viewed them as pretty Neanderthal: not terribly enlightened or looking at the real world, not understanding why people paid us the fees to do construction management the way we did it. . . .

[We tried to] blend the best of those two cultures. In fact, the articulated strategy inside the company was that we could take some of the hard construction skills that existed in Western Empire and sort of migrate it into our office, for instance, in Los Angeles or Miami or Washington, D.C.; that the sum total of the two would be better.

It was inevitable in the case of Geren and EPR that those operations would report to the management of our architecture group. In other words, from day one, CRS was going to be on top of architectural design, and the presidents of EPR and Geren had no question the boss was going to be the guy in charge of Caudill Rowlett Scott. What I'm saying is, it was sort of like a piranha that ate one of those cultures, and the other one was sort of killed off by benign neglect.

In the case of Western Empire Constructors, if you compared it to the domestic operations of our CM group—our construction management group—it was about the same size. In other words, if you set aside the big work going on in Saudi that was CM-related and only talked about the lower forty-eight states' construction activities, it was essentially equal in size to our CM group.

So I think the fact Western Empire was to report to the construction management group was always implied. Then it became a fact, but [one that was] resented by the general contractor culture. Then it became a battle among two or three people at the top over who was eventually going to come out on top. . . .

I would certainly say that EPR and Western Empire were structured from day one to succeed. Did we pay too much money? No. Did we put so much money in the principals' pockets that they retired on day one and didn't come back to the office? No. Did we put stock options and other things in the hands of the second-level management of both firms that made them want to work hard for years toward financial success? Yes. We did all those things, and yet there was an absolute cultural disconnect over who reported to whom in all instances.

I believe in all of those [acquisition cases, with regard to] the financial and other structures, employment contracts, [and] noncompet[ing] arrangements, we treated the human animal like a horse where you have to use beatings and sugar cubes. Darryl Roberson at EPR had sugar cubes to hang around and be really successful, and there were [to be] beatings, takeaways if he had walked out the first day and said, "I'm counting my chips now, thank you very much." To me, I guess the lesson learned in all of this—in the acquisition of "people businesses"—is that you simply cannot protect yourself contractually against somebody that sort of retires in place, who shows up every day, goes through the motions, but his heart is not in it.

The analogy might be that we had situations in all three of those acquisitions where people just kind of retired in place. They weren't having fun anymore because they didn't respect or couldn't relate to the people to whom they reported, and it just went from bad to worse. The other part of the lesson learned in all this: In answer to the question, "Would you do it all over again?" the answer is probably "Yes," because again, we were a firm that was dying domestically, had no work, and had to buy our way back in. . . .

I don't mean to imply that the acquired party in all cases was wonderful, brilliant, omnipotent. At times, the crowd to whom they reported had good points—more often right than wrong, maybe. Long-term key employees doing a good job. [Then] they see somebody who is paid a million dollars because he was part of a two-hundred-man firm that really did well, has got all this money in the bank and is acting like an asshole, and they are making $50,000 a year and thinking, "What's in this for me? I've been here ten years. Is this the thanks I get for making this guy wealthy?" So, looking back on all three of those [acquisitions], I would say the lesson learned—probably more important than the people acquisition, all the numbers, all the structure, all of whatever—is that you have to truly believe there's a cultural fit.

Q: Is there a big cultural difference in Sirrine, then?

A: I'd say two major differences. It was by headcount a larger company than all of CRS at the time. It was an older company founded in 1902. Some 90 percent of the critical mass did things we didn't do. It was process engineering in markets we were not in. Only 10 percent or less was architectural in nature, and it really wasn't the same type of architecture we did, either in building type or geography. So, we really had a totally different type of organization. We could look at it in the cold light of day and say, "These guys are not going to report to our architects, or vice versa. They're just flat different." That's a major difference.

The other is, it was so large in critical mass. It was not dependent on one, two, or three personalities on either side [process engineering or architecture]. So much so, in fact, that for about the first two years after the acquisition, we did everything we could to downsize the company because they had significant overhead. It was very ossified management: great tradition, incredible technical depth, but very staid, conservative, heavy at the top. We actually went through two early retirement induced layoffs [and] two or three other major workforce reductions at the top.

In the greater scheme of things, within twenty-four months of when we acquired that company, more people left employment in the company than the total of EPR and Geren put together—five hundred to six hundred people. But its core was so strong, it obviously didn't matter. . . . Also, in that company there were six hundred shareholders, more or less. It was not a public company in that it was not publicly traded, but in the eyes of the SEC, it had over five hundred shareholders, and so it had to file all the same documents.

I guess having been through it, I'm more of a purist on terminology now. I don't think merger works. I think acquisition might. Merger implies two things of some degree of equality coming together to form something else. I think in the real world there are buyers and there are sellers; there are no mergers. With twenty-twenty hindsight, I think also [that] in all cases, we probably would have been better off—even if it was only damage control, taking a bad situation and making it less bad—if we'd been more decisive about having been the acquiring party. When in doubt, in other words, from day one, assert the fact that you're the buyer by removing two or three people and putting your own in. I'm a firm believer in [the idea that] were somebody to walk in and buy CRSS today, their first right is to replace me. They are the new owner in that instance. When you think about it, how outrageous is it for a new owner to not have the absolute right to my job?

The advice I'd give myself and others going forward: Acquire companies where there is a true cultural affinity, be willing to replace the very top people very quickly, and don't buy a company unless you believe you have on your staff—or can quickly get—somebody as good or better than the guy you're buying so the first day he blinks and gives you any shit, you can throw open the door and put a better person in his place. I say that candidly as a buyer and would believe that in my own case if I were the seller. The seller has either the right to my job from day one or the right to tell me exactly how they want me to do it. And if I don't feel comfortable in doing it that way, then I ought to walk out the door so somebody else can....

You take a Darryl Roberson, who was president of EPR. When he and Chuck Bowman ran their firm, I believe they were spiritual leaders and guiders of a band of people having fun and growing. They sold it [to CRS], put a bunch of money in the bank, and he [Roberson] took on the role of spiritual defender of all his employees against these goddamn Philistines from Houston who bought the firm. So he sort of went from leader to guerrilla fighter: "I'm down there in the trenches protecting your ass from those Philistines." That's a whole different role from being the grower of the firm.

Eighty-three through '86 was a long drought in the construction industry; the longest and worst period we ever had. It actually started in '82 and ended in early '87; a four-year period. By '86, '87—when things started getting better—I think we began to officially articulate to our shareholder audience, our board, and everybody that there was a period when acquiring service companies was important because we needed critical mass. In 1987, with twenty-five hundred to three thousand employees, we didn't need that anymore. We were big enough to compete with the big guys. We basically said, "We are not going to make design, engineering, or related service company acquisitions. We are going to take the money we make in the base business and apply it to this independent power and cogeneration business, which is very capital intensive, very long-term, nonpeople intensive, but has a potential to stabilize our earnings—thirty-year contracts, twenty-year contracts, finance, no corporate debt." We started doing that and have [had] very good success to date. Along the way, we expanded into something that was then—and many would say today—venture capital, which is acid rain abatement, a company that became known as NaTec. It was originally a joint venture with a company called Industrial Resources in Colorado.

Q: NaTec is not an acquisition then?

A: No. NaTec is actually sort of a creation. It was a fifty-fifty joint venture between us and a then publicly traded company. . . . But it was a bet that, long term, the acid rain abatement market would be large, and this dry sodium sorbent injection technology would play a role. . . .

I had a list of probably twenty-five to thirty companies that we analyzed. We made a pass at one or two, but by far the one in mind with the greatest potential was the J. E. Sirrine Company. . . . We had no market we really owned, like in the early days when education was huge. We dominated that market, but we didn't have anything we did that really differentiated us that well. At the time, I felt it was already the Fluors and Bechtels and the M. W. Kelloggs who did ammonia, urea, hydrocarbon, cat crackers, ethylene. The big petroleum process industry was already dominated by giants, and there weren't any of those within the realm of our means to acquire. We did look at some in the gas processing business. But of the ones we looked at, Sirrine was the best by far. I worked on it for two and a half years of my life. We made one pass at them—had the deal signed up, announced that it fell through—then came back a year later and made it happen.

I think one of the great strategic questions for the company is: Can there be viable growth of these two parts that have some similarities but have great differences? . . . There's a whole world of investors that really would like to own a design/construction services company. There's a world that likes to buy independent power and cogenerations companies. There's a world that really believes that acid rain abatement is the whole thing of the future. But is there a world that likes all three at the same time? Probably not.

I think the focus for the next five years needs to be for each of our parts to be the very best of what we do. We may find that to be the best in the markets we serve, the company as we know it today ought to be two or three companies in the future, not just one. In other words, to be the very best, our architecture operation certainly doesn't need an independent power company as an affiliate, and vice versa.

In all candor, it's been my experience that you can take a very senior person in the architecture operation who ought to know a lot about what the rest of the company is doing, but the odds are he knows very little about the rest, and, sadly, he really doesn't care. [The] same would be true in engineering. . . . In our company, you have people whose affinities are primarily set along professional disciplines.

This next decade will have little place for the medium-size firms. The well-capitalized, globally oriented engineering and design firms and the very small "boutiques" will have the edge. The ones in between that just serve vanilla ice cream won't have a lasting impact. We're too big to be a boutique, so our challenge is to be bigger and well financed enough to be global in those special markets.

■ CHAPTER 12

CORPORATE CULTURE

■ TIB: 1 JANUARY 1981

One person in CRS (let's call him George) said the other day that our senior officers can't make decisions. That was quite an indictment.

George was dead serious. I was immediately put on the defensive. I said, "George, these guys were trained for team action and sometimes team decision is necessary." What I didn't say is that some of us use team as a crutch. "And there is another thing," I added. "George, do you remember that favorite expression that once permeated CRS? It was, 'Let's suspend our judgement until we know for sure we are right.'" Then I thought to myself, "Bull, that's indecisiveness." I'm sure George wasn't the least bit impressed with my response. I wasn't. The fact is: IF CRS IS TO CONTINUE TO GROW QUALITATIVELY AND QUANTITATIVELY, WHICH MOST OF US WANT, WE MUST BE DECISIVE—TAKE RISKS. GO AGAINST THE CONSENSUS.

IN SHORT, CREATIVE, ASSERTIVE LEADERSHIP MUST BE EXERTED AT EVERY LEVEL. POOLING OPINIONS ISN'T MAKING BOLD DECISIONS.

■ In a squib written in 1983, Bill Caudill drew attention to the fact that at CRS there were no reserved parking places for the officers, and there were birthday parties for everyone "regardless of their position on the organizational chart."[1] Those were signs, he said, of the firm's "appreciation and fair treatment of the worker, regardless of what he or she does."

From the very beginning, CRS, unlike some other architecture firms, was averse to displays of rank. In the years immediately after World War II it was still easy to find firms in which status was drummed into people's consciousness. Willie Peña recalls going into offices in which the chief draftsman sat at an elevated table, looking down on a long hall occupied by subordinate draftsmen all "lined up like rows of corn."[2] In some of those status-bound offices, there was an unwritten rule against designers' talking to working-drawings people. Strict organization by rank was equated with professionalism.

But CRS rejected that attitude, as did many others in the postwar era. More flexible, democratic, participatory ways of working were being instituted. In Cambridge, Massachusetts, when Walter Gropius and a group of young architects started The Architects Collaborative (TAC) in December, 1945, they, like Caudill Rowlett Scott a short while later, made a point of de-emphasizing hierarchy. The Architects Collaborative put all of its principals on an equal footing, allowing each partner and senior associate a voice in every project and paying each partner an equal salary and an equal share of the profits—this despite the fact that Gropius, as founder of the Bauhaus and head of the Harvard Graduate School of Design, was without question the firm's preeminent figure.[3]

In Texas, CRS preached the necessity of openness. "We had a leader, but he was not dictatorial," Peña observed. "We could each have our say." To be able to analyze action—seeing both the good and the bad and weighing them astutely—was held up as a "characteristic of a mature professional."[4]

Caudill liked to declare that CRS was composed of "good guys who know their stuff." By "good guys," he meant employees who were eager to work and willing to cooperate with one another. Though some strong-willed individuals—disparaged at the time or later as "prima donnas"—left CRS because the teamwork concept prevented them from following their own impulses as far as they wanted to go, many others enjoyed the firm's atmosphere. It was not automatic for people to pull together in harness, especially young designers just out of architecture school, where individuality was celebrated. Nevertheless, the people who flourished at CRS learned sooner or later to be team players. When CRS's Houston headquarters, the White House, was being planned in 1968, a psychologist from California gathered and summarized staff members' attitudes so that the new offices would meet the employees' needs and nurture their ability to work together. After the partners' annual meeting in 1969, Caudill exulted, "We are more team than TAC. Gropius, who invented the team, I think would have been more proud of CRS than his own firm."[5]

Many of the principals stayed with CRS for decades. Turnover among the rank and file, on the other hand, was heavy—not that this is unusual in architecture firms. Some young architects came to CRS intending to stay for only a couple of years and move on. It was said that CRS was a "graduate school" for a generation of architects. Turnover was also kept high by the practice, widespread among architecture firms, of quickly laying off staff when work subsided. Turnover and staff growth seemed to heighten the desire to define CRS's values and to promote those values among its employees. This was accomplished by many means, including sometimes-elaborate exercises in corporate introspection, such as companywide attempts in 1968, 1974, and again in the 1980s to define the firm's values and goals. Corporate goal setting prodded the staff to think about where the company was going or ought to go, and helped prevent employees from falling into a rut. The company made a consistent practice of talking and writing about goals and values. "We thought that if we put them down on paper, they became very real," Peña observed.

Bill Caudill's work area and busy bulletin board in the open-plan office environment of the "White House." *Photo courtesy Rondal Partridge.*

Leaders at CRS were expected to act as mentors, preparing employees for increasing levels of responsibility. At the same time, there was an awareness that "mentoring" goes only so far, that learners "must have the privilege of making mistakes."[6] By letting people try their wings—especially in branch offices, away from the constant presence of the top officers—CRS developed a succession of leaders who helped keep the firm vigorous.

INTERVIEWS

WILLIE PEÑA

[In the beginning,] we . . . all thought we were designers. Bill sat down and said, "Hold it, hold it, we've got to get organized here." He didn't like the way we were working. There was something wrong with the output, it was not consistent. . . .

We said, "Well, Bill, you're the best designer here, you be the designer." He said, "All right, now that that's settled, who's going to do *this?* Who's going to do *that?*" Well, John would do promotion and working drawings whenever he could because he was still teaching. Wallie would be working drawings for sure. I would do specifications [in] color. Bill was colorblind, so he depended on someone else to do color.

So, I took over exterior and interior color and programming. I also did supervision, but not working drawings. The first set of working drawings I did for the firm was so bad. It was the Weick house. That taught Bill that I was *not* a working drawings person. . . .

The idea was—and maybe Bill didn't verbalize it at the time, but he did later—[that] none of us were geniuses, but we could have a *team* of specialists which could equate to genius. In other words, [by] pooling our talents together, we might be a genius. Separately, we were not. . . .

The idea of specializing in roles . . . came about through the belief that the deeper you go into a subject, the more mastery of that subject you can obtain. And then, of course, if you put that mastery in the team, then you would have a team of experts. He [Bill] believed in football, everybody is a specialist. He also knew in team activity, diversity might suffer. It's a little more difficult than when you're dealing with just one man. He also believed in football [that] if you have one star, [you could] give him the ball every time, and he'll go with it. But, wouldn't it be great if you had a team with not just one star, but five stars? That would be superb. Now you're in the national league! But he said, "It takes a more sophisticated management to take care of a team with four or five stars." That's when management became important. . . .

He would quote a famous sportscaster who said that a good coach does not devise a play, plan, or whatever they call it and assign people to it. He has to take cognizance of who he has, and then designs the plan with the people in mind. He said: "Managers can't design people. They can design the organization plan." He knew I was a lousy working drawings guy. I knew I would never be as great a designer as Bill Caudill. He was my teacher. How could I outdo him? He knew, too, I was a good analyst. Wasn't it natural for him to push me toward analysis? Now he's got a job for me. He was a guy prone to analysis: "Let's cash in on that," not, "We need an analyst. Willie, you do it!" No, he would go with people's talents and assign them a job they could do well. . . .

I think you could see it mostly in the beginning days, but even toward the last, you could find a whole bunch of guys who claimed Bill was their mentor. Why? Because they could go to him and tell him, "I'm not happy," then he would find out, "What *makes* you happy?" He only regretted that people would come to him with that kind of problem at seven in the morning because that was *his* time. He really didn't want to be disturbed then. But at any other time, you could go to him. . . .

We didn't believe in free sketches. We believed if we were going to do the job, we had to start with some sort of program. Design the school, make it look like it should rather than start with a picture and sell that. So that was one professional value we had. Another—we got this from Bill and John—[was] to deal with people on some level of integrity. You never put something bad on paper. Who knows where that might lead? You dealt with them truthfully and didn't put bad things [opinions] on paper that could ricochet. John Rowlett, particularly, emphasized that in dealing with clients.

Q: Were the partners all single at the time?

A: No. Bill Caudill and John Rowlett were married. When there were just four, Wallie and I were the two single guys. For about three months, the firm didn't have any work, so Wallie and I didn't take any salary home for those three months because they [Caudill and Rowlett] had families. We had savings left from the war, etcetera, and felt we didn't need the money all that much. That was the kind of spirit in the firm: self-sacrifice without much to do about it [because it] seemed natural to do it. . . .

Bill believed in sharing. We should give some of it back. He said we should set aside a reasonable amount of money and just give it back to some worthwhile charity and not say anything about it. It was a very honest thing coming from the heart: as a firm, we should give something back.

HISTORY OF THE CRS TREE

The Limbs = Diversified Design Solutions (Character of CRS Architecture)

The Trunk = Straightforward, Economical Solution to Clients Problems (CRS Strength)

The Roots = CRS Commitment to

1. Problem-Solving Approach
2. Team Concept—Practice of Architecture
3. Architecture is for People

The Soil = People, Money, Land, and Material (Tom Bullock, 1960)

The Seed = To Produce a Better Architecture (John Rowlett with Bill Caudill, 1944)

LEWIS MAY

I've always been mesmerized by Caudill and by Caudill Rowlett and Scott. I had followed them in the journals for years. I was one of these odd landscape architects. I guess I still am, come to think of it. . . . But I really didn't enjoy the practice of landscaping; it was meaningless. So I wanted to join CRS. The dean immediately just freaked—he was an architect—[and said]: "Don't join them. You're a landscape architect, and they'll just eat you up," and so on and so on. So I came over to Houston and had two interviews, one with Harwood Taylor and one with Bill Caudill. Neuhaus & Taylor offered me a lot more money, and I took the CRS job. . . .

But you didn't do it for the money. It's so much fun—dozens of awards, hundreds of projects. It was absolutely very, very exciting for the first eighteen and a half years. . . . Up until the last six months, it was the finest practice of its kind in the country for a landscape architect. . . . [T]here were no rules, for one thing. The fact that we treated it not as a vocation, we treated it as a passion. There's not a thing we did in a project type that was not exploratory, pioneering. From graphics to interiors to landscape architecture to plain architecture, there was not any reason you could not excel to achieve, to be anything you wanted to be. I mean, as a landscape architect, I was the design principal named after Paul Kennon when I left the firm—the first nonarchitect ever. Again, that's a perfect example. You've got a six-hundred-person architecture firm, then you've got a landscape architect as a design principal. . . . Everybody was young. I think what made it great was there was this exploratorium that allowed you to reach great heights.

Also, I think the people I went to work for in 1972—and Tom and I have discussed this—were products of a different society, a different culture. [They were] people of their word. There was honor, there was integrity, there was ethics, [and] there was morals. Those are strange things in today's practice of anything. We've all sort of taken the butcher shop mentality of [get your] "paycheck and get out of here." When I joined the firm, it had forty-five people. . . . I would have no problems about going to Bullock or Wilkinson about an impropriety, or issues, or somebody who hadn't been given a raise that deserves one, or this student needs to be recognized—no one does that anymore. That's why I used to go to the office at five or six o'clock in the morning, and I'm not a morning person—I'd set my clock to go see Caudill. . . .

I'd find Caudill. I would walk through his bay, cough real loud, kick his trash can just to let him know I was here, but I would never approach his desk. I'm not saying he would growl; he wouldn't. I would go back to my desk and in about thirty minutes, he would take the bait and come back there, sit down, and talk to me. So, for the first three or four years of my career, I had this wonderful before seven relationship with Bill. You know Bill. He would talk about anything. . . . "Tell me about landscape." He was mesmerized by my drawings. He would touch them and feel them and take them home. We talked about drawing, we talked about architecture, we talked about landscape architecture. I would go there that early in the morning purposely to communicate with him. That's why it got as good as it was. Not because of Bill, but because there was recognition of any contribution, any idea. . . . Now the world looks for heroes. I'm not talking about CRS, but any culture in the world needs heroes. It's us, it's American. We had a whole office full of heroes then. We had Wallie with all his idiosyncrasies and Willie and Tiny and Bill. They were all bigger-than-life figures.

BILL CANNADY

Another thing I noticed Bill had at Rice as well as at the firm was his key group of support personnel who were always a secretary who could type real fast and understand *what* to type . . . also somebody who was sort of a word merchant, somebody outside the field, a writer as opposed to a secretary. He always had one of those close to him at Rice and at the firm. The other one was someone who was real good with either graphics—Bill was good on that, but he needed backup some of the time—or a photographer. That was his team. Everybody was to make money, but these guys were to make waves—stir up things that created opportunities for *other* people to make money. He was an extraordinary PR [public relations] person in that sense. Probably he was the best learner at the firm, and I know he was the best learner at Rice. He was willing to look at anything, read anything, think or talk about anything.

He would always sit right on the front row at a Rice lecture. [I] guess I told you the story about him and Lou Kahn. Kahn was talking at St. Thomas University in a building Philip Johnson designed, which is laid out like a perfect Greek amphitheater—a two-to-one ratio in a rectangle with a semicircular seating arrangement and a semicircular stage. It had one chair with Lou Kahn sitting in the middle of the stage. The room was packed, and we were sitting with Caudill in the third or fourth row, so it was at an eye-level, one-on-one relationship with Kahn. I was sitting next to Caudill, and he was right in the middle facing Lou Kahn.

Kahn would say something like, "Architecture is space," and stop. Well, Bill would grab into his pocket for pocket cards—making his typical lip-smacking noises—and start scribbling. Then he would put it all back in his pocket. Then Kahn would look at Caudill and say, "Space is light." Bill would jump back into his pocket, tear out the pocket cards, [and] scribble furiously again. You could tell the audience was either disturbed or chuckling about it. Kahn couldn't move forward with the lecture without Bill's reacting, so even *he* was beginning to get kind of concerned about what Bill's reaction would be to the next sentence. It was typical of Bill to be determined not to miss a thing that was relevant. Of course, *everything* Kahn said was relevant, so the whole thing had to be scribbled on these pocket cards. . . .

One thing people may not be aware of is Caudill's ego. He had a super ego. He also was very good at camouflaging it, giving you the impression of a modest, humble, stuttering country boy [who was] just like everybody else. He was as good as there was at playing that when he wanted to play it. I never intentionally tried to find out what was behind it, but I did.

There was an occasion at Rice on which he had appointed myself and Andy Todd [Prof. Anderson Todd] to be a committee of two to hire a new assistant professor. We were going to do the groundwork; he was going to do the hiring. We were to dig up the candidates. We spent a lot of time talking to him [Caudill] as well as others in the U.S. to find the best candidate possible. Like a lot of situations where you try to look at as many candidates as possible, it turns out Caudill actually had his favorite right from the beginning. He seemed to be just waiting for us to come around to that. The more we searched, the angrier he got about the fact he had already made his choice. It was an architect who at the time was a young designer at SOM [Skidmore Owings Merrill] in New York City. Andy and I went to New York, interviewed him, and came back with a not-too-glowing report. We had a first choice, a landscape architect from Berkeley, along with a second and third choice. As I remember, the second choice was a recent Yale graduate, editor of *Perspecta* magazine. Our third choice was the architect from SOM Bill wanted.

We gave him the report in his office, going over our choices in great detail. The more we talked, the angrier he got and the madder we got because we had put so much time into it. Toward the end of the discussion, I said something very bad: I made the comment that this landscape architect from Berkeley knew as much about architecture as anyone on the faculty. I didn't realize that included Caudill. He stood up and screamed as he slammed his fists on the table, "Goddammit, don't tell *me* about architecture." He pointed his finger right in our faces. We both literally fell out of our chairs on the floor. Bill's face was glowing red, white hair standing up—looked like God was coming down on us. That ended the discussion. The meeting was over, and we crawled out of his office. . . .

Bill's energy level was two or three times the average person's and was focused daily on creative things. When I was at Rice, I was the associate director of the school. He got to CRS too early for Bullock, which seemed to be one of their basic problems—i.e., Bill's leaving to go to Rice. For many years, Bill would show up at the school around noon. It became routine for us to meet about 11:30 and go have lunch and talk about ideas, etcetera. It was a pretty exciting relationship for a young guy right out of college. He treated me pretty much as an equal, and I had an opportunity to be involved in everything he was doing all those years at Rice.

At CRS, I felt it was a different arrangement. He seemed to have a lot more problems with time at CRS than he had at Rice. So when I moved over to CRS, I tried to reestablish that relationship with Bill but found it was actually easier with Tom and Herb than Bill because he had so many pressures on his time. I thought maybe I could have some time with him when he got to work in the morning. Work started at eight, so I went in at 7:30, but he was already there and involved in something. Then I went in at seven, and he was still already there and buried in his work. So I went in at 6:30, then at six. Actually, I found if I went in at about 5:30, I could beat him to the office and wait on him. I did that one time, and we had coffee and visited. But I decided, "This is not worth it." So I went back to regular hours. It was impossible to beat him to work and to get to him before he got to his work—because then it was impossible to drag him away from it.

Q: He always kept those hours. Hard to know whether he kept them because he couldn't sleep or because he liked getting to the office before everybody else so he could work undisturbed. I suspect it was the latter.

A: When he didn't want to be disturbed, it was hard to bust in on him.

Q: No. Even in that open plan office, Bill could put "partitions" up around himself, and you knew he didn't want to be bothered.

A: You could tell by the way he looked at you whether you could interrupt. If he was free, he'd take the time to talk with you. At CRS, there was very little time for that, and that's what I missed. Whereas at the university, he was very accessible.

JONATHAN KING

Before EFL had its own office, I had an office in the Ford Foundation with some orange crates full of books, reports, and pictures. I had asked Bill Caudill to come in when he was next in New York [and] he did a couple of weeks later, with Tom Bullock. Bill was an extraordinarily warm and open person. Rather than it being a fifteen-minute conversation, we ended up spending two or two and a half hours together. He told me everything I should read so that I'd know all about schools and everything I should look at, and gave me a list of all of CRS's best competitors so I'd know who else to talk to. Meanwhile, Tom Bullock sat there in silence—except for answering questions when questions were asked of him. That sort of set off a relationship that lasted quite a long time. Obviously, EFL needed to know who the players were in the school building landscape.

At that time, CRS, to me, represented two very interesting, somewhat divergent points of view. One was their background in research which came out of Bill's work here at Texas A&M, work that was still going on at that time—that was 1958. Ben Evans was down here keeping some of that going. It sort of lost its momentum, I think, as a result of the loss of Caudill as a faculty member. But at least there was a feeling that research could be done, which at that time was extraordinarily rare. I knew of some architectural research that was happening at MIT. Al Dietz was doing some things, and Marvin Goody was doing work . . . and the Texas A&M work. There was almost none going on that I was aware of in other places, other than history, which didn't seem germane to my problem at the time. So that got me interested in CRS.

Plus the fact that CRS was always pushing the edge on design. They were taking some of the theoretical work of the Modern Movement and trying to apply it to pedestrian buildings like schoolhouses and developing sort of post-Miesian notions like "lean and clean" for architecture. There was a kind of wonderful freshness in those buildings that may not be apparent now because when you look at the drawings and photos, they tend to look rather stark—maybe too lean and clean. When you look at the buildings now, they were all too cheap, so they haven't worn as well as buildings ought to wear. . . .

Q: You said something earlier about CRS always seemed to be pushing the design frontiers. Was it because of Bill, or because of the kind of people they were hiring?

A: I think it started because of Bill, and it then went on because of the kind of people they hired and the kind of atmosphere they surrounded themselves with. I grew up in New York City. It's an old place. If you want to do something in a new way, somebody tells you it was tried in 1644 and again in 1830, and it didn't work. If it did work, the Teamsters Union owned it, and you couldn't do it.

There was something about Texas at that time that said, "Well, hell, that's a good idea, let's do it now, let's not wait and see if it works someplace else." Like the open-plan school. When that idea was generated, CRS rushed in and did some open-plan schools, like Consolidated A&M over here. Some of those schools didn't work very well, and the reason they didn't work very well was that they were out in front of the client that was using them. And maybe they weren't all terribly good ideas anyway, but there was a willingness that if it makes some sense in terms of architecture and in the process of education, then let's see how it works. Let's not be timid about it. When new structural techniques came into play, CRS would try them. I don't know if you were ever in the Dow Center. . . . It had huge, ugly plastic beams that covered the entryway. They were pretty interesting. Again, they don't seem as wonderful now as they did then, but they tried them and tried them as soon as somebody could make those beams.

Q: What was unique that you could transfer to some other young firm now? Was it an attitude? Or was it specific to being in Texas at that time? Was it a couple of individuals?

A: Well, I think the attitude was supported by being in Texas. The individuals were critical. I mean, the fact that you could go to the top with somebody who wanted to try something. Wallie Scott wouldn't have been the first to try anything, but Bill had a vast curiosity, also ambition, to be ahead of the pack—not to do a slightly better conventional-mold school, but to reinvent the schoolhouse if there was an opportunity to reinvent the schoolhouse. Bill would love a client who had a new educational idea who said, "We're not going to teach in this way anymore, we're going to teach in that way." As a result, he would hitch an architectural answer to an intellectual query because most of the schoolhouses of the 1958 era—when I became cognizant of this field—were, as my boss, Harold Gores, used to say, "Just thirty, thirty, thirty down the hall." Nothing but boxes for thirty kids, thirty-by-thirty feet, a double classroom for the library, one and one-half for the kindergarten, and that was it. Somehow, that kind of rigid collection of boxes invented by New Englanders in 1848 just didn't seem the be all and end all of education in the latter half of the twentieth century.

Q: You started to talk about Bill.

A: Yes. Bill, I think, protected that atmosphere by letting people like Tiny try any ideas they could generate. As long as they could justify them and fight with him about them, they could do them. There was an open society within CRS, and this was both an intellectual commitment on Bill's part and a personal openness. . . . Bill had many sides. He was a reasonably sharp businessman. He looked at balance sheets and could read them all right. He had a wonderful, apparently naive quality that served him well when he was dean at Rice. He made everyone feel that if they didn't work twenty-six hours a day, Bill was going to be in bad shape and fall on his face. So he had all these people carrying the load for him, [working] harder than they had ever worked in their lives. It was a little like that at CRS, too. Somehow, everybody felt they just *had* to help Bill, that there was in him somewhere an apparent need for help and without all these "sword bearers" to protect him, he was going to be beat up. Somehow, everybody joined to help Bill. This was most apparent at Rice: His staff and faculty did better work than they had ever done before—and more of it. I felt that way in working with him . . . just got to keep him from getting into trouble, just have to chip in. That was part of his quality as a leader, certainly as the dean at Rice and at CRS. When he came back from Rice, I never felt he was entirely comfortable at CRS, never quite knew what he should be doing and how he should relate to these people who had been working when he wasn't there [full-time].

Bill was also one of the great promoters of modern times. I'm sure you've gotten that from Tom and others you've talked to. Tom would have been happy if Bill hadn't gone to Rice and had spent the time running around the U.S. getting schoolhouses and colleges for CRS. But Bill, I think, needed a different kind of challenge, and the Rice thing reflected that. I think he was very happy at Rice and certainly made Rice a much more exciting place when he was there.

I don't think he was uncomfortable with CRS moving into other things. He never struck me with being uncomfortable when we started up the Construction Management Group (I was part of that enterprise). As long as it wasn't architecture, it didn't bother Bill. It was a useful activity that somebody could do with a different label on it. He would get disturbed sometimes when he felt other considerations were pushing into the architectural arena. Bill was an immensely successful person. He succeeded beyond most people's fondest expectations. But he also felt a sense of failure because he was not a prime design person in the sense that Frank Lloyd Wright, Corbu, and Cesar Pelli were. When you said design in the United States, Caudill was not on the list of the top eight people. As he got older and older, I think he more and more felt bad about that and would wonder if he had devoted himself to design whether he could have leapt into that pantheon.

This photo of Bill Caudill with Rice University students was taken during his tenure as director of Rice's School of Architecture from 1961–69.

Q: But then that would contradict that whole effort about the team, right?

A: Well, Bill always had conflicts between the team and the ego. Architecture by team was something he was truly committed to, and he spent a lot of time thinking about it—wrote about it, as you know. He was genuinely concerned with that. But he also was a designer, and sometimes he felt that the designer should be the chairman of the team—at all hours of the night and day. If somebody would tell Bill we were going to do a building system, that it would be more efficient to do it this way than that way, and he thought it would be more elegant to do it that way than this way, you could have a knockdown with him for quite a while, and he'd go off mad, come back, and forgive you the next day. But not all team members were equal on his team. He wanted to be the captain.

DAVID THORMAN

A little anecdote on Bill Caudill: Back in the mid-'70s, we had several people trying to get planning [at CRS] as a fundamental service. We had Garland Anderson, Randy Sahni, Ray Martin, and we had others, [like] Gerry Pfeffer. We were trying to get into all sorts of planning: city planning and other types of projects. We went to an interview for a little $50,000 job in Rock Hill, South Carolina, just south of Charlotte. The team was comprised of myself as programmer, Ray Martin as manager, Garland Anderson as planner, and Bill Caudill. We were all excited because this was our first interview for a city planning job. We went into the interview, and it was in a small conference room, and we had our slides, etcetera. Bill looked around the room, and all the guys there were kind of city fathers. Bill said: "The only reason I'm here is that I've got gray hair. I'm not going to work on this project, but I've brought three of the brightest guys I know who are going to work on this project. I want them to tell you how they're going to do it." Then he stepped aside. Just the way he said that and the confidence it instilled in us was tremendous. He really didn't say anything more after that, just sat back and watched.

The interesting thing was after the interview, which took about an hour. As we were leaving and there were others coming in, they stopped us and told us to wait. So we went into a little room and waited for about ten minutes. They came in and said, "We've decided to hire you guys and have canceled the rest of the interviews." It's a nice story about a little project, but again, it shows the kind of leadership Bill had.

Can I philosophize a little about the firm?

Q: Sure, philosophize.

A: Looking back, there are a lot of things CRS has done very well. If I go back to the early '70s or late '60s when I first joined the firm and look at what our principles or concepts were for running an organization, what made us successful, the first was vision. Obviously, [it's] what Bill and the partners had. The second was good, solid management. If anything, the firm Caudill Rowlett Scott back then was known for its management. We had good project managers and, in our business, good concepts of how you manage. The whole idea of programming came out of this need for management and organization.

Q: Programming as a separate activity is an integral part of project management.

A: Absolutely.

Q: And yet, if it's done successfully, all those changes come in the programming phase, not in design.

A: That's right. It separates those things that need to be looked at in a very logical way from those that need to be looked at in a very creative way. It gets the fundamentals clear so there's no question about their getting mixed up in design ideas. Programming, the squatters approach, these are all management techniques. The reality is in the profession. Nothing has happened in terms of process since these things were put into place by Caudill Rowlett Scott twenty to thirty years ago. The concept of construction management, of fast track—all these management concepts were on the leading edge, and the company is still respected for them. . . .

Maybe it goes back to management. We always had good designers. We had a diversity of designers who were team players: Norm Hoover, Frank Lawyer, Tiny Lawrence. All of them worked with project managers as team members, and there was a healthy respect for what each brought to the team. I'm convinced a lot of the awards we won came because we allowed our designers to be very free in a somewhat structured environment—structured enough that they didn't have to worry a lot about detailing. That combination is really what made us successful.

I think a lot of those fundamentals [were] lost over the years for one reason or another. It occurs to me that back in those days, when the partners came to a point where a decision had to be made, they would get in a room, shut the door, and argue it through until they came to an agreement before they left the room. I'm probably saying this wrong, but the idea was similar to the squatters: you don't leave until you've made a decision. They would stay in the room until they reached a decision. They may have disagreed, but [they] *agreed* to disagree. . . . They were of one mind, and the company moved forward.

Today [May 14, 1991] I see a lot of meetings with no conclusion reached at the end. People leave and go in seventeen different directions. Again, it's a management principle. Programming is part of it, squatters is part of it, [it's] a whole communication style. Caudill used to preach that a one-page memo is all you need. If it's more than that, you're wasting everybody's time.

JAMES THOMAS

I joined CRS on February 1, 1961. . . . My first encounter with [someone] I knew was from CRS was when they were looking for Christmas cards. [I was working for] Wells Design . . . a place that had all the very nicest, finest contemporary furniture and accessories . . . in town. I was really surprised because, as far as I could tell, CRS had sent the office boy over to select Christmas cards. I later found out that the "office boy" actually was Charles Lawrence, director of design—a very young-looking guy. . . .

My office at CRS to begin with was in a corner of the design department, which at that point was a total of seven people, including Jim Gatton and a guy named Jack Yarborough who did design development. There were also Don Wines and Frank Lawyer and, later on, Dan Stewart. I'm not sure who else. It was a wonderful little group. . . . We could have the entire design department and their wives to Caudill's house for a spaghetti supper and all fit comfortably in his little living room over in Memorial Bend. . . .

I had my [second CRS] office in the design room. I'm not sure what precipitated my having to move, but I ended up moving into a little area right behind Bill Caudill's office which had been sort of a woodshop. . . . So I was sitting outside the back of Caudill's office when he took over the architecture department at Rice, and I was one of only two Rice graduates in the firm at that time . . . so I had a wonderful time. He bounced things off me about what he was doing, and of course he changed Rice forever. It had been leaderless when my classmates and I went through it, and he brought everything he had with him to Rice. A lot of people in Houston felt he used Rice as a promotional tool for CRS, and I'm sure that's true. On the other hand, since I sat outside his door, I realized that he got there at four in the morning, and he did eight hours of work at CRS. Then he went to the Rice faculty club for a lunch meeting every day, and he left Rice about eight o'clock. So he gave 100 percent at both places, and I think we should all be forever grateful to him for doing that. . . .

For many years after I left CRS . . . I missed the kind of excitement that Caudill, Bullock, Lawrence, and Paseur generated. . . . They were leaders in a profession in which leadership is not that obvious. I think they would have been a great success at almost anything they had undertaken.

I understood Caudill had written a book on design that Bullock and Paseur had explained to him was not a good book and that Caudill then wrote a wonderful book . . . called *Architecture by Team*. . . . At his age and his accomplishments, I imagine that he wanted to be and had every prospect of being remembered as an architect. But I think he really wanted to be remembered as a great designer. I always felt sad for him in that I don't think that he ever understood that he, probably more than any architect, changed the way architecture was practiced. He and his team—and Bullock certainly [was] in the middle of all that. I don't think Bullock has ever gotten the kind of recognition he probably deserves. . . .

I worked for a firm that changed the practice of architecture. . . . Caudill sent me a letter after I left CRS in '75 or '76 about how he was going to be planning a grand reunion of all the people who had worked at CRS and had left. I wrote him back a smart-ass letter saying that I wanted very much to help with that and knew a lot of other people did, too, [but] that I didn't know whether we would be able to rent the Astrodome or not. A bunch of us had received the letter and had all been very enthusiastic about it, but nothing happened. Later, at some AIA function, we asked somebody from CRS whom we had all grown up with what happened. He said when someone on the management team had gotten wind of Caudill's letter he presented this picture of all the former employees driving up in their Porsches and the current employees still in their Volkswagen bugs. This would be an unfortunate contrast, so the idea was dropped. It was kind of sad, I think, that the reunion actually happened at the memorial tribute for Caudill some years later. . . .

Looking back at CRS, it seems to me that one of the ways they kept a lot of us there for not a whole lot of money was that they kept a sense of excitement about architecture in general and the architecture we were doing very specifically. The team concept, to me, was really valid. It was not BS; it really did work. We were a team; we worked together. The level of excitement about your work kept you going even when you were exhausted. You had been on a weeklong squatters and were having to come to the office even on Saturday and Sunday to catch up [just] so you could go on another squatters the following week. The level of excitement was high, and the work was constantly presented to the whole firm in the different reviews and presentations and pinup boards, the whole works. I think all of us who were there at the time, when it was small enough for communications to still be fairly clear, think of it as a wonderful period of our lives. . . .

When you worked at CRS, you had the sense that you were working on something important. It was not just make-work, not just a temporary facility, not space planning for some little office. You were doing hospitals, you were doing schools; you were doing things that helped people learn [and] that would make a contribution to their lives. You really felt that was a major part of your work, and CRS management did a great deal to emphasize that. . . .

I was told years ago that the pocket card was invented by Caudill because he could not remember anybody's name. That his secretary would type on the cards first thing in the morning everyone he was expected to meet that day so he could just refer to the card and find out who he was, in fact, talking to. Of course, I thoroughly enjoy that aspect of things because I cannot remember anybody's name.

The classic, I think, was Willie Peña, who was equally bad about names. When we got this job at Abington High School outside of Philadelphia, Willie went up and spent many weeks programming the project and building up the fact that the world's greatest project architect, Jim Gatton, was coming up to be in charge of the project. Jim tells the story that he was there for the school board meeting, at which he was to be introduced, and Willie got up and started talking.

Jim began to notice that Willie was maybe talking a little bit longer and was a little more florid than he might have been just to introduce him. He finally became aware that Willie couldn't remember his name! Finally, Willie turned to Jim and said, "Buddy-bub, introduce yourself to the board." I always had a great soft spot for all those people like me that cannot remember names.

STEVE PARSHALL

My beginnings with the firm started in a university setting. I studied at the University of Illinois, and both professors I knew had made a comment about CRS. Then I was fortunate that Bill Caudill spoke at the university . . . about *Architecture by Team* and those principles. That was probably my first real awareness of the firm. That must have been in 1973.

After that, in grad school, I had an opportunity for an AIA fellowship on research communication. I was to do a case study of three companies. One was . . . CRS. I picked the three firms because of their research reputation. I had a format: I wanted to investigate how practice reached out, brought in research information, and applied it in architecture. . . .

When I arrived at CRS, I had three interviews: one with Bill Caudill, one with Wallie Scott, and a third with Willie Peña. All of them, obviously, were extremely inspirational, but the one with Willie was when I recognized the function of programming as a mechanism to find information, whether directly from the client or from research literature, direct interview—however you could reach out and grab it, bring it in, then determine how it would pertain to problem seeking, problem solving. . . .

A lot of this was Willie's own intellectualism as a person who read [and] investigated. He was always balancing theory and practice. The whole evolution of the programming methodology came about through his reading of books by Osborne, Joya, et al.—theory—and then saying, "All right, here's the reality of day-to-day practice. Now how does that make sense?" . . . Willie was an intellectual craftsman—and not just him, but he's an example. He reached out. Of course, CRS fostered that kind of environment, and that's why the reputation was there and why I identified the firm for the case study.

After that opportunity, I finished the architectural curriculum and went into business school during what was probably the last great recession in the '70s. Maybe recession is justification—I was offered the opportunity for a joint degree in business, so I went into business school. . . . Business curriculum had a requirement that you do a six-month work-study [program]. I wrote to CRS and asked to be an intern. They replied they'd like to think about it, but the workload was such, etcetera, etcetera. I sent in my résumé anyway, and [I] believe it ended up on Charles Lawrence's desk.

I got a letter back, and the word used was "preceptorship." I didn't know what the word meant, but I learned that when Caudill was at Rice, they adopted the Preceptorship Program here [at CRS]. So I was invited to come down as a preceptee, and my preceptor was Charles Lawrence. On my first day—Charles is not a very tall fellow, and I'm not a very tall fellow—he put his arm around me, looked me in the eye, and said, "You and I are going to go a long way in this corporation!" So we had that in common. . . .

I did a little of everything—building models, etcetera. In September, Willie was going to write the second edition of *Problem Seeking*. Since I had been down there before, and Charles knew I had an interest in programming, he said, "Why don't you work with Willie as his research assistant on this next edition of *Problem Seeking*?" So I jumped into that. . . . When I first came to the firm, the programming group sat right next to the library. That's why it was named the Peña Library: because of the value Bill and Willie put on library and archival resources. . . .

The other thing I had done was keep a journal for the purpose of the preceptorship or internship. I began daily entries in the journal on everything: how the office was arranged, how people interacted, the daily storytelling, so to speak, when Willie would sit down or Wallie Scott. They were always telling stories, and these reinforced the principles of the practice. While working on the book, I was writing these observations.

The book itself [*Problem Seeking*] was a challenge. It began by Willie telling me to read an article—he would choose [it]—and give him an abstract. Then we moved into working with graphics. So I became a jack-of-all-trades. It was a very intense period—Bill and Willie working together. They pushed on each other very hard, and the intensity level was pretty dramatic. There was one incident that probably originated the famous comment about Peña's "Alamos." He had that personality. I won't say he was explosive, [but] he got upset with the graphic designers [that day].

There was a picture of John Focke in the *Problem Seeking* book. It's over the theory of the left brain [versus the] right brain. The picture was divided, and the graphic designer thought that was grotesque, and she refused to do it. There had been a series of days of avoidance, and Willie walked over [and] wanted to know how she was progressing, and this issue came up. There were other graphics they weren't satisfied with. Bill and Willie were very demanding. So Willie had one of his "Alamos." If you've been in the "White House" [CRS's headquarters on the West Loop], you know it's visually broken up from Bay 12 all the way down to Bay 6, so when he had that kind of eruption, it stopped the whole office. And then, shortly after, that graphics designer wasn't with the company anymore. I don't know whether she quit or was fired.

After an event like that, Bill, Willie, and some of the others had a way of going back and making up. [The] next day, Willie felt embarrassed and ashamed, and he came back in and reconciled. I guess I'm saying that one could see the balance in their personalities. It wasn't all drive, demands, emotion; there was finding the balance and putting things back in order. But Willie effectively shut down the office for a short period of time. . . .

Willie came to me and said the company wanted to start a stand-alone research function, and he [Caudill] needed an assistant. Caudill was going to hire somebody right out of college—a technologist—and he had all these specifications, but for some reason, he asked me. He knew I had an interest in research, but Willie said something like, "Caudill needs to be organized." That's a knack I have. It made a good team arrangement, [but] it was a turning point for Willie because he was letting go of somebody he had mentored: "You're not going to be a programmer anymore." It was almost a sacrilege to do something else. . . .

My work in research was essentially with another mentor: Caudill. Different demands, communication. Caudill would be at the airport or halfway there, think of something, and call you up: "One more thing; think about *this*." It was a great time. A time when Caudill was focused on transition of the firm. . . .

One of his ideas was a "brain drain." You think of losing talent to another company when you hear that word, but we used it to mean that we wanted to sit down [and] drain our brains, think up ideas. So Caudill set up these formats—one with Frank Lawyer, Jim Gatton; some for different markets like convention centers; one on design-build. "How do we design-*build?* We don't want to do Austin Company *design*-build." . . .

Looking back on it, I realized that these people have left the company. I think Caudill knew that would happen. . . . So it was truly a brain drain in the sense that before we lost the knowledge, Caudill got it on tape. He probed it, pulled it out of people. It was a two-edged sword: If they left, we had captured something; if they didn't, the process itself might have refocused a new interest for some of these individuals. Of course, right in the middle of that research era was Bill's death. After that, we kept the research going, and that's when Bullock started to come into it because he fostered the research, the next plateau. . . .

Wallie was the master of business development. . . . When Wallie did an interview, he put everybody at ease and made the whole team walk on water. He made me a hundred times what I thought I was. The long and short of it all is that I learned the selling process from Wallie—again, on-the-job training, mentorship, so to speak.

We got [the project with] Motorola, and then Intel called. Now Wallie was gone—my first interview! I started with the slides, and I'm going on—the client stopped me and said, "Would you tell me who CRS is?" I can [still] see it today. I know we're going to have some of our young people—just as I did—go out to sell at their first opportunity, and they'll forget the first thing. The first thing Wallie did was to say who we are and who he brought with him. You learn in the field, you were given the chance to make that mistake. Thank God nobody else from the firm was there [with me that day]!

Once you learn to sell, you're valuable. It's a different value to the company. You've got people who produce work, but that's very different from people who go out in the marketplace and close. There's a difference between marketers, sellers, and closers. I got it figured out: this closing stuff suddenly puts you in another class! In CRS, there's a demand environment for people, and we can't get enough of the people who are in demand. It's what I call the "Cloning Syndrome." Our marketers will come back and say, "I want so and so to go get in front of this client." Wallie was very good at that. He was also very good at listening to his clients, talking with his clients. He had a high anxiety level. Boy, if he felt uncomfortable, something was wrong, and he worked at it: "I don't feel good about this; it's not right." Very intuitive. . . .

These were highs; I remember a low. This was the Solar Energy Research Institute—my first or second [project] in the company. I was assistant programmer on this project. We put out the report, and there were errors in the map. At that time, we were still typing lists and lists of numbers on Wang computers that were just word processors.

I put out the report, [and it] went to the Solar Energy Research Institute in Denver. Of course, research scientists are very demanding clients. They are very precise. So the long and short of it was that a letter came back to the firm that this product was no good [because] there were numerical errors in the map. In fact, the letter was sent to Bill Caudill, and I remember it was about 7 A.M. one day. Caudill's work pattern was that he always went in at six or seven in the morning. I was sitting at my desk before the day started, and he walked over, had this letter. He said, "Here's your blank-blank job!" Now, that's a low, isn't it? Here's what he told me: He asked if I had ever heard his old plumber's wisdom: "You think you feel bad now? The old plumber's wisdom is you can never feel as bad as a plumber who has fallen into a sump pump." Instead of getting fired on the spot, he was picking me up and saying, "Go back in." I thought I had failed absolutely and was ready to jump off a bridge. . . .

The more I work on some of these government and military projects, the more I think these guys who came out of World War II—Caudill, Rowlett, Bullock, Peña—were very pragmatic people. That doesn't mean they weren't innovative, didn't have a better idea, didn't have contrarian points of view, but they were extremely disciplined educators and loved architecture. They got excited over a schoolhouse with poles and a lift slab. Wallie would talk about elegance, minimum use of means, of materials, etcetera. If anything, design in that aesthetic was their own aesthetic. . . .

I always believed we had very high standards in our practice. . . . As I've gone through my career there [at CRS], I've gotten into predicaments and would ask myself: "What would Bill Caudill have done?" I came to an interesting conclusion: First, he would not have gotten into this place!

A priest in college once talked about ethics and said, "Ethics tell you what to say no to." Very simple definition. If you watch Bullock, Peña, Caudill, there are very crisp things they say no to. It's not that they were not opportunistic, exploratory, eager, but they kept themselves out of trouble because they had a very clear code about what they did, why they did it, and the things they don't do. Some were just good business sense. . . .

A lot of things people assume are conventional wisdom, the CRS partners had contrary viewpoints about. Willie was talking about the commingling of programming and educational consulting. The educational consultant takes on a performance criterion and gives professional advice. They [partners] always kept their distance from that, saying, "We are not educators." Yet Rowlett was an educator, [and] Peña and Caudill knew more about education than most. In fact, Willie said that a lot of times we knew more about education than the educational consultant on a project. But they never called themselves educational or performing arts consultants. They had a very clear ethic about what they were and what they weren't. . . .

The one characteristic Bill brought to the company—I think Bullock had it on a different plane—was the ability to make a right turn or a 180-degree turn. Because of their personal will and strength, they could push something that had tremendous inertia. . . . Turning a company is different from maintaining its course.

RALPH CARROLL

I started to work under an old fellow named Jim Gatton. The first job he put me on was the Port Neches Elementary School, which Jim had designed. He was the designer, project manager, doing the working drawings. He set me up as draftsman and told me what to draw. It was during that period that I met a young fellow in the firm who would come in once in a while, bring[ing] in a couple of blue-line prints of this elementary school Jim had designed with red marks all over it. He said he had been down talking to the client, and they wanted to change things. I finally said, "Jim, who's this young pup who keeps telling me what to do with your design?" [Jim replied,] "Oh, Ralph, that's Wallie Scott!" . . .

Probably Bill is the one who said, "This is going to be 'architecture by team.'" That was the title of his book. Other architects were practicing the "ego architecture," but Bill decided we were going to involve the students, professors, administrators, and we were going to do architecture by team. It was a timely philosophy, and it more than affected our ability to get schools. I think it affected the mentality of the firm. Bill didn't set himself up as *the* ego designer. Tom wasn't *the* manager. Herb wasn't *the* manager. It was truly architecture by team. That, along with the desire to communicate quickly and efficiently with clients, the squatters idea, snow cards—good grief, how many firms use those techniques now? All of that was, I guess, a bit of a revolution, and it allowed the firm to evolve into something totally different. . . .

That's the only explanation of why CRS was different. It was at the founding—that dedication. Unlike so many firms that became father-daughter-son firms—that kind of thing was verboten at CRS, again because Bill and John decided, "We're not going to do that." So young architects starting with the firm had a chance to become real members of the firm and grow with it. They didn't have to worry about someone's son coming in and taking their job away many years later. That happened in many firms and proved to be disastrous for them, but that couldn't happen here. Bill, Herb, Frank, [and] Tiny were good at bringing young people along [and] educating them. Herb did a magnificent job in educating a project manager. Me! I'm not sure they consciously did it, but they did it. . . .

Every architectural project manager in the world, including me, has bemoaned the fact that designers just don't understand cost. They keep designing something that's over the owner's budget, [and] then we have to come back and redo at our cost, and that hurts. There's one guy with CRS, Tiny Lawrence, a super nice guy. If he could understand what the budget was and what it really meant, he would design to it. . . .

I remember once we had a project in Cook County: Moraine Valley Community College. The chief administrator wanted this to be an open-plan college, and the budget was very limited. We did the programming, and I talked a little to Tiny about it, and he said: "Ralph, I still can't grasp this. Can you put together some kind of palette, give me some parameters?" So I worked at a palette of material. Not just square footage or cubic footage, but some material we could work with that I got from Byron Stennis. The estimator said: "Yeah, you could do this. If you stay within the square footage, you can make it." I gave all this to Tiny and his team, and he did it. An open-plan community college was unheard of! This was open classrooms, not just offices. Tiny did a magnificent job, and it was completely within the budget as it all turned out. His ego didn't get in the way. If the only thing you could afford was mud and straw, he would do you a nice design of mud and straw. That was Tiny.

JACK DEBARTOLO

I went to high school in Waxahachie, a church school. Met a beautiful girl and I married her as soon as I could. It took me five years! I was an undergraduate student at the University of Houston. Got my bachelor of architecture there. Upon completion of that, Pat and I were getting married, and I applied for grad school at Columbia and went to New York. But I always wanted to come back to Houston. I only wanted to work for two firms in Houston. I had done my research. I was trying to get a job at Mies's office, but it was difficult because the salary was so poor, even though I was accepted.

I had read a lot about squatters. Tom Bullock will forget this, but I presented my thesis at the Houston Club when he was at the same speakers' table to present Jones Hall. He asked me to hold these boards while he spoke to them with his gentle way he had and his big cigar. I was totally humiliated but impressed. He told me to come see him sometime when I had got it together.

The open and interactive thinking of everybody was real stimulating. Before Bill wrote *Architecture by Team,* he used to give us papers on things he was thinking and speaking about—some of the early TIBs. I began to catch on that one and one could be more than two. I saw that as a global thing at CRS because no one was too selfish to give you their idea or tell you where to go, what to do. Help you out, so to speak, including the very senior people. I always felt very much part of whatever I wanted to be part of. If I didn't want to, I didn't have to. But if I wanted something, I could find it—just be willing to go ask.

My main contact after the first couple of years there was Bill. I got to work with him one on one, and that lit my fire. He always had time for me and gave me his very best. Frank [Lawyer] did, too. I poured in 100 percent and always got 100 percent back. There was never a limitation placed on me. I could do anything I was willing to do. I think about that a lot because a lot of people today say, "What do you want me to do?" I'd steal the bacon. I can remember taking Tully Stadium from Frank and redesigning parts of it. Frank would look at it with a strange expression like, "Why are you doing this? But it's pretty interesting." I always felt that openness that permitted you to think freely. . . .

JANE STANSFELD

[I worked at CRS] from '73 'til February '92. It was a long time, almost twenty years, but I always tell everybody I had two years off for good behavior! I had a daughter in 1979 and a daughter in 1983 and had about nine or ten months off for each one. That's one of the very good things CRS did for me. When I had my first daughter in 1979, there was really no law then about giving maternity leave and that kind of thing.

Q: There wasn't even a standard procedure.

A: Right. I had never been sick between '73 and '79, so they gave me every hour of sick leave I had accumulated during that period, all the vacation I had accumulated, so I had two or three months of paid time off. Then they just said, "Take as long as you want, and when you want to come back, there will be a job for you."

So I came back [and] did a little part-time work for three or four months. I thought it would be wonderful to work part-time: have a daughter to look after for half a day, then work half a day. After three or four months, I found I was really working a full day anyway, so [I] just went back full-time. CRS was so wonderful to accommodate everything I wanted to do. . . .

I had a daughter in 1983, [and] they were wonderful again. This time, we scheduled the project I was working on around my delivery date, so we finished construction documents about a week before I was due. After being off eight or nine months, Paul Kennon called me up and said: "Don't you think it's time you came back? We've got a nice project starting up. Would you like to come back *now?*" So I did. Without laws telling you what you must do—that's the way it ought to work.

Q: It was civilized.

A: It was very civilized, very nice. I thought CRS did a wonderful thing for me.

Q: How did you adjust, coming over from England? You must have gone to architecture school there.

A: I was registered in England when I came over. I was very English. In the first project team meeting we had after I joined CRS, we were all in the room together. The project architect had figured out who was going to do what, and he assigned [an area] to each person: "Cryer, you're going to do the fire stairs." "So and so, you're going to do the floor plans," etcetera. When it got round to me, all that was left was the exterior detailing. He looked at me and you could tell he was thinking, "My God, I'm left with a *woman*—an Englishwoman at that—to do the very important detailing!" He said, "I don't know what to do now," and I said, "I'm a registered architect, you [can] give me the roof."

In those days, CRS didn't have nearly so much close coordination with the team on the boards and what was going on in the field. Occasionally, the team from the field came in and told us what happened. Over the years, certainly in the '80s, CRS was getting more into exchange between the field and the production teams. I think that was a good thing.

Very early on when I was at CRS, we had a little group of us, and we used to give each other reading assignments. We'd read a certain book and all get together at lunch once a week and discuss the book we'd read. It was always books about architecture; the social impact of architecture and things like that. I think lots of people were doing that kind of thing in CRS in those days. We were, as Bill called us, "eggheads." He knew everything going on in the office, and he knew we had just been focusing on that particular topic, so he asked us to give him some ideas for a speech, which for me as a young junior in the office was just wonderful . . . that Bill Caudill would ask us for ideas. We gave him some ideas, [and] after the speech, as a thank you, he invited us all to lunch at his house. . . . So we all went. We all thought that was wonderful, unbelievable. We were so happy. That sort of thing doesn't happen nowadays. That charm and personality of CRS, you don't feel that [kind of] warmth anymore.[7]

I worked very closely with Paul on all the large projects: the IBM project, the 3M project, Chrysler Technology Center, the Bell Northern Research Facility, and International Bank of Georgia. I worked on a lot of projects with Paul. I had almost feelings of hate about working with Paul because he always excited you, always stretched you, and you always felt wonderful to be working with him. But you got worked so damned hard, pushed to the limit. Sometimes you began to doubt whether you had any family left.

As for Paul, he seemed to be able to split his time between family and work. His family didn't get much of him, and sometimes I felt my family didn't get much of me, either. But I enjoyed working with Paul a lot. He got as much as he possibly could from everybody. Everybody was a team member. I was a strong technologist and a manager, and he always pushed my technology and allowed me to give input on the technology and took it, which I thought was wonderful. I thought all the squatters we went to with him were big events. I really enjoyed the experience. . . .

My fondest memories of CRS were the incredible amount of thought. CRSers were thinkers and produced something that was better than they had ever done before. For example, picking a piece of glass for a building. I've seen other firms choose glass because it looks pretty, [or] because the color is right. But at CRS we'd pick a piece of glass because of its performance, because of the light that went through it, because of all the things that related to that piece of glass. Looking back at the IBM project, the last one I worked on at CRS in a big way, we had the largest amount of heat mirror glass ever installed in the U.S. Why? Because it was the best deal on glass at the time, and it looked good.

We always thought in-depth about what we were doing and not superficially. That is one of the things I even miss now.

■ CHAPTER 13

PARTNERS

■ TIB: 15 OCTOBER 1982

A CRS alumnus and a bit of a philosopher says: "THERE AIN'T NO BICYCLES BUILT FOR TWO IN THIS BUSINESS."

CRS was founded on the team concept—working together toward the same goals. But often each team member has his own perception of what the goal should be: award winning projects, projects with utility first and aesthetics second, projects that come in every time below the construction cost but above the profit goals.

How do we get more than one on the bicycle? The trick is to get a consensus among the team members. The goal then becomes an award winning project that hasn't sacrificed utility for aesthetics, that was built within the budget, that won't drive the user into bankruptcy to own and operate, and that brings a profit to CRS.

■ The original partners—Bill Caudill, John Rowlett, Wallie Scott, Willie Peña, Tom Bullock, Ed Nye, Charles Lawrence, and Herb Paseur, now referred to as the founders—not only got CRS off the ground, but also provided much of the firm's leadership for many years. The eight were the glue that held the firm together for most of its existence.

The original eight in 1966. ***Left to right:*** **Wallie Scott, Herb Paseur, Tom Bullock, Charles Lawrence, Ed Nye, John Rowlett, Willie Peña, and Bill Caudill.**

INTERVIEWS

PHIL WILLIAMS

I think first, it was the duality with Bill and John. They were a very complementary pair. Bill had this notion of how to create with this burst of energy and really get a problem solved, [and he could] do it *with* the client, creating a kind of fervor about it that was very productive, instantaneous, and explosive. John was a patient, fatherly kind of guy—I guess even when he was young—who saw the long-term, understood the value of indirect promotion and building relationships. So he had a steady, long-term, balancing effect on Bill's spontaneity. . . .

The tripod became the firm's geometric representation of stability with the three basic factors. But then Willie entered into it and added the thoughtful, analytic, problem-solving approach, an almost by-the-numbers kind of approach in sharp contrast to Bill's spontaneity. So we had Bill's spontaneity, John's long-term view, and Willie's attempt to be analytical—all of which made a very, very stable, creative firm. As long as those three had the environment where they could exploit those talents and pass them on to the next generation and make the next generation feel responsible for them, it was really an ongoing, productive outfit.

WES HARPER

Caudill was such a salesman. I think it was natural for him to sell ideas. It was his natural way of relating to the market. For example, when you return from a trip, the first thing you do is write a letter to everyone you dealt with—each school board member, the superintendent. I think that was just Caudill's way of doing things, and he insisted that we all do it. He had a perspective and ability—others would flag on it. In the Oklahoma City office, we'd start doing our own thing and not be as good about client relations. All of a sudden, after he came up for a visit or some contact was made, that practice would be regenerated. So I think a lot of that energy came from Caudill himself. Of course, it got translated by Bullock and the others. . . .

This candid shot of Bill Caudill was taken by client George Zimbel while they were participating in a tour of schools sponsored by EFL in 1962.

John was kind of low pressure, laid back. He seemed to have the ability to go out and talk to school board members who were farmers and relate to them where they were at. He would drive his old car out there—not a big, expensive car—[and] he would talk to them across the fence. He had the ability to make people at that level feel comfortable.

Part of the firm dynamic was that they had this strong, central kind of trust: team, philosophy, research, being the best, publicizing themselves, having a national image. At the same time, they had a lot of people who were low key and could relate to clients at many different levels of expectation.

There was a story told about the University of Miami job at Coral Gables. There were five or six architects—I've forgotten their names—invited to come and make a presentation for that project. One of the big-name architects came just before John on the schedule of interviews. The story went he [the big-name architect] came into the board room and made a fifteen-minute power presentation: "If you hire me, I'll do you a building that will get the attention of everybody in the country, but I've got to be on a plane in fifteen minutes." And he was out the door and gone. John Rowlett came in right after and said, "I'm here, gentlemen, for as long as you want. Here's our firm's work. What do *you* want to talk about?" He gave them the feeling [that] if they wanted to talk all day and all night, he was available, and he got the job. . . .

One thing that really impressed me: We invited Caudill to come back up here to the school [Texas A&M]—must have been in the late '70s, a year or two before he died.[1] We invited him to come up here and talk to our students. By then, I had seen some of the articles in the magazines about the firm: its philosophy, where they came from, etcetera. Old Caudill talked to those students in his very enthusiastic, convincing way. He talked about . . . team versus prima donnas, doing good architecture, about drawing and graphics being an important part of quality, about design isn't everything, specialization.

Honest to God, it's as if he could have made the same speech in 1955 that he made in 1979! That guy never changed his tune. He was born understanding that, and while it has gone through variations and increased [in] understanding, the basic philosophy and approach has remained exactly the same from the very beginning. I was really impressed with that: the sheer determination to do it, and this huge organization of people with the *same* goal. That's a pretty astounding thing to do, particularly when it's ideas you are producing. You're not making cars or some [other] product.

Obviously, CRS architecture has a certain institutional trim. Maybe it didn't generate a following like Michael Graves or somebody like that, but in that sense, I think it was very successful. As a human organization, I think they pulled off something really unique, [and] I appreciate having been a small part of that.

WILLIE PEÑA

When he [Bill] first came into our sophomore classroom/laboratories [at Texas A&M], he was brand-new—just graduated from MIT, had to buy new clothes. He bought some outlandish clothes with a big hat—like Frank Lloyd Wright—big trousers. And he was stuttering. He couldn't get three words out because he was nervous.

The class got together—Dan Perkins and a whole bunch of the guys—and said: "We've got to go to Mr. Langford and tell him to get us another prof.[2] This is going to be terrible!" He was really bad nervous. Nobody did anything about it, though—or if they did, I didn't know about it. The next time, he was a lot better, and subsequently, we got used to it. . . .

In 1955, when he did the Edward R. Murrow show, he asked Mr. Murrow at the beginning for a little bit more time: "you see, I stutter." He didn't stutter that much. There was a class of stutterers in Chicago who were just by chance watching this TV program with a stutterer on. It was an inspiration to them, and they wrote to tell him that if he could do it, they could do it.

Bill never blamed anyone for it. He didn't blame the schools or say they hadn't taught him that, this, or the other. He didn't blame his mother. He acknowledges her as having developed his character. In effect, he got his drive from his mother: "Bill, get yourself a paper route," "Bill, get yourself a corner to sell papers," that kind of thing. She had the work ethic very much in her and poured it into Bill. . . .

In every firm, there has to be a good guy. John was ours. He was good at promoting. [He was always] charming [and] gracious to our clients. He believed in friendships [and] kept up his contacts with school people. He was our first contact with educators. So John was into promotion, but from the very beginning, we acknowledged Bill as our leader. . . .

TOM BULLOCK

The people by 1955, having stepped on each other, in certain ways duplicated efforts. I think it became more apparent we'd have to specialize. I would

Bill Caudill, the stuttering young man who wanted to hide himself at the rear of some drafting room, found himself up front, effectively communicating with large client groups such as this one at Colorado College in 1961.

have to stay with management, which didn't disturb me at all because I didn't know anything about it, so [I] didn't have anything to be scared of. . . . So we specialized in things. [We] weren't all around critiquing everybody's designs. . . .

John was really my teacher and the one who gave me tremendous opportunities, like the move to Oklahoma where he shoved the responsibility at me, delegated a lot.

Bill would say: "Bullock, don't show me your analysis. I don't want to see that. What do you *think,* Bullock? *Tell* me." He had an almost unbelievable confidence in what I thought. For that reason, he scared the hell out of me because you're never right all the time. He backed me all the way, and I think there was a bond there; bonding with our partnership, throughout the partnership. It was unbelievable! . . .

Bill Caudill, ***left,*** **and Wallie Scott about 1953.** *Photo courtesy Gulf Photo.*

Wallie was the Roger Staubach of architecture on interviews. Wallie is the coldest fish in the world on meeting someone for the first time, but he can walk into a directors' meeting and warm them up like nobody's business. He was a winner. He would tell you, too. Losing is the lowest point you can have—primarily losing a job, an opportunity, a project we thought we could really do something about. It's not just getting a job. . . .

The nice thing about it [going public] was we had Bill Caudill, Willie Peña, and the original partners—along with others—still working the design business we always had, so Herb and I . . . could separate ourselves from the traditional business and "go to school" on going public, which we did. Herb and I, as architects . . . didn't have to worry about what Bill, Wallie, Willie, et al. were thinking. . . . Nor did they have to figure out what we were doing. We were so well acquainted with each other, it worked. . . .

I was fortunate in meeting Herb in 1955. He was hired as a designer. About 1961, I nominated him for a general partnership because he was so good at client service, and in 1965 or '66, I recommended that he take on my job as CEO—or COO [chief operating officer] at that time—of the company. Within four or five years, he convinced me and led the movement to go public. That was the way we should expand: not only the traditional way of more offices and services, but expand our business.

In '71, he became the president/CEO of the public corporation, and I joined him as chairman of the board on a full-time basis. At that time, I didn't realize Herb had a long-range plan. He felt—and I think he still does—that a CEO of any business tends to run out of steam after ten years, and I believe he set his sights on that because in 1981 he decided to retire—ten years later. In that ten years, he was in the forefront of all the acquisitions and our changed ways of doing business.

He was the kind who would knuckle down and do whatever you needed and [do it] very well. . . . When the need for client service arose, he took over that job. When I needed somebody to take over after ten years as managing partner, he took that on. . . . He's not a person who makes snap decisions, but once he makes up his mind, that's it. Herb decided that we ought to look at the kind of growth we would need in the '70s, and I credit him with our going public in 1971. Herb and I were really a two-man partnership separated from the rest of the company for ten years in a downtown Houston office. . . .

Herb Paseur as the firm's top executive in 1974.

[Bill and Wallie] were the only two partners besides Herb and I who were on that board [the public corporation's board of directors]. Bill recognized major change in our life [and] also recognized that it provided liquidity for the original founders, but he would not put that first. Bill would go hungry, go without any resources to keep architecture number one. But he saw the opportunity as well to expand the business. . . .

TINY LAWRENCE

John seemed to have stability and an air of sterling character and understanding of the profession. . . . All of this made him very wonderful as an emissary for CRS.

Wallie was a balanced professional in that he had design power, and he knew how to put a building together. And he was good with clients and their presentations, so he had a nice, even keel. He was probably a person who could have gone out and been a one-man office and done very well.

Willie is probably the purest of all of this from the standpoint of architectural morality and theory, and he's probably the only intellectual in the whole bunch. So he brought maybe a deeper, philosophical look into who we were and where we were going and why and brought us up sharp when we sort of wandered from the path he thought we ought to be heading in.

Tom is—it's strange, but I think of Tom in the same categorical series as Bill because he was not as strong a designer as Bill, but [he possessed] all the other aspects of having a deep insight into the facets of our profession and how you make things work and looking ahead to where we should go. Tom had a capability that Bill didn't have: consistency, which is kind of interesting. He seemed to me to have the ability to generate spirit in the firm and make the group feel like where they were going and how they were getting there was fun and exciting. And my perception is that he could do that better than any of the rest of them. . . .

Herb . . . you've got to love somebody who's got design in his blood sitting there making business decisions.

Me? I think of myself as a designer who is capable of conceiving and developing and selling a strong piece of design. . . .

We did have, I think, a rather common core of ethical and moral values. . . . And all of us enjoyed music in various forms. Willie loved classical music. Willie, I guess being the intellectual, loved all kinds of music, but he preferred classical. And Wallie and Tom and I loved music out of the big band era and on into the '50s. Bill liked music and played. Of course, Wallie played saxophone; Tom played the trumpet. No, it's the other way around: *Wallie* played trumpet.

It certainly involves teamwork if you play. I don't play an instrument, so I wouldn't fit in this mode. . . . And Bill was from a different era, but he liked jazz music from an earlier age. He played piano and, I think, trumpet at one time. But I think there was some easy camaraderie because of that. I mean, when we would get together socially, [we would] enjoy music and play the hell out of it as loud as our wives would let us, and act silly. And I think that helped a certain amount of bonding as a team.

FRANK LAWYER

Peña is a marvel. . . . a great communicator. . . . . Clients loved him because he had a great sense of humor, worked hard, got *them* to work hard, and they loved it and felt they had some input.

Ed Nye . . . [is] a very solid engineer. I never went to him with a ques-

From left: **Ed Nye, Wallie Scott, and Willie Peña in 1957.** *Photo courtesy Roland Chatham.*

tion he couldn't in some way find an answer for. He wouldn't put you off. He would stop what he was doing and work with you. . . . He was very quiet, never looked for attention, never did anything to get attention. He was sure a solid person, and the firm needed his maturity and good thinking. . . .

JONATHAN KING

Wallie was an immensely likable person, very interested in money. He loved selling jobs, loved the notion of money coming into the firm, loved the stock exchange, loved making money on it. He was interested in everything about money except spending it. . . . He just had no interest in what money can buy. [His] only interest in money [was] as an abstract, intellectual thing.

He was a person who related to common people—not to use the word in a condescending sense. We would go into a selection committee meeting, and Wallie would look around the room, and they all liked him. . . . You couldn't help believing Wallie Scott. . . .

By the time I got to CRS, John [Rowlett] was sort of declining in influence in the firm, and his interest in architecture was declining. He did a lot of things like play poker with school board members, promote jobs. . . . He was the consummate gentleman. [He once] told me over several martinis that if he hadn't been able to sell work, they all would have starved to death long ago at CRS.

[Tiny Lawrence] was the finest designer at CRS. [He had] an incredible sense of detail. I think he definitely exceeded Caudill. . . .

By the time I knew Tom, he was the president of CRS. It didn't make a lot of sense to me when Bill brought this meek fellow in [to my office at EFL] who never said anything, and [Bill] said, "This is our president." Tom sat there, and Bill talked. But he was the president, and I guessed the board of directors had elected him. He had changed a lot by the time I went to work for CRS and hasn't been quiet since!

I felt when I was there, he was also the most discerning critic of CRS design in the office. . . . Sometimes, he would come into the juries we had on our projects and lambaste us for doing second-rate Perkins and Will work or Bruce Goff look alikes. He could always kind of get into the nerve center, the problems of buildings. He could look at those buildings and tell us we were straying from the CRS line and doing third-rate work: "Throw the damn thing out and start over!" I always thought he was smarter about that than anybody else in the place with the possible exception of Herb Paseur, [who was] also a pretty good designer.

CHUCK THOMSEN

I would say in the later years, Bill became a guru, a father figure, sort of an inspirational person who stood for what was noble in the profession. And Tom and Herb became the business leaders of the company, with Tom on the entrepreneurial side creating acquisitions or new companies, which Herb would have to figure out how to make effective. . . .

Herb was kind of the transitional player between the original innovators who had these great ideas and delivered on them and the larger company that was led by a person who deployed the resources of the organization to those people who would continue doing those things, the creative organization. . . .

He was a man of extraordinarily good judgment who never let his ego get in the way. He never got in a situation where he felt like he had to compete with his people. Most of the rest of us have to resist being a star. . . . Herb was perfectly happy to sit quietly and not say a thing and decide whether this person or that person or that person ought to be supported in their efforts. He didn't much care what the efforts were as long as they were professional, profitable, and legal.

I was trying to put together a presentation—one of my first presentations to the investor community. I didn't know what I was doing. I went after it like I was trying to sell work to a client because that's what I had been doing for ten years. Herb looked at all that and said, "Chuck, the more you tell somebody, the less control you have over what they remember." That's the way he managed. [He was] a man of few words that you tended to remember. . . . You never questioned whether or not he was telling you the truth. Sometimes, Herb didn't tell you everything, but you knew what he *did* tell you was the truth as he believed it to be. That was characteristic of all the partners.

Bill was fair. [He] had a lot of integrity, but was very open—he wouldn't keep things to himself. . . . I remember when his first wife [Edith] died. Everybody called to ask, "What can I do?" He wrote a memorandum to everybody in the company saying, "Everybody is bothering me about 'What can I do?' There *isn't* anything you can do. My grief is severe. The nicest thing you can do is let me work. Work with me just like you always have." Now, here's a guy who puts his guts out on the table.

He got his AIA Fellowship and Gold Medal by just being himself. Bill was very much that way. So when there were personality conflicts in the company, Bill would run and drag them out in the sunlight for people to examine. We used to tease him about being Mary Worth. The same thing over at Rice: Bill Lacy would call him "Mother": "Be careful, Mother will get after you for that!" Bill mothered us in every way. He cared about us as individuals. [He] wanted to help our careers, advised us—kick you in the butt and then pick you up and dust you off. He'd be abrasive and stimulating on one side, and [be] supportive emotionally, financially, [or] whatever on the other side. He was all those things. He was the glue that stuck the company together, and I think Tom learned that.

Tom was more political than Bill, a little more opaque in some ways than Bill. Sometimes, you really didn't know what was going on in Tom's head, but he had that same recognition. [I] don't know whether he learned it from Bill or whether it was intuitive, instinctive.... Call it both, mutually supportive. He had this clear recognition that the way you build a great company is by building great people, and proceeded to do just that. . . . Some big things I would credit Tom with is having a lot of vision of what the world might be like, the country might be like, how to arrange a board of fine people, how to take a company public, how to start up a new business, how to go national and international. It was Tom who wanted to move the company to Houston from Bryan. I think Tom, more than anybody, was the change maker.... He really was the visionary of the company.... I think more often than not, Tom was the instigator and Herb the implementer.

The CRS leaders were kids out of small-town, middle-class families with stars in their eyes [and] almost a naive belief in their ability to do great architecture. They knew [that] in order to succeed they would have to have a better idea, a better way of doing things because they weren't going to get any work from their fathers' friends on the golf course.

In CRS, the way you shot down an idea in a meeting was to say, "There's nothing new about that." It's part of the fiber of the company to imply that if you haven't figured out a better way to do things, it wasn't a good idea....

Bill used to say he ran CRS like a school and ran his school [Rice] like a firm. The truth of the matter was that he did try to get some hard-nosed management aspects of running an operation in at Rice, and he did try to get some aspirations and vision and principles plugged into CRS.

RAY BAILEY

I think it was one of those rare combinations where if personalities among the core group were in conflict, it was never open. It seemed like a very good group that kind of reinforced each other and looked at the big picture....

JOE DENMAN

It must have been something like 1977 when Tom made contact about joining the [CRS] board, and I told him I just couldn't at that particular time. But in 1980, he made a second contact, and in May of 1980, I did go on the board.... I'm not sure who made the motion for me to join the board, but behind the scenes, Tom Bullock had told everybody, "Don't *anybody* second the motion." So I'm sitting there, and no one seconded the motion! I'll never forget it. A few years later, we pulled the same trick on a friend of ours.

BOB DOUGLASS

I had turned in my first expense statement. . . . after countless squatters, etcetera, and it ran into the thousands of dollars. I first gave it to Jim [Falick], and he actually got pale when he saw this. He held it like this and said, "Come with me." He marched ahead, I marched behind, this paper in front, down to Herb's office. I think Jim put it on the desk and said, "What do you want to do about *this?*" Herb looked at it and said, "Pay it, of course. Bob, you need to learn to turn these in on time. We do it every other week. I want you to write a thousand times, 'I will turn my expense account in on time.'" He handled it wonderfully well. Jim expected me to get fired, I'm sure.

We had just gotten this new kind of typewriter called an MTST—the forerunner of the word processor. So I went down and had whoever ran that machine cut me a thousand "I will turn my expense statement in on time" assignment and gave it back to him. He laughed about it.

JIM FALICK

There are lots of stories about Wallie: He's been the guy in the back room who is technically good; they would never let a client see him and locked him in a closet; he became a partner because he had a car—all sorts of funny stories. On the other hand, Wallie went to interviews.... [and] said, "I'm the 'S' in CRS," and he'd always smile. He had a stock of jokes and was the warmest individual you could imagine, and everybody liked him. He was totally unknown in the firm, but you could put him in front of a board, and they just *liked* him.... [C]ertainly half or more of my success was due to traveling with him, listening to him, and watching him, for I realized what it took....

Whatever anybody's titles were, it was Tom who ran the firm. Whether he ran it by ownership or, as I think, by influence, the power of his personality and what he wanted to achieve and was willing to do to other people for not wanting to.

LEWIS MAY

[T]hese people were fairly secure in their own personal ids and egos. I know Caudill pretended not to be, but they were possessed, they were driven; they took risks; they changed models; they changed roles.

JANE STANSFELD

I swam with Bill a lot, particularly during the time I was having my daughters. I used to swim at lunchtime, and he used to swim at lunchtime at the Dads' Club. Bill would swim his lap, put his little pine needles up—he had them all laid out neatly in a row so he knew how many laps he had done. He would swim another lap and move another one. He was a very slow swimmer.

I remember hearing one of the other ladies in the pool—there were usually quite a few people in the pool—talking to him about architecture. She thought architects were crazy, etcetera. She was obviously having something done to her house. Bill never let on he was *the* big man in one of the biggest architectural firms in town. He just let her go on and on in this tirade about architecture. I was swimming in the next lane laughing my head off. He was like that. He could talk to anybody and always brought himself to the level of the person he was talking to. [He] never adopted a tone of superiority. That lady was talking about architecture, and he was right down with her, never lorded it over her at all.

JOHN STAMBAUGH

[For Bill, writing] was a method of expression. He felt so many things, and his inability to express himself at times . . . rather than try to stumble through words—which sometimes didn't come easy—he could write and distribute them. Not that he didn't talk a lot; he talked a lot! Everybody thought his stuttering was a personality trait, a positive thing, not a negative. . . .

Just being around him would stimulate you. . . . Hardworking—worked 'round the clock many times. When we went to South America, he sat behind me [in the airplane] because he didn't want to leave the lights on while I was trying to sleep. We left at midnight from Mexico City, [and] he spent the whole plane trip to Lima, Peru, writing his concepts of what we saw in Mexico City. He worked all night back there. That's the way he did things: so involved with whatever he did and excited by it.

John was a gentleman, a real quiet, reserved personality. No doubt, he recognized Bill's superiority in all regards but tried to complement him as best he could. . . . He was a special assignment person. They sent him on foreign and domestic trips to do things for the firm.

Herb was soft but strong. He could implement things well. [He had] good business sense, good judgment. He studied figures, didn't just look at them superficially. He was profit oriented.

He controlled costs. [He was] very strong, he and Tom both. [It's] hard to choose between the two. Tom has a little more compassion, more understanding of people individually. Tom is so sensitive to people, and Herb lacked that sensitivity but [was] equally qualified in all other regards. . . .

On the wall of Stambaugh's office is this statement: "It was my childhood friend, John Stambaugh, who warned us back in 1950 that we could no longer operate as four self-minded dilettantes. John was a team man. He played third base with me in school, played a virtuoso tenor sax with me in those dance bands.

"'You remind me of four kids in four separate canoes gliding beautifully about in four directions on a smooth lake,' he charged. He could have been more charitable and said 'four prima donnas,' which we really felt we were. Members of our team had not yet learned to say *we.*

"Stambaugh posed this question: 'What will happen when the water gets rough?' And it did, we had many storms. Thanks to the counseling of Stambaugh, who has given us management and financial advice from the very beginning of the firm, we tied our canoes together—legally and organizationally—and were able to weather the storms. He also helped us create a team dedicated to common goals, stemming from a common philosophy. Not just a firm of individuals sharing a common office—John taught us to say *we.*"

Bill Caudill sent that to me and had it put into its present form there. It was a very fine thing for him to say. I guess that was the way I felt at the time, but they certainly performed as a team.

TOM BULLOCK

[After] Bill went to Corning, [we] had a hell of a time getting him to come back to Texas, even to Bryan, his home here in College Station, and particu-

John Rowlett, *seated at center,* reaches retirement in 1973. He is flanked by Caudill, *left,* and Scott, *right.* Standing, *from left,* are Nye, Paseur, Lawrence, Bullock, and Peña.

larly Houston. He didn't like the idea of coming to Houston. He'd been offered the deanship at Cornell, [which was a] big deal—Oklahoma boy from Texas going to Cornell. [It was a] big temptation for Bill, and he seriously considered it. . . . Bill had other opportunities when he was in Corning.

Earlier I said Bill was agreeable to letting some of us decide whether we would sell the company and him to Perkins and Will and all of that. Bill wasn't in the mood to give us much say on this, as I remember. I did play a strong part in convincing Bill to come back to Texas. I don't know whether

I pulled John Stambaugh's string at the time; might have to convince Bill. I don't think he would have played a real strong part because Bill could talk him into what *Bill* wanted to do. My point at the time was that we needed Bill Caudill to do what we needed to do, the things Bill said we should do. For Bill to leave—it wasn't abandonment, that wasn't it. [I] didn't want him to feel guilty, but damn, there was a better future in CRS than there was at Cornell. That was the key, and it had to be sold on that basis, not just that "We need you," but "There is a better future for Bill Caudill in CRS." We did that, and I remember when Bill made that decision, he did move directly to Houston—never moved back to Bryan–College Station.

We had an office at 3400 Montrose, [a] tall building. We were on about three floors with pieces on each floor. . . . So Bill came to work in that environment. Tiny Lawrence, Bill, and I bought houses out in a newly developed area out on Memorial called Memorial Bend. We shared a ride every now and then. I had some of my hottest arguments with Bill after he moved back to Houston on the subject of "Why the hell did I come to this place?" I had to continue convincing him because there was a time when we moved to Houston that the business was in bad shape. We didn't have a lot of business and [we] had made that big leap. We were all suffering, all ready to say, "Why in hell did we allow this to happen?" So there was a little insecurity there on all our parts; certainly Bill was part of that. [It was] not just me, though I did play a big part in convincing Bill—twisting his arm, hitting him on the head, anything to keep him—because without Bill playing a role in the continuing development of CRS, it would have been very difficult.

Now within a couple of years, he went to Rice University as dean—full-time there, full-time with CRS, really half-time each. But that gave him the fulfillment I think he was looking for if he had gone to Cornell. He wasn't looking for the job as dean. He was a known quality at that time, and word had got out that Bill was in Houston, and I think the architect alumni at Rice played a part in pointing the new president, [Kenneth] Pitzer, in Bill's direction to give him that job.

Q: What if Bill Caudill hadn't been part of it at the beginning but everybody else had?

A: A number of us played the role of being the glue for the company. I took credit for it just from my position. Bill did, too, and others. We're all "sticky" people and stuck together. If Bill had not been there, it would certainly have been completely different. I think many of us would have left. When I was in Oklahoma City, I had a chance to spin off with some local people. I didn't seriously consider that, but all of us would have had that opportunity and probably would have done it.

He was a great person, a magnet—with kids, adults, all of that. No question about it: Any number of us could have left, and the firm would have changed some, but it would not have disappeared. I think if Bill had left, it would have disappeared. Let's put it that way. If Bullock had left, it would have changed, but it would not have disappeared.... We were great; he was greater.

He was the kind of guy who said: "Don't ever say anything bad about a client. I don't care *how* bad he might be, don't ever say it. If you do, you've got to put it in writing and send it to him."

He would come and sit at the Rowlett Lectures [at Texas A&M]—we started those in '78 or '79 when John died. Bill went to every one of them. He'd sit in the audience and never say a word. People didn't know he was there. What a hell of a loss! This guy could just get up and say something and all of the sudden, zip, and everybody would be listening. He had a great ability to do that.

Also, the fact that Bill had great trust in his partners, great trust.... My point is that we had a true democracy in our company.

■ CHAPTER 14

AFTER THE BREAKUP

One wonders if the profession will ever see a CRS again. Rarely a day slips by without me wondering how it all happened in the hopes I might recreate at least a portion of it in my own office. I know, of course, that the answer lies not in a single person, but in a team.

As deeply rewarding as were my fifteen years in the remarkable CRS environment, questions persist. . . . What more is there to say about a place that generated such a passion for humanizing architecture? Can an architectural firm be so fundamentally committed to change as was CRS and yet survive? Or is the legacy of the theory, the processes and the culture the ultimate form of survival?

To paraphrase what is still the best architectural mission statement I have ever encountered: we DID create some good architecture; in various ways, we profited enormously from the experience; and we certainly had a great deal of fun along the way.

—James M. Wright, A.I.A., principal,
Page Southerland Page,
Washington, D.C., 15 Feb 2001

■ The end of CRS began, it could be argued, in 1983. Alarmed by the petering out of the Saudi building boom, the holding company CRS Group that year acquired J. E. Sirrine, a South Carolina process engineering firm that operated mainly in the United States—a market that CRS had shifted away from during the years of dynamic overseas growth. The combined corporation, CRS Sirrine—later CRSS—was more an engineering than an architectural firm in terms of both staff size and income.

One of the many subsidiaries established by CRS, CRS Capital, developed into an independent power company specializing in cogeneration plants—a line of business that was even farther removed from architecture. It was hoped that those activities, and the other acquisitions discussed in previous chapters, would give CRS a bright domestic future.

The most significant outcome, however, was that within a few years, the parts became more valuable than the whole. The new financial reality could not long be ignored. Starting in the summer of 1994, CRSS began to divest itself piece by piece. The architecture group was sold that year to St. Louis–based HOK, a global firm that had collaborated with CRS on schools in the early days and later on work in Saudi Arabia. Sirrine was sold to Jacobs Engineering in Pasadena, California. So was CRSS Constructors, the thriving construction management group. The independent power group CRSS Capital was swallowed up by U.S. Tractebel, a subsidiary of the Tractebel Group, a Belgian company that develops independent electric and gas projects. The firm that had evolved disappeared, although components of it remained active in the design and construction world. In fact, CRSS Constructors and CRSS Capital have each continued to use the CRSS name.

So the story came full circle: CRSS, a company that aggressively established or acquired subsidiaries during its rise to prominence, was itself consumed in the marketplace, leaving behind only its one-time subordinates.

There is, however, another way to look at this. For although CRS no longer exists as an independent and functioning firm, it left a legacy of ideas and processes that continues to influence the way architecture is practiced. From the very beginning, what set CRS apart from other firms was its devotion to the process of architecture and construction. Caudill and Rowlett and their later colleagues were never primarily stylists. They were idea people, interested not only in the esthetics of the buildings, but in the best methods for finding out what problems the building must solve, and in designing processes for addressing those problems.

"Problem seeking," or programming, was CRS's biggest single idea to influence the profession. Before CRS, architects coined phrases such as "form follows function," but it remained for CRS to do the hard work of figuring out exactly what all those functions were and how they could be effectively accommodated. In any complex project, there are multiple functions, goals, and conditions that must be understood and woven into a coherent design. Over a period of many years, CRS devised state-of-the-art methods for organizing the process and propounded the use of those methods by the entire profession.

The intuitive side of architecture was buttressed by a rational system that helped designers avoid producing arbitrary or incomplete solutions to their clients', and society's, problems. Without the techniques that make up programming, it is hard to imagine how architecture could have dealt with the ever more complicated requirements of buildings in the twentieth century. A designer cannot sit down at a drafting board or a computer and produce a workable hospital or a major educational facility without first having the needs well investigated and sorted out. It took the persistence of CRS to develop the capabilities that contemporary society demanded.

The firm was a leader and innovator, pushing the design and construction industry toward construction management, fast-track scheduling, and better ways of working. In an editorial tribute, *Architectural Record* observed that CRS insisted on giving its clients "the best functioning solutions to the program that commitment and research could provide; construction costs in line with budget; and a building that would be ready on schedule."[1] But CRS did more than that: It presented the methods for achieving those results to the profession as a whole. The processes that CRS pioneered have been widely adopted and absorbed. It is interesting to look around the architectural profession today and discover many firms running their projects through a "studio" kind of organization under a core of three people representing design, management, and technology. This is, of course, Bill Caudill's "troika," which brought divergent talents and concerns together with the aim of producing well-balanced results.

Nor was CRS a "form giver." It was not a Le Corbusier or a Frank Lloyd Wright or a Louis Kahn. But the need for form givers is limited. What is needed more than a proliferation of new forms is a way of producing large quantities of good architecture, and that was CRS's forte. The firm knew how to organize and gear up for a mass society that required large numbers of well-designed but not overly expensive buildings quickly. Although it won scores of awards and honors, CRS never aspired to be a "boutique" or "high design" firm. It wanted to produce good architecture consistently and to devise effective means for doing so. This it succeeded in doing.

John Rowlett died in 1978. Bill Caudill, the firm's intellectual leader, died in 1983. He was posthumously awarded the AIA's Gold Medal in 1985. Wallie Scott died in 1989. Other early CRS leaders were still living as the twenty-first century began, but they had stepped down long ago. Tom Bullock retired as chairman of CRSS in 1989, and the last design leader of great stature was Paul Kennon, who died unexpectedly in January, 1990. Kennon had not

It was a CRS tradition to take a group picture each year. This photo was taken in 1970 when CRS had approximately 240 people in three offices. By 1983, the CRS Group had grown to thirty-one hundred people with offices around the world.

groomed anyone to succeed him. He had trouble bringing others up to the point at which they would compete with him, so when Kennon died, there was no one to grab the reins. Perhaps if he had lived or if a dynamic successor had taken the reins, the architecture group CRS would be in business today, spun off as an independent entity. But architecture had ceased to be a major focus of the corporation as the 1980s progressed and the business evolved into one more focused on financial than professional challenges.

That said, not many architecture firms last as long as CRS did, or accomplish nearly as much. It will likely be a long time before CRS's influence fades away.

■ APPENDIX A

THE VOICES

Richard L. "Andy" Anderson, F.A.I.A.: Joined CRS in January, 1967, and worked on projects as designer and manager. Also assisted in marketing. Left the firm in September, 1971, and settled in Tucson, Arizona, where he teamed up with former CRSers Jack DeBartolo and Solomon Pan to form Anderson DeBartolo Pan, Inc.

Ray B. Bailey, F.A.I.A.: After graduating from the Massachusetts Institute of Technology with his master's degree in 1967, he joined CRS as a member of the design team. Worked primarily with Frank Lawyer. Remained with the firm for five years, leaving in 1972. Four years later, he started his own design firm, Ray Bailey Architects, Inc., of Houston, where a number of former CRSers currently are employed.

Robert A. Brooks, A.I.A.: Joined CRS in 1968 as an architectural programmer under Willie Peña. Went on to earn a reputation as a double specialist in both programming and education before departing the firm in 1973 and partnering with former CRSer Jim Collier in Brooks/Collier Architects four years later.

Thomas A. Bullock, F.A.I.A.: Hired into the firm by John Rowlett in 1948 while still enrolled as an undergraduate at Texas A&M University. The fifth partner, he served his entire professional life at CRS. He was the partner in charge of the Jones Hall project. For forty years he was the leading management voice in CRS. He served as managing partner/president from 1957 until the time the firm went public in 1971, after which he was board chairman until his retirement in 1989. He held his position as chairman of the CRSS Executive Committee until 1995.

William T. Cannady, F.A.I.A.: Joined CRS in 1967, when he was hired by Bill Caudill as a design group leader. A member of the faculty of the Rice University School of Architecture since February, 1964, he taught design and served as Assistant Director while Caudill was the director of the architecture school. Along with Bob Douglass, he invented the CRS "gaming" method of hospital facility programming. After eighteen months at CRS, he resigned from the firm in 1969 to pursue further academic work at the Bartlett School of Architecture, University College, London. He currently practices architecture in Houston and teaches a design studio as a professor at Rice University.

Ralph C. Carroll, A.I.A.: Joined CRS in 1957 as a member of the firm's original Bryan office. Served CRS projects in many capacities, most notably as construction supervisor.

Jack DeBartolo, Jr., F.A.I.A.: Joined the CRS design group in November, 1964. He became an associate partner in the late 1960s and assisted Bill Caudill in leading his design team. In 1970, he became the firm's senior vice president and took on the firm's design team leadership in health care, working with Bob Douglass, Jim Falick, Terry Tengler, and Solomon Pan. He left the firm in February, 1973, with aspirations of starting his own design firm. He then headed to Tucson where he teamed up with former CRSer Richard "Andy" Anderson to buy out William Wilde & Associates, where Anderson was employed at the time. Later, Pan also joined the firm, which eventually became known as Anderson DeBartolo Pan, Inc. He left ADP in 1995 at the time of its merger with Fluor Daniel to start his own firm, DeBartolo Architects, in Phoenix.

Joseph C. Denman, Jr.: A member of the CRS Board of Directors from 1980 until the firm's divestiture in 1995, his ties to CRS date back to 1948, when he worked part-time for the firm while attending Texas A&M University. After graduation, he took a job with Southern Pine Lumber Company in order to remain close to his roots in Lufkin, Texas. After the firm merged with Time, Inc., in 1973, he held the title of group vice president and director. He also held the title of chairman/president/CEO of Temple-Eastex, Inc., for a ten-year period prior to his retirement. He joined CRS's Board on a second invitation after declining a previous offer in 1977.

H. Robert Douglass, F.A.I.A.: Joined the firm in June, 1968, from Leo Daly as a specialist in medical facilities. His most significant contribution was his part in developing, along with Bill Cannady, the CRS "gaming" method of facility programming. He resigned in December, 1971, and later established his own successful health-care facility consulting practice, which was subsequently acquired by Deloitte and Touche. After earning his doctoral degree at Harvard, he returned to Houston and his consulting practice.

James Falick, F.A.I.A.: Joined CRS in June, 1965, and was instrumental in establishing a successful health-care facility specialization presence for the firm. He served in various capacities within the firm from executive vice president to director of marketing. He left in the summer of 1975 to establish the Falick/Klein Partnership, a Houston architectural firm that specialized in health-care facilities. He is currently a consultant in health-care architecture.

John W. Focke, F.A.I.A.: Joined CRS in the summer of 1968, beginning a twenty-two-year career with the firm. With Willie Peña, he coauthored the first edition of *Problem Seeking.* He helped develop trademark CRS concepts such as *fast track* and systems building. After departing the firm in 1990, he became a principal with Ray Bailey Architects.

James B. Gatton, F.A.I.A.: Started working full-time for CRS in January, 1957—albeit on a one-year trial basis that hinged on the stipulation he be allowed to "do everything." Though very much a generalist in his early years with the firm, he later found his specialties in schools, office buildings, and large assembly facilities. In fact, the one-time antispecialist eventually became renowned, both in and outside the firm, as CRS's leading project manager. He closed out a long and prosperous career with the firm as a member of CRSS Architects, Inc.

W. Weston Harper, A.I.A.: Hired by Tom Bullock in 1955, he joined the CRS branch office in Oklahoma City doing elementary school design oriented toward the efficient use of natural environment. He worked on the second and third additions to Norman High School, among other school projects, before moving to the Houston office in September, 1959, where he became a project architect under Herb Paseur's guidance. As in Oklahoma, he worked primarily on schools, including the University of Miami at Coral Gables, before leaving the firm in 1964 to accept a teaching position in the Texas

A&M College of Architecture. He served as department head from 1969–73, and taught at Texas A&M for thirty years before retiring in 1994.

Thomas A. Hooker, A.I.A.: Joined CRS in November, 1965, as a project designer. He was loaned to the American Association of Junior Colleges from 1968 to 1971, where he helped push that organization to the national forefront of community college planning. Upon returning to CRS, he was assigned to the firm's new Los Angeles office as director of development. He resigned in March, 1974, but returned briefly to CRS in the early 1990s. He is currently a principal with Wiginton Hooker Jeffry in Dallas.

G. Norman Hoover, F.A.I.A.: An eighteen-year CRS veteran, he joined the firm in July, 1964, and became one of its principal designers. He left the firm in 1983 to work in the architectural design group at 3D/International.

James M. Hughes, A.I.A.: A senior vice president of CRSS, he joined the firm in 1959 during its first year in Houston. He became CRS's community college specialist and was instrumental in establishing the firm's reputation as a leader in this building type, both in the U.S. and abroad. He retired in 1985 after a twenty-six-year career with the firm.

Jonathan King, Hon. A.I.A.: Joined CRS in 1970 as senior vice president, partner, directory of systems building, and educational specialist. He had become known to the architectural and educational communities during his years as vice president an treasurer of the Ford Foundation's Educational Facilities Laboratories (1958–1970), and he was recognized for his innovative thinking and effectiveness in developing building systems for school and college construction. While at CRS, he helped to bring the cost, quality, and time benefits that had been gained in the construction of schools to housing, prison, and hospital design. He left CRS in 1976 to become Professor of Architecture and Director of the Architectural Research Laboratory at the University of Michigan. He retired in 1986, and built a house designed by Bill Caudill on Fripp Island, South Carolina. In 1992, he returned to Texas to become Visiting Professor of Architecture and Director of the CRS Center at Texas A&M University. Throughout his career, Jonathan was known for his wit and for his love of mentoring bright young men and women. He died in 1997 soon after his retirement from Texas A&M.

Charles E. Lawrence, F.A.I.A.: The seventh of the original eight founding partners, he joined CRS in 1951 as a designer. Guided by a strong belief in the essential relationship between structure and architecture, he sought to make structure a prime contributor in his designs. He ended his thirty-year career by retiring in 1981, but continued to collaborate with CRS to complete design projects such as the Orange County Performing Arts Hall in California, and the United States Embassy in Saudi Arabia. He now designs industrial architecture.

Franklin D. Lawyer, F.A.I.A.: After receiving his M.A. at Granbrook, he arrived in College Station in 1952 to take on a dual role as a full-time teacher at Texas A&M within the College of Architecture and as a part-time designer at CRS. Four years later, he left academia and joined the firm full-time, specializing in schools. He headed the design teams on a great many of the firm's prize-winning buildings and was involved in over 150 squatters. He retired in 1984, and within a few months, he found himself teaching inside the walls of one of the projects he had helped design: the University of Petroleum and Minerals in Saudi Arabia, an appointment that lasted seven years. He and his wife Betty are now living in Wimberley, Texas.

Lewis T. May, FASLA: A CRSer from 1972 to 1991, this talented landscape architect/planner and CRS spokesman rose to the level of design principal before leaving the firm. His landscape design graces many of the firm's international projects. He currently heads a studio at Page Southerland Page in Houston.

Mike A. Myers: A member of Texas governor John Connally's team, he served as the state's liaison to CRS for the duration of the HemisFair project, completed in San Antonio in 1968. As president of Myers Financial Corporation in Dallas, he was later invited to join the CRS Board of Directors in 1980. He remained on the board until the firm divested completely in 1995.

Edward F. Nye, P.E.: A college friend of Bill Caudill's in the 1930s at Oklahoma State, he joined CRS as its sixth partner in January, 1956. He headed CRS's structural engineering operation, working in close collaboration with its architects.

Steven A. Parshall, F.A.I.A.: Joined CRS in September, 1976, on a six-month "preceptorship" while an undergraduate at the University of Illinois, working and learning with Charles Lawrence and Willie Peña. Upon earning his degree, he returned as a full-time programmer with CRSS Architects, later heading up the firm's research and CRS's advance planning group as well. He currently is a senior vice president with HOK and serves as practice director for HOK Consulting.

C. Herbert Paseur, F.A.I.A.: The eighth and final founding partner of CRS, he joined the firm as a designer in May, 1955. He later moved into project and firm management, and led the firm into many new frontiers, including public ownership. He served as president and CEO of CRS, CRS Design Associates, and the CRS Group, Inc., before retiring in 1981. He remained on the CRS board until the firm's complete divestiture in 1995.

William M. Peña, F.A.I.A.: He was hired by Bill Caudill as CRS's "first employee" in 1948. He became the firm's fourth partner in 1949. He came into the firm to do design/working drawings but quickly found his niche in color, public relations, and programming. Along the way, he helped invent the CRS concept of squatters. The "Prince of Programming," as he became known, Peña was the principal author of the various editions of *Problem Seeking*, which is widely recognized as the definitive work on programming.

David N. Scoular: He was hired in 1970 by Jim Falick as a member of the firm's fledgling health facilities group. As a result of that duo's one-two marketing punch, CRS became the hottest health-care design firm in the country almost overnight. He left CRS in 1974. He later served as a consultant for Stanford for a ten-year period thanks to a relationship developed during his CRS days with Larry Crowley, then vice president of the Stanford Medical Center. Most recently, he served as director of planning for the Baylor College of Medicine within the Texas Medical Center in Houston.

John F. Y. Stambaugh: A friend and associate of Bill Caudill's from elementary school on, he was never an official CRS employee. Nevertheless, he played a crucial role in shaping the firm's future. He devised CRS's early system of accounting and developed a system of forecasting, as well as a revolutionary time-control formula that served as a guide for all of the firm's projects and their billing. He also implemented an annual share ownership evaluation process used by the partners to determine, among other things, salaries. In addition to shepherding CRS's early financial programs, he established his own successful accounting firm, Frazier and Torbet, which was later acquired by Touche Ross and Company.

Jane M. Stansfeld, F.A.I.A.: Educated and registered as an architect in England, she joined CRS in 1973 as a member of the design group. She ultimately moved into project management, helping to produce, most notably, the Chrysler Technology facilities. She attained the status of vice president before leaving the firm in February, 1992, to join Lockwood Andrews and Newnam, Inc., of Houston—a subsidiary of Leo A. Daly. Elevated to F.A.I.A. in 1993, she is now a senior vice president at Page Southerland Page.

Joe B. Thomas, P.E.: Joined CRS in February, 1961, as an interior designer and the first person hired following a four-month layoff period. The consistent quality of his work gained much recognition for the firm's projects. He resigned in January, 1973, and accepted a partnership position in S. I. Morris. He was later affiliated with Ray Bailey Architects.

Charles B. Thomsen, F.A.I.A.: Joined CRS on a part-time basis in 1965 while also teaching at Rice University. Three years later, he entered the firm full-time. He was responsible for the development of construction management as an architectural service of CRS, a service that became known as CRS/CM, CM Associates, and ultimately CRSS Constructors, Inc. When Herb Paseur retired in 1981, Thomsen became president and CEO of CRS. He resigned just over one year later, and moved on to a fulfilling career with 3D/International, Inc., where he currently serves as both chairman and CEO.

David F. Thorman, A.I.A.: Joined CRS in November, 1965, and worked in design production, primarily on schools, in his first months. He subsequently moved into the firm's project management program, headed by Willie Peña, where he discovered his specialty. In 1973, he took over management of the Programming and Planning Group, serving as project manager on many of the firm's subsequent projects. In the late 1970s, he started the firm's first interiors division. He left CRS in November, 1980, but returned in January, 1986, as manager of the firm's Advanced Planning Group. Two years later, he migrated into business development for education full-time, and obtained the billion-dollar Dade County project, the largest domestic project up to its day for CRS. Still later, he became the sales manager for CRSS Constructors, Inc., where he was responsible for all sales activity for the eight offices across the company.

Bruce W. Wilkinson: Joined CRS in November, 1978, as Chief Financial Officer. He was promoted to president and CEO in March, 1982. During his tenure until the firm's divestiture in 1995, he presided over the firm's acquisitions, as well as its membership, including its initial listing in 1985, on the New York Stock Exchange.

Donald B. Wines, A.I.A.: Joined CRS in August, 1957, as a designer in the Oklahoma City office headed by Rowlett, Bullock, and Paseur. He transferred to the Houston office in mid 1959, taking on design assignments in a variety of building types. He was a participant in the CPM project in Saudi Arabia as one of the initial three-man squatters team for site selection in December, 1965 (with Lawrence and Finlay). Until 1967, he continued to work on this significant project through master planning, basic design, and design development. Thereafter, he made the transition to building type specialist in elementary through secondary schools. In February, 1969, he spearheaded an on-site management team for CRS's prestigious Baltimore City Public Schools building project. He held the title of vice president before he left CRS in 1970.

Philip C. Williams, A.I.A.: Joined CRS in August, 1957, as a member of the drafting and design development team in the Oklahoma City office. He was instrumental in establishing the firm's reputation as a leader in city and university planning. He left CRS in August, 1972, and later headed up Stanford University Facilities Planning office.

■ APPENDIX B

AWARDS

DATE, PROJECT NAME, AWARD, AWARDED BY, PROJECT CITY, PROJECT STATE

1950, Huston Elementary School, Award of Merit, American Association of School Administrators/AIA, Blackwell, Oklahoma

1950, School Administration Building, Award of Merit, Texas Society of Architects, Alvin, Texas

1951, Westwood Elementary School, Award of Merit, American Association of School Administrators/AIA, Stillwater, Oklahoma

1951, Westwood Elementary School, Top Award, Better School Design Competition, *The School Executive,* Stillwater, Oklahoma

1951, Will Rogers Elementary School, Top Award, *The School Executive,* Stillwater, Oklahoma

1952, Albany Elementary School, Award of Merit, Texas Society of Architects, Albany, Texas

1953, Lamar Junior High School, Top Award, *The School Executive,* Laredo, Texas

1953, Sam Houston Elementary School, Top Award, *The School Executive,* Port Arthur, Texas

1954, Norman High School, First Honor Award, American Institute of Architects, Norman, Oklahoma

1955, A&M Consolidated High School, First Honor Award, Texas Society of Architects, College Station, Texas

1955, A&M Consolidated High School, Honorable Mention, Better School Design Competition, College Station, Texas

1955, Florence Black Elementary, Award of Merit, American Association of School Administrators/AIA, Mesquite, Texas

1955, J. R. Moore Junior High School, Top Award, *The School Executive*, Tyler, Texas

1955, Jane Phillips Elementary School, Award of Merit, American Association of School Administrators/AIA, Bartlesville, Oklahoma

1955, New Austin Elementary School, Award of Merit, American Association of School Administrators/AIA, Edna, Texas

1956, Benjamin Franklin Junior High School, Citation, *Progressive Architecture,* Dallas, Texas

1956, Bettes Office Building, Citation, Progressive Architecture, Oklahoma City, Oklahoma

1956, J. R. Moore Junior High School, Honor Award, Texas Society of Architects, Tyler, Texas

1956, St. Joseph's Academy, Citation, *Progressive Architecture,* Brownsville, Texas

1957, Brazos County Courthouse, First Honor Award, American Institute of Architects, Bryan, Texas

1957, Five Primary Schools, Award of Merit, Texas Society of Architects, Andrews, Texas

1957, San Jacinto Elementary School, Award of Merit, American Institute of Architects, Liberty, Texas

1957, School Administration Building, Honorable Mention, School Executive, Alvin, Texas

1957, Underwood Elementary School, Top Award, *The School Executive,* Andrews, Texas

1958, Odem Elementary School, Citation, American Association of School Administrators/AIA, Odem, Texas

1958, Underwood Elementary School, Award of Merit, Texas Society of Architects, Andrews, Texas

1959, Robert E. Lee Senior High School, Citation, American Association of School Administrators/AIA, Tyler, Texas

1959, San Angelo Central High School, Award of Merit, American Institute of Architects, San Angelo, Texas

1959, San Angelo Stadium, Award of Merit, Texas Society of Architects, San Angelo, Texas

1959, St. Joseph's Academy, Honorable Mention, Better School Design Competition, Brownsville, Texas

1960, Brazos County Courthouse, Award of Merit, Texas Society of Architects, Bryan, Texas

1960, San Angelo Central High School, Award of Merit, Texas Society of Architects, San Angelo, Texas

1960, San Jacinto Elementary School, Award of Merit, Texas Society of Architects, Liberty, Texas

1960, Spring Woods High School, Award of Merit, American Institute of Architects, Houston, Texas

1960, St. Joseph's Academy, Award of Merit, AIA Houston Chapter, Brownsville, Texas

1960, St. Joseph's Academy, Award of Merit, Texas Society of Architects, Brownsville, Texas

1960, St. Joseph's Academy, Citation, American Association of School Administrators/AIA, Brownsville, Texas

1961, Donart High School, Citation, American Association of School Administrators/AIA, Stillwater, Oklahoma

1961, Dow Center, Award of Merit, Texas Society of Architects, Houston, Texas

1961, Paul L. Dunbar Elementary School, Citation, American Association of School Administrators/AIA, Gary, Indiana

1961, Paul L. Dunbar Elementary School, Top Award, Better School Design Competition, Gary, Indiana 1963, Carlsbad High School, Award of Merit, Texas Society of Architects, Carlsbad, New Mexico

1963, Chippewa Middle School, Citation, American Association of School Administrators/AIA, Saginaw, Michigan

1963, First National Bank, Honor Award, Texas Society of Architects, Giddings, Texas

1963, Montrose Elementary School, Citation, AIA Houston Chapter, Laredo, Texas

1963, Montrose Elementary School, Honor Award, Texas Society of Architects, Laredo, Texas

1963, Olin Hall of Science at Colorado College, Award of Merit, Texas Society of Architects, Colorado Springs, Colorado

1963, Robert E. Lee Senior High School, Honorable Mention, AIA Houston Chapter, Tyler, Texas

1963, Spring Woods High School, Second Place Award, Construction Specifications Institutional Award for Excellence in Specifications, Houston, Texas

1964, Blackwell Senior High School, Citation, American Association of School Administrators/AIA, Blackwell, Oklahoma

1964, Bullock Residence, Honor Award, Texas Society of Architects, Houston, Texas

1964, Jesse H. Jones Hall for the Performing Arts, Second Place Award, Construction Specifications Institutional Award for Excellence in Specifications, Houston, Texas

1964, Mexia General Hospital, Honorable Mention, Construction Specifications Institutional Award for Excellence in Specifications, Mexia, Texas

1964, Olin Hall of Science at Colorado College, Award of Merit, AIA Houston Chapter, Colorado Springs, Colorado

1964, Recreation Center, Award of Merit, Texas Society of Architects, Clear Lake City, Texas

1964, William Fleming High School, School of the Month Award, *The Nation's Schools,* Roanoke, Virginia

1965, Abington High School, Food Service Honor Award, *Institutions Magazine,* Abington Township, Pennsylvania

1965, Blackwell Senior High School, School of the Month Award, *The Nation's Schools,* Blackwell, Oklahoma

1965, Spring Woods High School, Award of Merit, Texas Society of Architects, Houston, Texas

1966, Bullock Residence, Award of Merit, AIA Houston Chapter, Houston, Texas

1966, Maine Township High School South, Citation, American Association of School Administrators/AIA, Park Ridge, Illinois

1966, Nixon Senior High School, Award, Texas Society of Architects, Laredo, Texas

1966, Roy E. Larsen Hall (Harvard University), Citation, American Association of School Administrators/AIA, Cambridge, Massachusetts

1966, Southern Colorado State College Library/Classroom Building, Award of Merit, U.S. Office of Education, Pueblo, Colorado

1967, Blackwell Senior High School, First Honor Award, Office of Civil Defense, Blackwell, Oklahoma

1967, Jesse H. Jones Hall for the Performing Arts, Honor Award, American Institute of Architects, Houston, Texas

1967, Jesse H. Jones Hall for the Performing Arts, Honor Award, Texas Society of Architects, Houston, Texas

1967, Klapper Elementary School (P.S. 219), Chamber of Commerce Award, Borough of Queens, Flushing, New York

1967, Klapper Elementary School (P.S. 219), Citation, American Association of School Administrators/AIA, Flushing, New York

1967, Roy E. Larsen Hall (Harvard University), Honor Award, Texas Society of Architects, Cambridge, Massachusetts

1967, Southern Colorado State College Library/Classroom Building, Honor Award, Texas Society of Architects, Pueblo, Colorado

1967, Southern Colorado State College Library/Classroom Building, Honor Award, Western Mountain Chapter–AIA, Pueblo, Colorado

1968, Caudill Rowlett Scott Office Building, Citation, *Progressive Architecture,* Houston, Texas

1968, Claremont College Four Colleges Science Building, Honor Award, AIA Pasadena Chapter, Claremont, California

1968, Jesse H. Jones Hall for the Performing Arts, Honor Award, AIA Houston Chapter, Houston, Texas

1968, Lake Ann Elementary School, Citation, American Association of School Administrators/AIA, Reston, Virginia

1968, Pearl River Middle School, Citation, American Association of School Administrators/AIA, Pearl River, New York

1968, Quincy Vocational-Technical Institute, Citation, American Association of School Administrators/AIA, Quincy, Massachusetts

1968, Skill Center, Citation, American Association of School Administrators/AIA, Flint, Michigan

1968, University of Miami Science Building, Honor Award, AIA Houston Chapter, Coral Gables, Florida

1968, University of Miami Science Building, Honor Award, Texas Society of Architects, Coral Gables, Florida

1968, William Rainey Harper College, Citation, American Association of School Administrators/AIA, Palatine, Illinois

1969, Claremont College Four Colleges Science Building, Honor Award, Texas Society of Architects, Claremont, California

1969, Eastwick High School and George Pepper Middle School, Silver Medal Award, AIA Philadelphia Chapter, Philadelphia, Pennsylvania

1969, Texas Senior High School, Outstanding School Architecture Award, Texas Association of School Administrators and School Boards, Texarkana, Texas

1969, Winona High School, Citation, American Association of School Administrators/AIA, Winona, Minnesota

1970, Anniston Educational Park, Citation, American Association of School Administrators/AIA, Anniston, Alabama

1970, Anniston Educational Park, Special Award, Council of Educational Facility Planners, Anniston, Alabama

1970, Caudill Rowlett Scott Calendar, Award of Excellence, Tulsa Art Directors Club/Graphex 70, Houston, Texas

1970, Caudill Rowlett Scott Calendar, Silver Medal, Tulsa Art Directors Club/Graphex 70, Houston, Texas

1970, Caudill Rowlett Scott Letterheads, Special Judges Award of Distinction, Tulsa Art Directors Club/Graphex 70, Houston, Texas

1970, Caudill Rowlett Scott Office Building, Award, Communication Arts Magazine Awards Program, Houston, Texas

1970, Caudill Rowlett Scott Office Building, Design Award, Prestressed Concrete Institute, Houston, Texas

1970, Claremont College Four Colleges Science Building, Design Award, Prestressed Concrete Institute, Claremont, California

1970, Dodge City Community College, Honor Award, American Association of Junior Colleges/AIA/USOE, Dodge City, Kansas

1970, First Hutchings–Sealy National Bank Barricade, Award of Distinction, Tulsa Art Directors Club/Graphex 70, Galveston, Texas

1970, Jackson-Via Elementary School, Citation, American Association of School Administrators/AIA, Charlottesville, Virginia

1970, Manhattan Community College, Special Award, Council of Educational Facility Planners, New York, New York

1970, North Orange County Junior College (Cypress Campus), First Honor Award, AIA Houston Chapter, Cypress, California

1970, North Orange County Junior College (Cypress Campus), Remodeling Award, American Association of Junior Colleges/AIA/USOE, Cypress, California

1970, North Orange County Junior College (Fullerton Campus), Award of Merit, American Association of Junior Colleges/AIA/USOE, Fullerton, California

1970, Winona High School, Outstanding School Architecture Award, Texas Association of School Administrators and School Boards, Winona, Minnesota

1971, A. J. Cox Elementary School, Outstanding School Architecture Award, Texas Association of School Administrators and School Boards, Guilford, Connecticut

1971, Anniston Educational Park, First Honor Award, Texas Society of Architects, Anniston, Alabama

1971, Birch Elementary School, Award of Commendation, Texas Society of Architects, Merrick, New York
1971, Birch Elementary School, Citation, American Association of School Administrators/AIA, Merrick, New York
1971, Birch Elementary School, Outstanding School Architecture Award, Texas Association of School Administrators and School Boards, Merrick, New York
1971, Blackwell Senior High School, Citation, National School Board Association, Blackwell, Oklahoma
1971, Caudill Rowlett Scott Office Building, Architectural Graphics Award, Prestressed Concrete Institute, Houston, Texas
1971, Caudill Rowlett Scott Office Building, First Honor Award, AIA Houston Chapter, Houston, Texas
1971, Caudill Rowlett Scott Office Building, First Honor Award, Texas Society of Architects, Houston, Texas
1971, Dodge City Community College, Honor Award, Texas Society of Architects, Dodge City, Kansas
1971, Eastwick High School and George Pepper Middle School, Citation, *Progressive Architecture,* Philadelphia, Pennsylvania
1971, Eastwick High School and George Pepper Middle School, Design Award, *Progressive Architecture,* Philadelphia, Pennsylvania
1971, Jackson-Via Elementary School, Outstanding School Architecture Award, Texas Association of School Administrators and School Boards, Charlottesville, Virginia
1971, Joliet Junior College, Honor Award, American Association of Junior Colleges/AIA/USOE, Joliet, Illinois
1971, Long Beach High School, Award of Merit, Concrete Industry Board of New York, Long Beach, New York
1971, Long Beach High School, Silver Archie Design Award, Long Island Association of Commerce and Industry, Long Beach, New York
1971, North Orange County Junior College (Cypress Campus), Honor Award, American Association of Junior Colleges/AIA/USOE, Cypress, California
1971, Sauk Valley Community College, Award of Commendation, Texas Society of Architects, Dixon, Illinois
1971, Sauk Valley Community College, Award of Merit, AIA Wisconsin Chapter, Dixon, Illinois
1971, Sauk Valley Community College, Citation, Illinois Association of School Boards, Dixon, Illinois

1972, Brazosport College, Award, AIA Houston Chapter, Freeport, Texas

1972, Caudill Rowlett Scott, Architectural Firm Award, American Institute of Architects, Houston, Texas

1972, Energy Control Center (Houston Lighting and Power), Award of Merit, AIA Houston Chapter, Houston, Texas

1972, Energy Control Center (Houston Lighting and Power), First Honor Award, Texas Society of Architects, Houston, Texas

1972, Student Housing State University College at Brockport, Award of Merit, Automation in Housing, Brockport, Texas

1973, Baltimore Management Planning (Baltimore Public Schools), Outstanding School Architecture Award, Texas Association of School Administrators and School Boards, Baltimore, Maryland

1973, Brazosport College, First Honor Award, Texas Society of Architects, Lake Jackson, Texas

1973, Brazosport College, Honor Award, AIA Houston Chapter, Lake Jackson, Texas

1973, Brazosport College, Landscape Design Honor Award, Southwest ASLA, Lake Jackson, Texas

1973, Capital National Bank's United Gas Facility, Interior Architecture Award, AIA Houston Chapter, Houston, Texas

1973, Caudill Rowlett Scott Office Building, Interior Architecture Honor Award, AIA Houston Chapter, Houston, Texas

1973, Desert Samaritan Hospital, Honor Award, Texas Society of Architects, Mesa, Arizona

1973, DeVry Institute of Technology, Special Citation, American Association of School Administrators/AIA, Phoenix, Arizona

1973, Fodrea Community School, Special Citation, American Association of School Administrators/AIA, Columbus, Indiana

1973, Hyatt Regency Hotel and Parking Garage, Interior Architecture Honor Award, AIA Houston Chapter, Houston, Texas

1973, Prima Community College, Honor Award, Texas Society of Architects, Tucson, Arizona

1973, Royal Palm Elementary School, Outstanding School Architecture Award, Texas Association of School Administrators and School Boards, Fort Lauderdale, Texas

1973, Student Housing, State University College at Brockport, Selected, First Federal Design Assembly, Brockport, New York

1974, DeVry Institute of Technology, Architectural Award for Excellence,

American School and University Architectural Competition, Chicago, Illinois

1974, DeVry Institute of Technology, Design Award, American School and University Architectural Competition, Chicago, Illinois

1974, DeVry Institute of Technology, Distinguished Building Award, AIA Chicago Chapter, Chicago, Illinois

1974, DeVry Institute of Technology, Honor Award, Texas Society of Architects, Chicago, Illinois

1974, Edwin J. Thomas Performing Arts Hall, Architectural Award for Excellence, American School and University Architectural Competition, Akron, Ohio

1974, Edwin J. Thomas Performing Arts Hall, Design Award, American School and University Architectural Competition, Akron, Ohio

1974, Edwin J. Thomas Performing Arts Hall, Honor Award, Texas Society of Architects, Akron, Ohio

1974, Mission Viejo Elementary School, Outstanding School Architecture Award, Texas Association of School Administrators and School Boards, Aurora, Colorado

1974, Mission Viejo Elementary School, Special Citation, American Association of School Administrators/AIA, Aurora, Colorado

1974, Student Housing, State University College at Brockport, Architectural Award for Excellence, American School and University Architectural Competition, Brockport, New York

1974, Student Housing, State University College at Brockport, Design Award, American School and University Architectural Competition, Brockport, New York

1974, Trenton State College Student Union, Honor Award, AIA New Jersey Chapter, Trenton, New Jersey

1975, Brazosport College, Award of Merit, AIA Southern California Chapter, Lake Jackson, Texas

1975, Bulkeley High School, Outstanding School Architecture Award, Texas Association of School Administrators and School Boards, Hartford, Connecticut

1975, Chaparral High School, Citation, American Association of Junior Colleges/AIA/USOE, Las Vegas, Nevada

1975, Edwin J. Thomas Performing Arts Hall, Design Award, Concrete Reinforcing Steel Institute, Akron, Ohio

1975, Edwin J. Thomas Performing Arts Hall, Honor Award, Prestressed Concrete Institute, Akron, Ohio

1975, Fodrea Community School, Architectural Award of Excellence, American Institute of Steel Construction, Columbus, Indiana

1975, Fodrea Community School, Award of Merit, AIA Southern California Chapter, Columbus, Indiana

1975, Fodrea Community School, Best Design for Low-Rise Construction, American Iron and Steel Institute Design in Steel Award, Columbus, Indiana

1975, Fodrea Community School, Honor Award, Texas Society of Architects, Columbus, Indiana

1975, Irwin Union Bank and Trust Company Branch Bank, Honor Award, Texas Society of Architects, Columbus, Indiana

1975, Ivan G. Smith Elementary School, Architectural Award of Excellence, American Institute of Steel Construction, Danvers, Massachusetts

1975, Ivan G. Smith Elementary School, Outstanding School Architecture Award, Texas Association of School Administrators and School Boards, Danvers, Massachusetts

1975, North High School, Citation, American Association of Junior Colleges/AIA/USOE, Minneapolis, Minnesota

1975, Salanter-Akiba-Riverdale Academy, Citation, American Association of School Administrators/AIA, Bronx, New York

1975, Salanter-Akiba-Riverdale Academy, Design Award, New York State Association of Architects, Bronx, New York

1975, Salanter-Akiba-Riverdale Academy, First Honor Bard Award, City Club of New York, Bronx, New York

1975, Student Housing, State University College at Brockport, Citation, American Iron and Steel Institute Design in Steel Awards, Brockport, New York

1975, Student Housing, State University College at Brockport, Design Award, New York State Association of Architects, Brockport, New York

1975, Student Housing, State University College at Brockport, Honor Award, AIA New York Chapter, Brockport, New York

1975, Student Housing, State University College at Brockport, Residential Design Award, AIA New York Chapter, Brockport, New York

1976, Bulkeley High School, Special Citation, American Association of School Administrators/AIA, Hartford, Connecticut

1976, Columbus 37XESS Addition, Design Award, Progressive Architecture, Columbus, Indiana

1976, Fodrea Community School, Outstanding School Architecture Award, Texas Association of School Administrators and School Boards, Columbus, Indiana

1976, Howard Educational Park, Design Award, Greater Wilmington Development Council, Wilmington, Delaware

1976, Hyatt Regency Hotel and Parking Garage, Design Award, AIA Houston Chapter, Houston, Texas

1976, Ivan G. Smith Elementary School, Honorable Mention, Texas Society of Architects, Danvers, Massachusetts

1976, Ivan G. Smith Elementary School, Special Citation, American Association of Junior Colleges/AIA/USOE, Danvers, Massachusetts

1976, Maple Hill School, Outstanding School Architecture Award, Texas Association of School Administrators and School Boards, Hackensack, New Jersey

1976, Mercy Hospital, Honorable Mention, Texas Society of Architects, Bakersfield, California

1976, Pine Bluff High School, Outstanding School Architecture Award, Texas Association of School Administrators and School Boards, Pine Bluff, Arkansas

1976, Salanter-Akiba-Riverdale Academy, Outstanding School Architecture Award, Texas Association of School Administrators and School Boards, Bronx, New York

1976, Thomas E. Leavy Activities Center and Harold L. Toso Pavilion, Special Mention, Texas Society of Architects, Santa Clara, California

1976, Tompkins Cortland Community College, Special Citation, American Association of School Administrators/AIA, Dryden, New York

1976, University of Petroleum and Minerals, Award of Merit, Texas Society of Architects, Dhahran, Saudi Arabia

1977, American High School, Award of Excellence, American Institute of Steel Construction, Miami, Florida

1977, American High School, Outstanding School Architecture Award, Texas Association of School Administrators and School Boards, Miami, Florida

1977, *From Infancy to Infinity,* Bronze Medal, Houston Art Directors Club, Houston, Texas

1977, CRS Poster Invitation, Communications Arts Award, Communication Arts Magazine Awards Program, Houston, Texas

1977, Heritage High School, Special Citation, American Association of School Administrators/AIA, Lynchburg, Virginia

1977, Howard Educational Park, Urban Design Award, Wilmington Chamber of Commerce, Wilmington, Delaware

1977, Hyatt Regency Hotel and Parking Garage, Award of Merit, AIA Houston Chapter, Houston, Texas

1977, James E. West Alumni Center, Western Los Angeles Regional Chamber of Commerce Award/Public or Community Buildings, Los Angeles Regional Chamber of Commerce, Los Angeles, California

1977, Jonesboro High School, Outstanding School Architecture Award, Texas Association of School Administrators and School Boards, Jonesboro, Arkansas

1977, Maple Hill School, Special Citation, American Association of School Administrators/AIA, Hackensack, New Jersey

1977, Salanter-Akiba-Riverdale Academy, Merit Award, Texas Society of Architects, Bronx, New York

1977, Texas Eastern University, Award of Merit, Texas Society of Landscape Architects, Tyler, Texas

1977, Texas Eastern University, Honor Award, Texas Society of Architects, Tyler, Texas

1977, Thomas E. Leavy Activities Center and Harold L. Toso Pavilion, Special Citation, American Association of School Administrators/AIA, Santa Clara, California

1977, Trenton State College Student Union, Award of Merit, AIA New Jersey Chapter, Trenton, New Jersey

1977, University of Maiduguri Logo, Graphex Nine Bronze Medal, Graphex Nine, Maiduguri, Nigeria

1977, University of Maiduguri Logo Stationery Package, Award of Design, Graphex Nine, Maiduguri, Nigeria

1977, University of Maiduguri Logo Stationery Program, Certificate of Merit, Art Directors Club, Maiduguri, Nigeria

1977, University of Petroleum and Minerals Campus Graphics, Award, Best in Environmental Graphics, Dhahran, Saudi Arabia

1977, "University of Petroleum and Minerals, Design and Master Plan Brochures (2)," Award of Design Excellence, Graphex Nine, Dhahran, Saudi Arabia

1977, Wake Forest Fine Arts Center, First Honor Award, Texas Society of Architects, Winston-Salem, North Carolina

1978, Bracewell and Patterson, Interior Architecture Award, AIA Houston Chapter, Houston, Texas

1978, Cuyahoga Community College, Honor Award, American Society of Landscape Architects, Cleveland, Ohio

1978, Fodrea Community School, Interior Architecture Award, AIA Houston Chapter, Columbus, Indiana

1978, Thomas E. Leavy Activities Center and Harold J. Toso Pavilion, Design Award, Texas Society of Architects, Santa Clara, California

1978, Thomas E. Leavy Activities Center and Harold J. Toso Pavilion, Honor Award, Texas Society of Architects, Santa Clara, California

1978, Wake Forest Fine Arts Center, Interior Architecture Award, AIA Houston Chapter, Winston-Salem, North Carolina

1978, Wyoming Valley High School, Special Citation, American Association of School Administrators/AIA, Kingston, Pennsylvania

1979, Campus Plan Book (Texas Women's University), Award of Excellence, Houston Art Directors Club, Denton, Texas

1979, Columbus 37XESS Addition, Honor Award, Texas Society of Architects, Columbus, Indiana

1979, Columbus 37XESS Addition, Honorable Mention, AT&T Building Awards Program, Columbus, Indiana

1979, Fodrea Community School, Interior Architecture Award, Texas Society of Architects, Columbus, Indiana

1979, Irwin Union Bank and Trust Company Branch Bank, Interior Architecture Honor Award, Texas Society of Architects, Columbus, Indiana

1979, Solar Energy Research Institute National Headquarters, Certificate of Commendation, Department of Energy, Golden, Colorado

1979, Solar Energy Research Institute National Headquarters, Owens-Corning Energy Conservation Award, Owens Corning Fiberglass Corporation, Golden, Colorado

1979, Southwestern Bell Accounting Center, Merit Award, AT&T Building Awards Program, Houston, Texas

1979, State and Mapleton Bank, Interior Architecture Award, Texas Society of Architects, Columbus, Indiana

1980, Bastrop Federal Correctional Institution, Owens-Corning Energy Conservation Award, Owens Corning Fiberglass Corporation, Bastrop, Texas

1980, Columbus 37XESS Addition, Architectural Award for Excellence, American Institute of Steel Construction, Columbus, Indiana

1980, Columbus 37XESS Addition, Architectural Award of Excellence, American Institute of Architects, Columbus, Indiana

1980, Columbus 37XESS Addition, Honor Award, American Institute of Architects, Columbus, Indiana

1980, Federated Shopping Center, Merit Award, Texas Society of Landscape Architects, Pasadena, Texas

1980, Houston Zoo Big Cat Facility, Merit Award, Texas Society of Landscape Architects, Houston, Texas

1980, Shell Oil Company Woodcreek Offices, Houston Lighting and Power Energy Conservation Design, Houston Lighting and Power Company, Houston, Texas

1980, Shell Oil Company Woodcreek Offices, Owens-Corning Energy Conservation Award, Owens Corning Fiberglass Corporation, Houston, Texas
1981, Bastrop Federal Correctional Institution, Design Award, Texas Forestry Association, Bastrop, Texas
1981, Herman Miller Seating Manufacturing Facility, Architectural Award for Excellence, American Institute of Steel Construction, Holland, Michigan
1981, Herman Miller Seating Manufacturing Facility, Honor Award, Texas Society of Architects, Holland, Michigan
1981, IBM Branch Office, Award of Distinguished Architecture, Reliance Development, Houston, Texas
1981, James E. West Alumni Center, Honor Award, American Institute of Architects, Los Angeles, California
1981, Mercy Hospital Interiors, Interior Architecture Honor Award, Texas Society of Architects, Bakersfield, California
1981, Shell Oil Company Woodcreek Offices, Achievement Award, Specifying Engineer, Houston, Texas
1981, Stephen C. O'Connell Center for Student Activities, Design Award, Precast Concrete Institute, Gainesville, Florida
1981, Stephen C. O'Connell Center for Student Activities, Interior Architecture Honor Award, Texas Society of Architects, Gainesville, Florida
1981, Stephen C. O'Connell Center for Student Activities, Owens-Corning Energy Conservation Award, Owens Corning Fiberglass Corporation, Gainesville, Florida
1981, Thomas E. Leavy Activities Center and Harold J. Toso Pavilion, Interior Architecture Honor Award, Texas Society of Architects, Santa Clara, California
1981, University of Petroleum and Minerals, Timberform Design Awards Program, Facility Housing and Playground, Dhahran, Saudi Arabia
1982, Herman Miller Energy Center, Honor Award of Distinction, Great Lakes Fabricators and Erectors, Zeeland, Michigan
1982, IBM Branch Office, Honor Award, Texas Society of Architects, Houston, Texas
1982, Mercy Hospital (Phase I), AIA Component Award, Texas Society of Architects, Bakersfield, California
1982, Mountain Bell Processing and Accounting Center, Honor Award, American Institute of Architects, Albuquerque, New Mexico
1982, Stephen C. O'Connell Center for Student Activities, Honor Award, Texas Society of Architects, Gainesville, Florida

1982, Stephen C. O'Connell Center for Student Activities, Lumen Award, Illuminating Engineering Society, Gainesville, Florida

1983, Carver-Hawkeye Arena, Facility of Merit, *AP&F* Magazine, Iowa City, Iowa

1983, Carver-Hawkeye Arena, Honor Award, American Institute of Architects, Iowa City, Iowa

1983, Carver-Hawkeye Arena, Honor Award, Texas Society of Architects, Iowa City, Iowa

1983, Carver-Hawkeye Arena, Owens-Corning Energy Conservation Award, Owens Corning Fiberglass Corporation, Iowa City, Iowa

1983, Herman Miller Seating Plant, Honor Award, American Institute of Architects, Holland, Michigan

1983, IBM Branch Office, Design Award-Energy Conservation, Houston Lighting and Power Company, Houston, Texas

1983, Jacksonville Convention Center, Award of Merit, APA Florida Chapter, Jacksonville, Florida

1983, Jacksonville Convention Center, Unbuilt Design Award, American Institute of Architects, Jacksonville, Florida

1983, Pasadena Town Square, Honor Award, Texas Society of Architects, Pasadena, Texas

1983, Stephen C. O'Connell Center for Student Activities, Interior Architecture Honor Award, AIA Houston Chapter, Gainesville, Florida

1983, Gulf Tower, Council Honor Award, American Consulting Engineers, Houston, Texas

1983, Gulf Tower, Excellence Award, Consulting Engineers Council of Texas, Houston, Texas

1983, Thomas E. Leavy Activities Center and Harold J. Toso Pavilion, Merit Award, American Institute of Architects, Santa Clara, California

1983, Wharton Center for the Performing Arts, Award, Masonry Institute of Michigan, East Lansing, Michigan

1984, Carver-Hawkeye Arena, National Honor Award, American Institute of Architects, Iowa City, Iowa

1984, Consolidated Diesel Engine Plant, Honor Award, Texas Society of Architects, Rocky Mount, North Carolina

1984, University of Petroleum and Minerals, Award of Merit, Texas Society of Landscape Architects, Dhahran, Saudi Arabia

1985, Arizona State University Research Park, Planning Award, National Association of Industrial Office Parks, Tempe, Arizona

1985, Center Tower, Award, NAIOP of Orange County, Costa Mesa, California

1985, Individual Honor to CRSS' Founder William Caudill, Gold Medal, American Institute of Architects, Houston, Texas

1985, Landscape Architecture in Saudi Arabia, Honor Award, American Society of Landscape Architects, Saudi, Arabia

1985, National Bank of Georgia, Best Architectural Award, Fulton County, Atlanta, Georgia

1985, National Bank of Georgia, "Citation for 'Most Beautiful Building,'" *Business Atlanta* Magazine, Atlanta, Georgia

1985, Orange County Performing Arts Center, Award of Accomplishment, Orange County Business Development Association, Costa Mesa, California

1985, University of Washington Teaching Hospital, Award for Excellence, Washington Precast Concrete Industry, Seattle, Washington

1986, 3M Divisional Headquarters, Honor Award–Environmental Management, National American Prairie Conference, Austin, Texas

1986, 3M Divisional Headquarters, Honor Award–Landscape Design, National American Prairie Conference, Austin, Texas

1986, 3M Divisional Headquarters, Merit Award–Master Plan and Analysis, Texas Society of Landscape Architects, Austin, Texas

1986, ARCO Oil and Gas District Offices, Award for Outstanding Architectural Design and Achievement, Texas Society of Architects, Houston, Texas

1986, Arizona State University Research Park, Honor Award, Industrial Development Research Council, Tempe, Arizona

1986, Carnegie-Mellon University, Firm Excellence Award, Texas Society of Landscape Architects, Pittsburgh, Pennsylvania

1986, Fort Drum Design Guide and Master, Honor Award, Texas Society of Landscape Architects Plan, Fort Drum, New York

1986, Galleria-Post Oak Master Plan, Honor Award, Texas Society of Landscape Architects, Fort Drum, New York

1986, GTE Directories Headquarters, First Place Award, ASID/Houston Chronicle, DFW Airport, Texas

1986, InterFirst Tower, Design Award, Concrete Reinforcing Steel Institute, Fort Worth, Texas

1986, Orange County Performing Arts Center, Masters Award, Ceramic Tile Institute of America, Costa Mesa, California

1986, Sonoma Mission Inn, Interior Design Award, *Restaurant Hospitality*, Boyes Hot Spring, California

1986, Three Houston Center, Award of Excellence, Houston Lighting and Power Company, Houston, Texas

1986, University of Washington Teaching Hospital, Regional Award (SPECTRUM '86 Design Competition), Ceramic Tile Distributors Association, Seattle, Washington

1986, Van Mosman Merchandising Offices, Honor Award–Interior Architecture, American Institute of Architects, New York, New York

1986, Yukon-Kuskokwim Delta Regional Hospital, Award for Outstanding Architectural Design and Achievement, Texas Society of Architects, Bethel, Alaska

1987, 113M 33 Maiden Lane, Lumen Award Citation, Illuminating Engineering Society, New York, New York

1987, Austin Center/3M, National Arbor Foundation Project Award, National Arbor Foundation, Austin, Texas

1987, Crowell and Moring Law Offices, First Place Award, ASID/*Houston Chronicle,* Washington, D.C.

1987, CRSS Dallas Office, First Place Award, ASID/*Houston Chronicle,* Dallas, Texas

1987, CRSS Dallas Office, Interior Architecture Award, Texas Society of Architects, Dallas, Texas

1987, IBM Clear Lake Product Display Area, Lumen Award Citation, Illuminating Engineering Society, Houston, Texas

1987, IBM Clear Lake Servery, Lumen Award Citation, Illuminating Engineering Society, Houston, Texas

1987, Jeddah Corniche Master Plan, Merit Award—Landscape Planning and Analysis, American Society of Landscape Architects, Jeddah, Saudi Arabia

1987, Shaw Pittman Potts and Trowbridge, Second Place Award, American Bar Association Journal, Washington, D.C.

1987, Yukon-Kuskokwim Delta Regional Hospital, Citation, *Modern Healthcare,* Bethel, Alaska

1988, Center Tower, Merit Award–Gold Nugget Awards Program, Pacific Coast Builders Conference, Costa Mesa, California

1988, Crowell and Moring Law Office–Library, First Place Award, Professional Office Design, Washington, Washington, D.C.

1988, CRSS Dallas Office, Designer's Offices, *Interiors* Magazine, Dallas, Texas

1988, Culver Academy, First Place–Historic Preservation, American Society of Interior Designers/Houston Chronicle, Culver, Indiana

1988, Lake Travis ISD Administration Building, Honor Award, AIA Fort Worth Chapter, Lake Travis, Texas

1988, Orange County Performing Arts Center, Merit Award–Gold Nugget Awards Program, Pacific Coast Builders Conference, Costa Mesa, California

1988, Shaw Pittman Potts and Trowbridge, Honorable Mention–Support Staff, Professional Office Design, Washington, D.C.

1988, Southwest/West Regional Library, Merit Award, AIA Fort Worth Chapter, Fort Worth, Texas

1989, 3M Corp's Austin Center Research and Development Facility, Honorable Mention, ASID/Houston Chronicle Interior Awards Contest, Austin, Texas

1989, CRSS Dallas Office, Designer of the Year–Scott Strasser, *Interiors* Magazine, Dallas, Texas

1989, Ota Housing, Honor Award, AIA Houston Chapter, Tokyo, Japan

1989, Riaro Hair Salon, Merit Award, AIA Dallas Chapter, Houston, Texas

1990, Astrodome Hospitality Suites, First Place, ASID/*Houston Chronicle* Interior Awards Contest, Houston, Texas

1991, Caudill Rowlett Scott Office Building, Honorable Mention, ASID/Houston Chronicle Interior Awards Contest, Houston, Texas

1991, Cummings E/MI Laboratory, Citation, American Architects/Houston Design Awards, Columbus, Indiana

1991, IBM-Austin, Urban Design Award, American Architects/Houston Design Awards, Austin, Texas

1991, Joiner Rowland Suro Keoppel Advertising Agency, Interior Architecture Award, American Architects/Houston Design Awards, Dallas, Texas

1991, Orange County Performing Arts Center, Merit Award, AIA Orange County Chapter, Costa Mesa, California

1991, Orange County Performing Arts Center, People's Choice Award, AIA Orange County Chapter, Costa Mesa, California

1991, Plaza Tower, Honor Award, AIA Orange County Chapter, Costa Mesa, California

1991, Stendig Showroom, Interior Architecture Award, American Architects/Houston Design Awards, Dallas, Texas

1993, Jesse H. Jones Hall for the Performing Arts, 25-Year Award, AIA Houston Chapter, Houston, Texas

1994, Jesse H. Jones Hall for the Performing Arts, 25-Year Award, Texas Society of Architects, Houston, Texas

1995, Caudill Rowlett Scott Office Building, 25-Year Award, AIA Houston Chapter, Houston, Texas

■ NOTES

CHAPTER 1. PIONEERS

1. Commentary by Bill Caudill written Apr. 2, 1964, in *The TIBs of Bill Caudill,* ed. Roseanne Terry Elisei, 7.
2. Commentary by Caudill written June 10, 1966, in ibid., 8–9.
3. Nicholas Lemann, "The Architects," *Texas Monthly,* Apr., 1982, 151.
4. William M. Peña, telephone interview by Philip Langdon, June 30, 1999.
5. Walter McQuade, "The Little Red Schoolhouse Goes Modern," *Collier's,* Sept. 9, 1950, 42–43, 65–67. Perkins and Will of Chicago and CRS were the two firms commissioned to produce school designs displayed in "New Schools, Economy Too," *Life,* Feb. 1, 1954, 74–80.
6. Charles Lawrence, telephone interview by Philip Langdon, Mar. 20, 1999.
7. William Wayne Caudill, "Space for Teaching: An Approach to the Design of Elementary Schools for Texas," *Bulletin of the Agricultural and Mechanical College of Texas,* Aug. 1, 1941, 4.
8. Ibid.
9. William M. Peña, telephone interview with Philip Langdon, May 19, 1999.
10. Robert Gutman, quoted in Philip Langdon, "When Bigger Is Better: Lessons from America's Largest Firms," *Architectural Record,* Aug., 1998, 58.
11. Scott is quoted in "Caudill Rowlett Scott: Vanguard in Architecture," an unpublished 1971 oral business history compiled at the University of Texas at Austin School of Business. The manuscript is in the CRS Center Archives at Texas A&M University. (Hereafter cited as "Vanguard in Architecture.")
12. William Wayne Caudill, *Architecture by Team,* 98.

CHAPTER 2. ABOVE THE GROCERY STORE

1. Unless otherwise noted, all quotations in this chapter by John Rowlett, William Caudill, and Wallie Scott are from "Vanguard in Architecture."
2. Bullock interview, ibid.
3. Peña interview, June 30, 1999.
4. Jay Baker and Barrie Scardino, "Flying High," *Cite: The Architecture and Design Review of Houston* (spring, 1998): 25.
5. Caudill, "Space for Teaching."
6. Peña interview, May 19, 1999.

7. McQuade, "Little Red Schoolhouse," 65.
8. Peña interview, May 19, 1999.
9. Ibid., June 30, 1999.
10. Former CRS staff member, professor of architecture at Columbia University, and later the first dean of Texas A&M University's College of Architecture.
11. A distinguished school architect from San Francisco.
12. Perkins and Will was a second-generation firm in Chicago specializing in schools.
13. Headed a large office in Lewiston, Maine, that designed simple but elegant schools.

CHAPTER 3. PROGRAMMING AND SQUATTERS

1. Charles Lawrence, interview by Philip Langdon, Feb. 28, 1999.
2. "Courthouse and Jail, Brazos County, Texas," *Architectural Record,* Jan., 1957, 149–54; A. S. Ware, "Brazos County Plans Courthouse for Service and Convenience," *County Progress,* June, 1954, 5–7, 11. The courthouse has since been substantially altered, marring its original design.
3. A French term, *charette* is derived from the intense final effort of students to complete their solutions to an architectural problem at the École des Beaux Arts in Paris. The term appeals to many architects enamored of traditional and European ways, but in the small Texas and Oklahoma towns where CRS started practicing in the late 1940s and early 1950s, the word *charette* would have seemed pretentious and hopelessly out of place—and it would have been a dubious choice for a modernist firm that had explicitly rejected most of the École's major tenets. Squatters was, by comparison, an ugly coinage, but it was direct and all-American.
4. Robert Gutman, professor of architecture at Princeton University, to Philip Langdon, June 28, 1999.
5. Peña interview, June 30, 1999.
6. Ibid.
7. William M. Peña, Kevin A. Kelly, and Steven A. Parshall, "Squatters Revisited," *Tennessee Architect* 3, no. 4 (winter, 1980): 17–18.
8. William M. Peña with William W. Caudill and John Focke, *Problem Seeking,* 1977.
9. William M. Peña and William W. Caudill, "Architectural Analysis: Prelude to Good Design," *Architectural Record,* May, 1959, 5. This was one of the earliest comprehensive explanations of programming as practiced by CRS.
10. Peña et al., *Problem Seeking,* 80.
11. Peña interview, June 30,1999.
12. Gropius was chairman of the Architecture Department at the Harvard Graduate School of Design, founding partner of The Architects Collaborative (TAC), and previously head of the Bauhaus.
13. From the dedication of the new school building in Blackwell, Oklahoma, Apr. 25, 1950.
14. Caudill, *Architecture by Team,* 317–18.

CHAPTER 4. "LEAN, CLEAN, LOGICAL"

1. Caudill, *Architecture by Team,* 97.
2. Ibid., 37.
3. Ibid., 55–56.
4. Ibid., 27, 119.
5. Charles Lawrence, telephone interview by Philip Langdon, Dec. 15, 1999.
6. Frank Lawyer observed: "We had three or four design teams, and we worked closely with a client and with the site and the materials. So I don't think you could look at a building and say 'CRS did that.'" The results, he said, were too varied for a corporate "signature" to emerge (telephone interview with Philip Langdon, Dec. 1, 1999).
7. Donald Canty, "The Curious Walls of Larsen Hall," *Architectural Forum,* Mar., 1966, 52.
8. Henry Winkelman, telephone interview by Philip Langdon, Nov. 24, 1999. Winkelman was a CRS designer from 1967–76.
9. Ada Louise Huxtable, "They Finally Got It Right," *New York Times,* Oct. 21, 1973.
10. Allan Jalon, "Sound Advice," *Center Stage, Los Angeles Times,* Sept. 21, 1986, 100–104.
11. The origins and results of the University of Petroleum and Minerals commission are described in Charles E. Lawrence's *Saudi Search,* 48–61.
12. Christopher Olson, "Chrysler Constructs the Ultimate Advantage," *Building Design and Construction,* 1992.
13. Paul Kennon died on Jan. 8, 1990, before the final architectural plans for the Bush Library were completed. James M. Wright of CRS succeeded him as the library's design director.
14. Willie Peña, telephone interview by Philip Langdon, June 10, 1999.

CHAPTER 5. COMMUNICATIONS

1. Elisei, *TIBs of Bill Caudill,* 81.
2. Ronald M. Reel, "CRS Design Associates," *Bankers Monthly,* Aug. 15, 1971, reprint in CRS Archives; Robert Levering, Milton Moskowitz, and Michael Katz, *The 100 Best Companies to Work for in America,* 57. In 1984, *Engineering News-Record* ranked CRS Sirrine as America's number one firm in revenue in both design and construction management.
3. Educational Facilities Laboratories was a nonprofit organization created by the Ford Foundation in 1958 to foster research and experimentation in school facilities.
4. Hughes joined the firm in 1959 and retired in 1985 as a senior vice president of CRSS. He commented on the stationery in an interview conducted July 22, 1991. CRSS was split up and sold in 1994 and 1995.
5. Parshall interview, Mar. 27, 1992.

CHAPTER 6. MARKETING

1. Quoted in Douglas E. Gordon, "The Evolution of Professional Practice," *Architecture,* Dec., 1987, 126.
2. Caudill, memorandum of May 17, 1954, CRS Archives.
3. Tom Bullock, telephone interview by Philip Langdon, July 9, 1999.
4. Ibid., July 7, 1999.
5. John Lyon Reid, F.A.I.A., of Reid and Tarics, was a distinguished San Francisco school architect. Larry Perkins, of Perkins and Will, was a well-known second-generation school architect from Chicago.
6. Mann was the Ronald L. Skaggs Endowed Professor of Health Facilities Design at Texas A&M.
7. Scoular was the director of planning for the Baylor College of Medicine in Houston.
8. Anderson DeBartolo Pan merged in 1996 with Fluor Daniel to become ADP Fluor Daniel.
9. France was administrator of Texas Children's/St. Luke's Hospital in Houston.

CHAPTER 7. GOING NATIONAL

1. In 1950, the Oklahoma City area had a population of 323,000, whereas Bryan had 18,102 inhabitants and College Station had 7,925.
2. Peña interview, June 30, 1999.
3. The American Association of School Administrators met yearly in Atlantic City, which had sixty thousand empty hotel rooms in the winter. That was before casino gambling was allowed.

CHAPTER 8. GOING GLOBAL

1. Walter McQuade, "The Arabian Building Boom is Making Construction History," *Fortune,* Sept., 1976, 114.
2. Tom Bullock, interview by Philip Langdon, Mar. 5, 1999.
3. McQuade, "Arabian Building Boom," 114.
4. Lawrence, *Saudi Search,* 9. The Lawrence quote in the sidebar titled "The Sand That Wouldn't Hold" is from this same source.

CHAPTER 9. GOING PUBLIC

1. Michael Baker III, "Public Ownership in the Engineering and Architectural Design Professions," typewritten report ca. 1981, CRS Archives, 1.
2. Oliver R. Witte, "Learn from the Public Giants," *Building Design and Construction,* July, 1978, 48.

3. Tom Bullock, E-mail to Philip Langdon, Aug. 28, 1999.
4. The firm's revenues jumped from $6.5 million during the fiscal year prior to the 1971 public offering to $31.4 million in the fiscal year ending June 30, 1977, as reported in Witte, "Learn from the Public Giants," 48.
5. Weld Coxe, *Managing Architectural and Engineering Practice,* 5–6. In the years since publication of that book, Coxe has held to the idea that architectural firms need to focus on projects, and that they can best do that when they are privately owned.
6. The biggest publicly traded firm as of 2001 was HLM Design, a Charlotte, North Carolina, based firm that went public in 1998. It had over four hundred employees, most of them in architecture, some in engineering.
7. William Fanning, telephone interview by Philip Langdon, Sept. 2, 1999.
8. Bullock interview, July 9, 1999.
9. Anderson interview, Aug. 24, 1993. In 1996, ADP merged with Fluor Daniel to become ADP Fluor Daniel.
10. Nye interview, Jan. 27, 1993. The division of CRSS began in 1994.
11. Wilkinson interview, Jan. 20, 1992.

CHAPTER 10. FAST-TRACK, BUILDING SYSTEMS, AND CONSTRUCTION MANAGEMENT

1. Except where otherwise noted, all information about Chuck Thomsen and CM in this introduction is from E-mail messages from Thomsen to Philip Langdon, Aug. 26, and Sept. 6 and 20, 1999.
2. A 25–50 percent reduction in design and construction time was attributed to fast track by two CRS vice presidents, Malcolm Tengler and Jack W. Smith, in their article "A Fast-Track to Quality, Speed and Economy in Hospital Construction," *Building Systems Design,* Nov., 1971, 20.
3. Rita Tatum, "Young CM firm corrals clients with candor," *Building Design and Construction,* Oct., 1975.
4. Tatum, "Young CM firm."
5. For insight into the psychology of dynamic, high-achieving groups like CM, see Warren Bennis and Patricia Ward Biederman, *Organizing Genius: The Secrets of Creative Collaboration,* 196–218. Bennis and Biederman say such groups have this in common: They are young, charged up, full of talent, "on a mission from God," optimistic rather than realistic, and never bureaucratic. See also Charles B. Thomsen, *Managing Brainpower.*
6. "DeVry Institute of Technology," *American School and University,* Feb., 1977, 51–56; "DeVry Institute, Bell & Howell Schools, Chicago, Illinois," *Architecture Record,* Feb., 1973, 134.
7. William B. Foxhall, *Professional Construction Management and Project Administration.*

CHAPTER 11. GROWTH

1. Weld Coxe, telephone interview by Philip Langdon, Feb. 7, 2000.
2. Chuck Thomsen, confidential memo to Paul Kennon, Mar. 15, 1982, CRS Archives.
3. Thomsen, who was fired in 1982, later had a career at the Houston firm 3D/International, becoming its chairman and CEO.
4. Alvin Toffler, *Future Shock.*
5. NaTec was established to help reduce industrial pollution at electrical generation plants and other plants as well.
6. Wilkinson interview.

CHAPTER 12. CORPORATE CULTURE

1. Jan. 15, 1983, TIB on "human values" in *The TIBs of Bill Caudill,* ed. Roseanne Terry Elisei (Houston: CRSS, 1984), 108–109.
2. All quotes from Peña are from a phone interview with Philip Langdon, Oct. 27, 1999.
3. Walter Gropius et al., eds., *The Architects Collaborative, 1945–1965,* 8, 12, 14–15.
4. TIB from March 21, 1972, in Elisei, ed., *TIBs of Bill Caudill,* 10.
5. Caudill TIB, July 29, 1969.
6. Caudill TIB, Oct. 15, 1972, in Elisei, ed., *TIBs of Bill Caudill,* 41.
7. Stansfeld interview, Oct. 20, 1993.

CHAPTER 13. PARTNERS

1. Caudill died of a heart attack June 25, 1983, at the age of sixty-nine.
2. Ernest Langford, head of the Department of Architecture at Texas A&M.

CHAPTER 14. AFTER THE BREAKUP

1. "Caudill Rowlett Scott (1946–1994)," *Architectural Record,* Sept., 1994, 9.

■ BIBLIOGRAPHY

Aeck, Richard L. "Use of Structural Steel in the Georgia School System." Paper presented at the Structural Steel for Schools Symposium, Birmingham, Ala., April, 1959, file 3000.0177, CRS Center Archives, College Station, Texas (hereafter CRS Archives).

Agostini, Edward J. "Facilities Planning and the Management Process." *Building Research: Journal of the BRAB Building Research Institute,* July-September, 1972. CRS reprint, CRS Archives.

———. "Pre-Design Programming: Some Do's and Don'ts." *Kliment's Reports,* May, 1975. CRS reprint, CRS Archives.

———. "Programming: Demanding Specialty in a Complex World." *Architectural Record,* September, 1968. CRS reprint, CRS Archives.

Agricultural and Mechanical College of Texas, Department of Architecture, School of Engineering. "19 Questions, 19 Answers: School Planning Seminar." Research Report, October, 1948, Architectural Research at Texas A&M College Engineering Experiment Station (hereafter ARTAMCEES), CRS Archives.

Bay, Alfred Paul, M.D.; Matthew Dumont, M.D.; and William Wayne Caudill. "The Bridge: A Report on Mental Health Facilities from Caudill Rowlett Scott." CRS Research Report no. 13, January, 1966, CRS Archives.

Bennis, Warren, and Patricia Ward Biederman. *Organizing Genius: The Secrets of Creative Collaboration.* Reading, Mass.: Addison-Wesley, 1997.

Bezman, Michel, and Paul N. Deltz. "The Second Generation of HVAC Equipment for Systems Bidding," *Building Systems Design,* April-May, 1973, 10–12.

Bickle, Larry W. "What to Do 'Til the Doctor Comes." *Building Operating Management,* September, 1979.

———, and John Emry. "Schools by Design." *American School Board Journal* 160, no. 8 (August, 1979): 37–38.

Brooks, Robert A. "Planning Better Schools: The Educator-Architect Thing." *National Elementary Principal,* September, 1972.

Bullock, Thomas A. "Design Applications in Modern School Construction." *Glass Digest,* November, 1957, 46–47, 88–90.

———. "Regional Offices with Central Production." *Architectural Record,* February, 1960.

———. "Organization for Efficient Practice: Caudill, Rowlett & Scott, Architects-Planners-Engineers." *Architectural Record,* November, 1960.

———. "Post-Recession Construction Markets." *Dodge National Forum* 4, no. 1 (1980): 4–9.

———, and Herbert Paseur. "Form Allows Function." *American School and University,* 1958–59. CRS reprint, CRS Archives.

Bullock, Thomas A., William M. Peña, and John W. Focke. "Universal Building Systems Research Interim Report #2." June 20, 1969. CRS Archives.

Cagley, James R. "Systems Building Saves Time and Money." *Civil Engineering ASCE: Environmental Design and Engineered Construction,* April, 1973.

———, John Alamont Pierce, and Paul N. Deltz. "Systems Building: Need and Response." *Building Systems Design,* November, 1971, 16–19.

Carlson, C. A., and Wallie E. Scott Jr. "Joint Ventures and Associations: Lessons Drawn from a Firm's Experience." *Journal of the American Institute of Architects* 56, no. 6 (June, 1976).

Caudill, William Wayne. *Toward Better School Design.* New York: F. W. Dodge, 1954.

———. *Architecture by Team: A New Concept for the Practice of Architecture.* New York: Van Nostrand Reinhold, 1971.

———, Frank D. Lawyer, and Thomas A. Bullock. *A Bucket of Oil: The Humanistic Approach to Building Design for Energy Conservation.* Boston: Cahners Books, 1974.

Caudill, William Wayne, Willie Peña, and Paul Kennon. *Architecture and You: How to Experience and Enjoy Buildings.* New York: Whitney Library of Design, an imprint of Watson-Guptill Publications, a division of Billboard Publications, 1978.

Caudill, William Wayne, with Charles Schorre and Jeffrey Conroy. *From Infancy to Infinity.* N.P.: Wall, n.d.

Caudill, William Wayne. "An Approach to Design of a High School." Res*earch-Arch*itecture Research Report no. 4, n.d., CRS Archives.

———. "Space for Teaching: An Approach to the Design of Elementary Schools for Texas." *Bulletin of the Agricultural and Mechanical College of Texas,* August 1, 1941.

———. "A Bibliography on School Architecture." Research Report no. 1, July, 1948, ARTAMCEES, CRS Archives, 20.

———. "Building for Learning." *School Management,* January, 1949, 4–5, 18.

———. "Toward Better Schools . . . Through Long Range Programming." *Architectural Forum,* October, 1949, 94–97, 164, 168.

———. "Your Schools: An Approach to Long-Range Planning of School Buildings." *School Executive,* pt. 1, August, 1950, 25–28; pt. 2, September, 1950, 54–57; pt. 3, October, 1950, 68–73; pt. 4, November, 1950, 58–61; pt. 5, December, 1950, 46–47.

———. "What Will the War Do to School Building Programs?" *School and College Management,* February, 1951, 2, 10.

———. "Colour in the Classroom." *Journal of the Royal Architectural Institute of Canada* 28, no. 5. (May, 1951): 123–24.

———. "What Characterizes a Good School Building?" *School Executive,* June, 1951, 19–22.

———. "Building Shapes: An Experimental Study for Natural Lighting, Sound Conditioning and Ventilation." *College and University Business,* August, 1951, 40–41.

———. "Form in Educational Architecture," *School Executive,* October, 1953, 79–93.

———. "Form in Educational Architecture." *Bulletin of the School of Education, Indiana University* 29, no. 6 (November, 1953): 45–51.

———. "What the School Board Member Should Know About School Buildings." *Texas School Board Journal* 1, no. 2 (September, 1954): 3–8.

———. "Housing the Secondary School of Tomorrow." *Teachers College Record* 56, no. 7 (April, 1955): 393–403.

———. "How Can School Buildings Aid the Educational Program?" *School Executive,* September, 1955, 11.

———. "It's All in the Ceiling!" *The Nation's Schools,* November, 1956, 69–72.

———. "Development of a Glass Gymnasium." *American School and University,* 1956–57. CRS reprint, CRS Archives.

———. "Form Follows Function." *NEA Journal,* March, 1957, 152–54.

———. "The Low-Down on Codes and Regulations." *School Executive,* February, 1958.

———."An Architect's View of West Germany." Research-Architecture Research Report no. 22, July 1, 1958, CRS Archives.

———. "Lift the Fog from School Design." *Educational Business,* August, 1958, 37–38.

———. "Big C: The Fourth of School Planning." *Bulletin of Pasadena Chapter AIA,* January, 1959, 7.

———. "Multi-Purpose Central Corridors." Research-Architecture Research Report no. 5, March, 1953, CRS Archives.

———. "Big C: The Fourth of School Planning." *Nation's Schools,* February, 1959, 142–44.

———. "How to Keep Going Forward." *Progressive Architecture* 40, no. 2 (February, 1959): 13.

———. "The Three C's of School Planning." *School Executive,* November, 1959, 56–59.

———. "Emerging Instructional Patterns and School Design." *American School Board Journal* 142 (January, 1961): 24–27.

———. "Journey Through an Indian Time Machine, as told to Martin Dreyer." *Houston Chronicle,* April 23, 1961, Travel sec., 11–12.

———. "The Preceptorship Program at Rice University." *Journal of the American Institute of Architects* 42, no. 3 (March, 1962): 55–57.

———. "Economies and False Economies in School Plant Planning," *Texas School Board Journal* 9, no. 1 (June, 1962): 24–27.

———. "A Three-Minute Course on . . . How to Plan a Schoolhouse." *Craft Educational Services Monthly Update,* November, 1962, 8–9.

———. "Fourteen Ways School Design Has Responded to Modern Education." *Nation's Schools,* January, 1963, 52–95.

———. "False Economies in Schoolhouse Construction." *Saturday Review,* May 18, 1963, 72–74, 84.

———. "Architects and People." *Arizona Builder/Architect,* June, 1963, 14.

———. "Shells and the Educating Process." CRS Research Report no. 8, July, 1963, CRS Archives.

———. "Shells and the Educating Process." *Producers' Council, Inc., Technical Bulletin 105,* September, 1963, 59–61. CRS reprint, CRS Archives.

———. "Visions of the Future: Audiovisual Presentations." Paper presented at the AASA, Centennial Convention and Work Conference, Atlantic City, New Jersey, February 15–19, 1964, 87–95.

———. "The Reasons Behind Innovations in Schoolhouse Design," *Architecture/West,* March, 1964, 20–21.

———. "Architectural Education Changes and Reforms: Spanning the Gap Between Theory and Practice." *Journal of the American Institute of Architects* 44, no. 5 (May, 1964): 23–28.

———. "What Makes a Campus More than its Buildings?" *College and University Business,* October, 1964, 55.

———. "Cultivate an Appreciation . . . for Architecture." *Texas Parent-Teacher,* November, 1964, 11, 13–14.

———. "In Education the Most Important Number is One." CRS Research Report no. 11, December, 1964, CRS Archives.

———. "The Case of the Hipbone." *Junior College Journal,* September, 1965, 20–23.

———. "What Works and What Fails in School Design." *Nation's Schools,* March, 1967, 85–116.

———. "Two for the Seesaw." *Journal of the American Institute of Architects* 47, no. 5 (May, 1967): 77–82.

———. "The Triad Theory: One Approach." *Journal of the American Institute of Architects* 48, no. 2 (February, 1968).

———. "Fighting the Practice Shock." *Rice University Review* (fall-winter, 1968): 37–40.

———. "Architecture in the Cause of People: Yesterday, Today and Tomorrow," *Architectural Record,* January, 1969.

———. "A Study—Memos from Russia 1969: Industrialization of the Building Process in Russia and England." CRS Research Report no. 19, February, 1970, CRS Archives.

———. "Russian Building Systems: The Architect Returns." *Progressive Architecture,* March, 1970. CRS reprint, CRS Archives.

———. "Forces Shaping Architectural Practice." *Florida Architect,* November-December, 1975, 20–23.

———. "First Draft Thoughts on Energy Conservation Through Design." February 21, 1978, CRS Archives.

———. "William W. Caudill on Lawrence B. Anderson." *Journal of the American Institute of Architects* 58, no. 7 (July, 1978): 86, 88.

———. "That Precious Tomato." *Creative School Designer,* September-October, 1978, 7.

———. "The Course of Architecture in a Decade of Discontinuity." Paper presented at a forum sponsored by the University of Houston Department of Architecture, December 3, 1979.

———. "Reconnaissance for the American Embassy, Riyadh, Saudi Arabia." CRS, February 25, 1980.

———. "Paper Architecture, Photo Period and Real Buildings." *Vision* (Hong Kong), April, 1983.

———. "Paper Architecture." *Texas Architect,* May-June, 1983, 66–71.

———, and Cleon Bellomy. "The Development of the Teaching Space Divider." *American School and University,* 1954–55. CRS reprint, CRS Archives.

———. "Spatial Approach to Planning the Physical Environment." *American School and University,* 1954–55. CRS reprint, CRS Archives.

Caudill, William Wayne, and Robert A. Brooks. "Review of Open Space Schools." *Journal of the American Institute of Architects* 52, no. 2 (February, 1972): 52.

Caudill, William Wayne, and Thomas A. Bullock. "Barriers and Breakthroughs." *American School and University,* 1956–57. CRS Reprint, CRS Archives.

———. "Some Thoughts Concerning Beauty." CRS Research Report no. 1, June, 1960, CRS Archives.

———, and Franklin D. Lawyer. "Seventeen Ways to Build for an Energy-Scarce Future." *The Nation's Schools,* July, 1974.

Caudill, William Wayne, Sherman E. Crites, and Elmer G. Smith. "Some General Considerations in the Natural Ventilation of Buildings." Research Report no. 22, February, 1951, ARTAMCEES, CRS Archives, 43.

Caudill, William Wayne, and Franklin D. Lawyer. "Johnny Goes to High School." *Systems for Educators* 5, no. 2 (November-December, 1958): 4–5.

Caudill, William Wayne, and E. E. Merrell Jr. "The Core: A Scheme for Facilitating Back-to-Back Classrooms." Rese*arch-Arch*itecture Research Report no. 6, n.d., CRS Archives.

———. "The Core: A Scheme for Facilitating Back-to-Back Classrooms," *American School and University,* 1953–54. CRS reprint, CRS Archives.

Caudill, William Wayne, and William M. Peña. "Economy in School Construction." *Catholic Building and Maintenance,* fall, 1954, 52–55.

———, and L. S. Richardson. "School Equipment Trends." *School Executive: School Administration in Review Special Reference Issue,* January, 1956, 95–97.

———, and Joe B. Thomas. "Air Conditioning of Schools." CRS Research Report no. 2, June, 1960, CRS Archives.

Caudill, William Wayne, and Robert H. Reed. "Geometry of Classrooms as Related to Natural Lighting and Natural Ventilation." Research Report no. 36, July, 1952, ARTAMCEES, CRS Archives, 53.

Caudill, William Wayne, and John M. Rowlett. "School Architecture in 1953." *School Executive,* January, 1954, 85–89.

———. "Selecting the School Site." Rese*arch-Arch*itecture Research Report no. 3, n.d., file 4000.1311, CRS Archives.

Caudill, William Wayne, and Wallie E. Scott Jr. "Can a Functional School be Beautiful?" *School Executive,* October, 1952.

———. "Quadruplex: A Scheme for a Four Classroom Unit." Rese*arch-Arch*itecture Research Report no. 1, n.d., CRS Archives.

Cherry, Edith. *Programming for Design: From Theory to Practice.* Boston: John Wiley and Sons, 1974.

Cherry, Ralph W. "Implications of Child Growth and Development for School Plan Design." *American School and University,* 1955–56. CRS reprint, CRS Archives.

Cocking, Walter D. "School Plants for Tomorrow." Rese*arch-Arch*itecture Research Report no. 18, July 7, 1956, CRS Archives.

Colbert, Charles R. "Today's Criteria of Design for School Buildings." Paper presented at the Structural Steel for Schools Symposium, Birmingham, Ala., April, 1959, CRS Archives, 4–6.

Convair-Forth Worth, a Division of General Dynamics Corporation, and CRS Team. "Investigating the Feasibility and Cost of Fallout Protection for a New Schoolhouse." CRS Research Report no. 7, July, 1961, CRS Archives.

Crites, Sherman E., and William Wayne Caudill. "Moving Air for Comfort." *Catholic Building and Maintenance,* fall, 1950, 23–25.

Coxe, Weld. *Managing Architectural and Engineering Practice.* New York: John Wiley and Sons, 1980.

CRS. "The Open University," n.d., CRS Archives.

———. "Junior High School Study: Analyses and Proposed Solutions to Problems in the Planning and Design of the Benjamin Franklin Junior High School, Dallas Independent School District," October 18, 1954, CRS Archives.

———. "Space is Where You Find it: A Study to Determine the Educational Potential of a Retired Government Testing Laboratory," 1968, CRS Archives.

———. "SL/TCH Hospital Room Inventory System," 1969, CRS Archives.

———. "Fast-Track and Other Procedures: A General Study of Design and Construction Management," November, 1969, CRS Archives.

———. "Space Inventory and Cost Analysis Simulation (SICAS): CRS Programming Inventory System," March, 1971, CRS Archives.

———. "Energy Estimate Analysis," September, 1978, CRS Archives.

———. "Program: Toward a Prototype Factory That Can Flex," April 1, 1982, CRS Archives.

———. "Ideas: Toward a Prototype Factory That Can Flex," May 14, 1982, CRS Archives.

———, and Herman Miller Research Corporation. "Scan: Toward a Prototype Factory That Can Flex," March 1, 1982, CRS Archives.

CRS Design Associates. *Industrialized Building Systems Investigation.* Chicago: Research Council of the Great Cities Program for School Improvement, August, 1975.

CRSS. *OFFICing: An International Round Table on Intelligent Buildings.* Houston: CRSS Research Division, January, 1988.

CRS Team. "The Design of the Brazos County Courthouse and Jail." Rese*arch-Arch*itecture Research Report no. 7, February 25, 1954, CRS Archives.

———. "Developing a Catholic Church-School Center." Rese*arch-Arch*itecture Research Report no. 8, July 5, 1954, CRS Archives.

———. "Programming School Building Needs." Rese*arch-Arch*itecture Research Report no. 9, September 4, 1954, CRS Archives.

———. "School Planning Clinic—San Angelo." Rese*arch-Arch*itecture Research Report no. 10, July 6–7, 1954, CRS Archives.

———. "Programming the San Angelo School Needs." Rese*arch-Arch*itecture Research Report no. 11, n.d., CRS Archives.

———. "Analyses and Proposed Solutions to Problems in the Planning and Design of the Benjamin Franklin Junior High School." Rese*arch-Arch*itecture Research Report no. 12, October 18, 1954, CRS Archives.

———. "Design of the Bettes Office Building, Oklahoma City." Rese*arch-Arch*itecture Research Report no. 13, September 26, 1955, CRS Archives.

———. "An Approach to Industrial Plant Design." Rese*arch-Arch*itecture Research Report no. 14, n.d., CRS Archives.

———. "Programming School Building Needs, Gainesville, Texas." Rese*arch-Arch*itecture Research Report no. 15, July 15, 1956, CRS Archives.

———. "Programming the Shattuck Schools." Rese*arch-Arch*itecture Research Report no. 16, n.d., CRS Archives.

———. "Programming Port Neches–Groves Schools." Rese*arch-Arch*itecture Research Report no. 17, July 30, 1956, CRS Archives.

———. "Programming Stillwater Schools." Rese*arch-Arch*itecture Research Report no. 20, January 1, 1957, CRS Archives.

———. "An Approach to College Design." Rese*arch-Arch*itecture Research Report no. 21, CRS Archives.

———. "The Practice of the Caudill Rowlett Scott Firm." CRS Research Report no. 12, November, 1965, rev. 1968, 1969, and 1972, CRS Archives.

———. "Pima County Junior College: An Approach to Campus Planning." CRS Research Report no. 15, September, 1967, CRS Archives.

———. "Educational Park: A Case Study Based on Planning and Design for Anniston, Alabama." CRS Research Report no. 16, July, 1968, CRS Archives.

———. "Probes-A Look at Criminal Justice Facilities." CRS Research Report no. 20, 1975, CRS Archives.

CRS Sirrine and WANG Advanced Systems Laboratory. "Probes: Office Technology and Management." Vol. 1, "Specifications for a Strategic Planning Process." June, 1984. CRS Archives.

———. Vol. 2, "Case Study." June, 1984. CRS Archives.

Denning, Robert A. "Campus Housing Appeals to Students at Low Cost." *American School and University,* June, 1975, 18–21.

Department of Architecture, Agricultural and Mechanical College of Texas. "Building for Learning." Research Report no. 3, July, 1948, ARTAMCEES, CRS Archives, 37.

"DeVry Institute, Bell & Howell Schools, Chicago, Illinois," *Architecture Record,* Feb., 1973, 134.

"DeVry Institute of Technology," *American School and University,* Feb., 1977, 51–56.

Dorsett, Clyde H., and James Falick. "Designs Link Mental Health Facilities with Community Activities." *HOSPITALS: Journal of the American Hospital Association* 38 (February 1, 1964): 34–36, 40–42.

Douglass, H. Robert. "Adventures in Hospital Design in a Foreign Setting." *AMA International Health Bulletin* 4, no. 1 (fall-winter, 1971).

Elisei, Roseanne Terry, ed. *The TIBs of Bill Caudill.* Houston: CRSS, 1984.

Evans, Benjamin H. "Natural Air Flow Around Buildings." Research Report no. 59, March, 1957, ARTAMCEES, CRS Archives, 15.

Falick, James. "Waste Handling in Hospitals." *Architectural and Engineering News,* November, 1965. CRS reprint, CRS Archives.

———. "Good Planning Can Make Hospitals Good Neighbors." *HOSPITALS: Journal of the American Hospital Association* 43 (July 16, 1967). CRS reprint, CRS Archives.

———. "Automation Should Not Just Fit Old Forms but Aid New Functions." *Modern Hospital,* October, 1969, 96–101.

———. "Cost Controls and the Design Process." *HOSPITALS: Journal of the American Hospital Association* 46 (February 1, 1972): 125–30.

———. "Designing Cheap Buildings is Expensive." *HOSPITALS: Journal of the American Hospital Association* 49 (February 1, 1975): 125–27, 129–30.

———. "Instant Architecture for Ambulatory Care: Build Fast but Build to Last." *Modern Hospital,* March, 1974, 59–62.

———. "How to Work with the Health Client." *Progressive Architecture,* July, 1974. CRS reprint, CRS Archives.

———. "Inmate . . . Patient . . . Patron." *Interiors,* November, 1972, 102–108.

———, and Scott S. Parker. "Coordination of Merged Facilities." *HOSPITALS: Journal of the American Hospital Association* 45 (February 1, 1971).

Falick, James, and James Thomas, "Interesting Interiors Equal Happier Hospitals." *Modern Hospital,* February, 1967.

Fleshman, Nancy Acker, Kirby Fonville, Renate Schweiger, and Leslie Wahl. *CRSS Stories: Motion in Only One Direction—Forward.* Houston: CRSS, 1992.

Focke, John W., and William M. Peña. "Problem Seeking: New Directions in Architectural Programming." CRS Research Report no. 18, November, 1969, CRS Archives.

Foxhall, William B. *Professional Construction Management and Project Administration.* New York: Architectural Record, 1972.

Gropius, Walter, et al., eds. *The Architects Collaborative, 1945–1965.* New York: Architectural Book Publishing, 1966.

Harris, Al, and William Wayne Caudill. "An Analysis of Two Multi-Purpose Corridor Types." *American School and University,* 1955–56. CRS reprint, CRS Archives.

Hartsfield, Robert J. "The Process is the Product." *Public Management* 52, no. 6 (June, 1970): 8–11.

Hensarling, Paul. "'Glass Walls' and the Instructional Program." *American School and University,* 1955–56. CRS reprint, CRS Archives.

Herndon, H. W., and William M. Pena. "Design for a Flexibly Graded Program." *School Executive,* April, 1957, 82–87.

Hiss, Philip H. "Practical Considerations." Paper presented at the Structural Steel for Schools Symposium, Birmingham, Ala., April, 1959, file 3000.0177, CRS Archives, 7–12.

Holleman, Theo R. "Air Flow Through Conventional Window Openings." Research Report no. 33, November, 1951, ARTAMCEES, CRS Archives, 45.

Hooker, Thomas. "Profile by Facilities Development." *Junior College Journal,* June, 1970.

———, and Allen A. Ambrose. "Architects Can Help You Win the Inflation Game." *Community and Junior College Journal* 43, no. 7 (April, 1973): 10–14.

Hughes, James, Robert H. Reed, and Julian Fisher. "Probes: A Search for Uniqueness of the Community College." CRS Research Report no. 14, January, 1967, CRS Archives.

Kennon, Paul A., Jr. "Exciting New School is Economical Too." *American School and University,* January, 1975, 20–22.

———. "The City as Cultural Artifact." *Architecture California* 8, no. 5 (May-June, 1986): 30–31.

———. "Town That Dreams." *The (Columbus, Ind.) Republic,* May 19, 1987, A-4.

———. "Caudill Rowlett Scott Sirrine History." In *Encyclopedia of Architecture: Design Engineering Construction,* ed. Joseph A. Wilkes and Robert T. Packard (New York: John Wiley and Sons, 1988).

———, Jay S. Bauer and Steven A. Parshall. "Evaluating Health Care Facilities." Pt. 1. *Journal of Health Administration Education* 6, no. 4 (n.d.): 819–31.

King, Brawley M. "Top Story Product Forum." *Top Story: The Sweet's Newsletter for Marketing Executives in the Construction Business,* December, 1981, 3.

King, Jonathan. "In Which the Bell Tolls." *Saturday Review Educational Supplement,* October 15, 1960. CRS reprint, file 3000.0222, CRS Archives.

———. "Teaching Facilities for Medical Education or Can We Have All This Plumbing and Architecture Too?" *Annals of the New York Academy of Sciences,* September 27, 1965, 655–60.

———. "New Developments Provide for Change." Paper presented at the Building Research Institute Fall Conference, September 29–30 and October 1, 1971, Washington, D.C.

———. "User Requirements and Performance Design." *National Bureau of Standards Special Publication 361,* May, 1972, 297–301.

———. "New Ways to Build, or, How to Get Your School Built Before You Retire." *National Elementary Principal,* September, 1972. CRS reprint, CRS Archives.

———. "From Process to Product." *Building Systems Design,* April-May, 1973, 3.

———. "Technology and Humanism: Not So Strange Bedfellows." *Building Systems Design,* April-May, 1973, 4–5.

———. "Buying Systems." *Industrialization Forum* 5 (1974): 3–8.

———. "Rust City: Experiment in College Housing." *AD,* June, 1975, 373–74.

———. "The Technology Behind Successful Campus Housing." *American School and University,* August, 1975.

———. "Evaluation: A Firm Undertakes Re-examination of its Work from the Users' Viewpoints." *Journal of the American Institute of Architects* 56, no. 8 (August, 1976): 29–30.

———, and Donn Carter. "Strong Case for New Facility." *American School and University,* April, 1974, 53.

King, Jonathan, and Todd Lee, "Systems Building: Where Do We Go from Here?" *Building Systems Design,* November, 1971, 35–40.

Kliment, Stephen A. "Revolution in Educational Facilities Requires Innovations in School Food Service." *School Lunch Journal* 23, no. 8 (September, 1969): 70–76.

———. "Editorial." *Architectural Record,* September, 1994, 9.

———, and Jack W. Smith. "Fast-Track: How it Slices Costs and Speeds up Construction." *American School Board Journal* 152, no. 8 (August, 1971): 14–19.

Krenitsky, Michael. "Approach to a University Library Design." *American School and University,* 1957–58. CRS reprint, CRS Archives.

Langdon, Philip. "When Bigger Is Better: Lessons from America's Largest Firms." *Architectural Record,* August, 1998.

Lawrence, Charles E. *Saudi Search.* Ed. Roseanne Terry Elisei. Houston: CRSS, 1986.

———. "The Planning Aspects of a Nuclear Science Center." *Journal of the American Institute of Architects* 39, no. 1 (January, 1959): 55–56.

———, Franklin D. Lawyer, and William Wayne Caudill. "Quality Profiles." CRS Research Report no. 10, June, 1964, CRS Archives.

Lawyer, Franklin D. "On-the-Spot Design of a Graduate School for Religion." *American School and University,* 1961–62. CRS reprint, CRS Archives.

———. "On-the-Spot Design of a School for Religion." CRS Research Report no. 4, September, 1960, CRS Archives.

———. "Probing the Future of Architecture." Address to the AAUW, Corning, N.Y., November 20, 1958.

Lee, Todd. "The Systems Built Schoolhouse and Beyond." *American School and University,* January, 1973, 22–24, 26.

Levering, Robert, Milton Moskowitz, and Michael Katz. *The 100 Best Companies to Work for in America.* Reading, Mass.: Addison-Wesley, 1984.

McCutchan, Gordon, and William Wayne Caudill. "An Experiment in Architectural Education Through Research." Research Report no. 32, November, 1951, ARTAMCEES, CRS Archives, 64.

Matsushita Electric Works and CRSS. *OFFICing: Bringing Amenity and Intelligence to Knowledge Work.* Japan: LibroPort, 1988.

Mattox, Robert F. "Planning the Campus by Computer." *Architectural and Engineering News,* March, 1968. CRS reprint, CRS Archives.

———. "Creating an Educational Environment." *Consulting Engineer,* March, 1969. CRS reprint, CRS Archives.

Moore, Hollis A., and William Wayne Caudill. "Schoolhouse Planning: Designed for the Early Teen-Ager." *Nation's Schools,* January, 1955. CRS reprint, CRS Archives.

Morhous, Francis E. "Year-Round Climate Control: Case Study of an Air-Conditioned High School." *School Executive,* March, 1959. CRS reprint, CRS Archives.

Nowak, Matthew A. "A Sound Survey of the Geometric School Plant." Research Report no. 64, September, 1958, ARTAMCEES, CRS Archives, 20.

Nye, Edward F. "Domes for Schools." *American School and University,* 1957–58. CRS reprint, CRS Archives.

———. "Bring Back Clean Air and Water." *San Jacinto Professional Engineer,* October, 1968, 2–3.

Olson, Christopher. "Chrysler Constructs the Ultimate Advantage." *Building Design and Construction,* 1992. CRS reprint, CRS Archives.

Parker, Scott S., and James Falick. "How to Make Consumers Real Partners in Planning." *Modern Hospital,* July, 1972, 103–106.

Parshall, Steven A., and William M. Peña. "Post-Occupancy Evaluation as a Form of Return Analysis." *Industrial Development,* May-June, 1983, 32–34.

Paseur, C. Herbert. "The Ancient King and His Three Wise Architects: An Illustrated Fable for All School Plant Planners." *Educational Business including School Equipment News,* November, 1958, 50–51.

———. "Campus Planning for 1970." *College and University Business,* November, 1958, 25–28.

———. "Flexibility in School Building Design or The Ancient King and His Three Wise Architects." *Journal of the American Institute of Architects* 39, no. 11 (November, 1959): 91–94.

———. "Decentralized School vs. Centralized School." CRS Research Report no. 3, July, 1960, CRS Archives.

———. "School: Michigan." *The Architects' Exchange,* January–March, 1962, 18–19.

———. "Science Hall Carries Utility Services in its Walls." *College and University Business,* June, 1963, 48–51.

———. "The Grasshopper Chase: A Teaching Tool." *Architecture/West,* March, 1964, 22–24.

———. "Architects Seek Wider Ecological Influence." *Houston Business Journal,* February 7, 1972.

———, and Thomas A. Bullock. "Zoned Approach to College Master Plans." *American School and University,* 1958–59. CRS reprint, CRS Archives.

Peña, William M., with William W. Caudill and John Focke. *Problem Seeking.* Boston: Cahners Books International, 1977.

Peña, William M. "Programming the Laredo Schools." Res*earch-Arch*itecture Research Report no. 2, n.d., file 4000.1311, CRS Archives.

———. "Architectural Analysis of a Proposed Typical Classroom . . . Blackwell Public Schools." *Report on Classroom Design,* May 28, 1948.

———. "Looking at the Inside." *Texas Outlook,* May, 1954, 9–11, 39.

———. "Programming the Bartlesville Schools." Rese*arch-Arch*itecture Research Report no. 19, October 4, 1954, CRS Archives.

———. "Predetermination of Natural Illumination by the Model Testing Method." *American School and University,* 1956–57. CRS reprint, CRS Archives.

———. "People and Program . . . Background for the Architect." *NEA Journal: 38th Yearbook,* 1959, 44–45. CRS reprint, CRS Archives.

———. "An Architect Designs with Air Conditioning." *School Executive,* March, 1959, 50–52.

———. "Sunday Seminar Excerpts." *Western Arts Association Bulletin* 44, no. 4 (September, 1960): 7–10.

———. "Organizing for Programming." *Building Research,* April-June, 1969, 8–11.

———, and William Wayne Caudill. "Architectural Analysis: Prelude to Good Design." *Architectural Record,* May, 1959, 178–82.

———. "Two Trips in Sixty." CRS Research Report no. 6, February, 1961, CRS Archives.

Peña, William M., and John W. Focke. "Performance Requirements of Buildings and the Whole Problem." *National Bureau of Standards Special Publication 361,* May 2–5, 1972, 43–55.

———. "Programming: Analysis as a Prelude to Design Synthesis." *Architectural Record,* October, 1975, 65.

Peña, William M., and Leroy V. Good. "Architectural Programming: Important Steps Before Design Can Begin." *Junior College Journal* (October, 1967): 34–37.

Peña, William M., and Joseph B. Thomas. "Myths and Facts about Ventilation." *American School and University,* 1963, 41–44.

Perkins, Lawrence B. "Visions of the Future: Audiovisual Presentations." Paper presented at the AASA Centennial Convention and Work Conference, Atlantic City, New Jersey, February 15–19, 1964, 96–103.

Pierce, John Alamont. "Specifications and the Systems Approach." *The Construction Specifier,* May, 1971, 55–59.

———. "The Performance of Performance Specifications." *The Construction Specifier,* May, 1972, 101–104.

Reed, Robert H. "Design for Natural Ventilation in Hot Humid Weather," in "Housing and Building in Hot-Humid and Hot-Dry Climates," Research Report no. 80, 1953, ARTAMCEES, CRS Archives, 11.

———. "Effects of Nearby Walks and Concrete Areas on Indoor Natural Lighting." *Illuminating Engineering,* July, 1956, 532–36.

———, and William Wayne Caudill, "Classrooms that Perform," *American School and University,* 1952–53. CRS reprint, CRS Archives.

Reed, Robert H., James Hughes, and Peter Piven. "The Urban Community College." CRS Research Report no. 17, November, 1969, CRS Archives.

Review of "Problem Seeking: An Architectural Programming Primer," by William M. Peña with William Wayne Caudill and John W. Focke. *Journal of the American Institute of Architects* 57, no. 12 (December, 1977): 80.

Richardson, L. S., and William Wayne Caudill. "Towards an Economical Flexibility." *American School and University,* 1954–55. CRS reprint, CRS Archives.

Rowlett, John M. "The Primitive Quality in CRS Architecture." CRS Research Report no. 9, April, 1964, CRS Archives.

———. "The Virtues of Primitiveness in School Architecture." *Bulletin of the National Association of Secondary School Principals,* March, 1965, 203–14.

———, and Thomas A. Bullock. "Relationship of Cost to the Geometry of a Building." *American School and University,* 1955–56. CRS reprint, CRS Archives.

Scott, Wallie E., Jr. "Architectural School Design." Paper presented at the Structural Steel for Schools Symposium, Birmingham, Ala., April, 1959, file 3000.0177, CRS Archives, 13–16.

Scoular, David N. "Stacking Up a Hospital in 390 Days." *Building Systems Design,* April-May, 1973, 6–9.

Smith, Elmer G., Robert H. Reed, and H. Darwin Hodges. "Measurement of Low Air Speeds by the Use of Titanium Tetrachloride." Research Report no. 25, May, 1951, ARTAMCEES, CRS Archives, 22.

Tatum, Rita. "Young CM Firm Corrals Clients with Candor." *Building Design and Construction,* Oct., 1975.

Tengler, Malcolm T. "Fast-Track Method Saves Time, Cuts Costs in Construction." *Hospital Topics: Today's Hospital Practices for Management, Medicine, Surgery, Nursing,* February, 1973. CRS reprint, CRS Archives.

———, and Jack W. Smith. "A Fast Track to Quality, Speed and Economy in Hospital Construction." *Building Systems Design,* November, 1971, 19–23.

Thomas, Joe B., and Gustave Akselrod. "CRS: The Computer in Energy Analysis." *Building Systems Design,* November, 1971, 22–29.

———. "Myths and Facts about School Air Conditioning." *ASHRAE Journal* (July, 1966): 46–50.

———. "Total Comfort Systems for Schools and Colleges." *ASHARAE Journal* (April, 1970).

Thomsen, Charles B. *Managing Brainpower.* 3 vols. Washington, D.C.: AIA Press, 1989.

———. *CM: Developing, Marketing, and Delivering Construction Management Services.* New York: McGraw-Hill, 1982.

———. "Architecture and the Information Machine." *Wisconsin Architect,* June, 1966, 43, 45, 47.

———. "Architecture/Tradition: The Computer." *Florida Architect,* January, 1967, 8–10, 16.

———. "Computing Educational Requirements." *Educational Equipment and Materials,* 1968, 65–66.

———. "The Construction Management Concept: A New Contractual Structure for Building." *Building Systems Design,* November, 1971, 40–43.

———. "Economic Optimization of Income-Producing Buildings with Computers." *Colloquium on Computer Applications in Real Estate Investment Analysis.* Monograph series no. 2. October, 1968. CRS reprint, CRS Archives.

———. "How High to Rise." *Journal of the American Institute of Architects* 45, no. 4 (April, 1965). CRS reprint, CRS Archives.

———. "How One Office Uses Computers." *Architectural and Engineering News,* June, 1966. CRS reprint, file 3000.0352, CRS Archives.

———. "Managing Large Projects: Knowing More Than How to Build." *Military Engineer,* September-October, 1981, 338–40.

———. "An Overview of Cost Management." *Architectural Record,* September, 1973. CRS reprint, CRS Archives.

———. "Putting a Campus Together with Systems." *College Management,* October, 1970. CRS reprint, file 3000.0450, CRS Archives.

———. "Schools in a Hurry: Merrick Systems Schools." *Progressive Architecture,* February, 1971, 78–79.

Toffler, Alvin. *Future Shock.* New York: Random House, 1970.

Trower, Michael H., and Edward F. Nye. "CRS: Management for Progress." *Building Systems Design,* November, 1971, 29–35.

———. "A Fast Track to Project Delivery." *Management Review,* April, 1973, 19–23.

Vezey, E. E. "The Feasibility of Using Models for Predetermining Natural Lighting." Research Report no. 21, January, 1951, ARTAMCEES, CRS Archives, 33.

Wadzeck, Garald. "Education Planning for an Ageless School." *American School and University,* 1957–58. CRS reprint, CRS Archives.

Whitcomb, Francis, and Stephen A. Kliment. "On Track with Fast Track." *Journal of the American Institute of Architects* 53, no. 2 (February, 1973).

White, Robert F. "Effects of Landscape Development on the Natural Ventilation of Buildings and their Adjacent Areas." Research Report no. 45, March, 1954, ARTAMCEES, CRS Archives, 16.

Wines, Donald B. "A Challenge Not a Choice." *High School Journal* 50, no. 2 (November, 1966): 73–78.

———. "The Direction of School Design." *Compact,* February, 1969.

Witte, Oliver R. "Learn from the Public Giants." *Building Design and Construction,* July, 1978.

Yarbrough, David B. "The Team Approach to Planning a College Science Building." CRS Research Report no. 5, September, 1960, CRS Archives.

Zingeser, Joel. "My House: Scattered Site Equity Housing." Unpublished report, 1970, file 3000.0452, CRS Archives.

Zucker, Elena M. "Fourth Annual Report on the BD&C 300." *Building Design and Construction,* July, 1980, 61–127.

INDEX

Page numbers in *italic* type indicate photos.

ISBN 1-58544-206-2
90000
9 781585 442065